D1539580

FORD MADOX FORD'S NOVELS

FORD MADOX FORD'S NOVELS

A CRITICAL STUDY

by John A. Meixner

UNIVERSITY OF MINNESOTA PRESS · MINNEAPOLIS

To the Hoffbergs

PREFACE

THE aims of this book are many. But on inspection they simplify to three — the description of Ford's fictional world; the analysis of his craft; and the evaluation of his accomplishment. Of the first two, little need be said; the book itself will define them. For the third, however, a few observations may have their value at the outset, as guides to the critic's approach.

In reading and rereading these novels, the author of this study has had experiences which have pleased him or not, and he has tried to find out why — to understand in an objective spirit the grounds for his response (including the bases of his preference), and to articulate them as overtly and as lucidly as possible. He has been interested in displaying the strengths of Ford's work and in accenting its genuine importance in twentieth-century literature. But he has not been unaware, as the reader will discover, of surprising limitations. In the past Ford has been harmed by neglect; in recent years he would seem to have suffered no less from excessive claims — claims which have been doubly damaging: in provoking antagonism or indifference (and thus obscuring his true achievements); and in not according his books that critical respect upon which, with his high, rigorous conception of the art of the novel, he himself would have insisted. A first-rate taste, Ford knew precisely what he *had*, and had *not*, achieved in his fiction. It is by balance, in the end, therefore, that Ford will be honored best.

But, of course, criticism that is thoroughly poised and detached is — finally — not possible. However objective the spirit in which the critic labors, the basis of his judgment must be subjective, dependent on his individual knowledge, experience, and sensibility. It cannot, indeed, be otherwise. Nor, in the end, is it even desirable. Without a point of view involved in the human condition, such writing must almost surely lack significance, color, and shape. Criticism has always been a kind of dialogue, in essence if not necessarily in form, between writer and reader. It is a conversation between minds of a different order which, if fruitful, sheds light that may not earlier have existed — a greater clarity, a quickened, more comprehending, even deepened, perception.

In this paradoxical faith, therefore — of the careful objectification of his own subjectivity — the author of this book has pursued his enterprise, with what creativity, penetration, and justice the individual reader must determine.

ACKNOWLEDGMENTS

In the writing of any such book as this, one's debts over a period of years steadily enlarge. And it is a pleasure, humanly and professionally, to acknowledge them in this place. First should come those whose influence was most central: Professor I. J. Kapstein of Brown University, who helped determine its organization, made valuable critical and stylistic comments, and who bracingly proclaimed that criticism itself should be a work of art; Professor James Franklin Beard, my colleague at Clark University, a trenchant, forthright, valuable commentator; and Dr. Carrie Hoffberg (now in the Department of Psychology, University of Michigan), who was extremely helpful as listener, encourager, and perceptive critic, and who has since emerged as a poet of remarkable power. In addition, the author is grateful to the diverse comments — critical, factual, or stylistic — of the following: Robie Macauley, editor of *The Kenyon Review*, in whose pages an abridged version of the discussion on the *Good Soldier* has already appeared, under the title, "The Saddest Story"; Professor Richard M. Ludwig of Princeton University; Professors Clyde K. Hyder, W. P. Albrecht, J. Neale Carman, and Robert G. Mahieu of the University of Kansas; Professor Samuel Middlebrook, Assistant Dean of the College, College of the City of New York; and, in particular, Professor Edward A. Bloom of Brown University. The writer has also profited from illuminating talks with Janice Biala, Ford's widow, and with Walter Allen, Edward Crankshaw, and Charles Kinross. And he is indebted to the support of David A. Jonah, chief librarian of Brown University, and to the enterprise of Robert Vosper, formerly Director of Libraries at the University of Kansas. Invaluable in the preparation of the final manuscript was Miss Jane Brookhart, now of San Francisco. And very helpful, at an earlier stage, was Mrs. Tilton Barron, of Worcester, Massachusetts.

To Mr. Allen Tate, the author owes a most special debt.

And, finally, he wishes to acknowledge the responsibility, skill, and resourcefulness of John Ervin, Jr., the director of the University of Minnesota Press, and of his staff — in particular, Miss Marcia Strout.

TABLE OF CONTENTS

FORD MADOX FORD'S NOVELS

i

FORD THE NOVELIST: ANGUISH AND CAT'S CRADLE

THE name of Ford Madox Ford runs through the fabric of the modern novel not unlike a master-thread, cutting importantly across the lives and careers of the chief novelists of his time. The list is almost a parade of twentieth-century fiction: Henry James — of whom Ford was disciple and persistent champion; Joseph Conrad — his intimate collaborator; D. H. Lawrence — whom Ford "discovered" and helped to launch so quickly; Ernest Hemingway — his editorial assistant on the *transatlantic review*; and James Joyce — a respecting friend, for whose *Finnegans Wake* Ford provided the famous provisional title, "Work in Progress."

Nor does the parade end, by any means, with such dominating figures. For Ford lived, down five decades, in continual, significant connection with a world of yet other important novelists — with writers like Stephen Crane, John Galsworthy, H. G. Wells, Wyndham Lewis, Glenway Wescott, Katherine Anne Porter, Caroline Gordon, Eudora Welty, Graham Greene, Robert Penn Warren, Jean Stafford (not to mention numerous worthy poets, most vividly Ezra Pound).[1]

In short, Ford's life was thoroughly engaged in the cause of contemporary literature, and the modern novel in particular. Probably no other single figure exerted a more meaningful and direct influence, practical and concrete, upon the fiction-writing of his time. Through his published work, his lectures, and, above all, his personal talk, he dedicated himself, in a less sophisticated age, to centering the attention of would-be writers on the overriding importance of knowing one's craft. And willingly he gave countless hours to the work of criticizing their manuscripts, of encouraging their labors, and of aiding them to publication. Ford's extraordinary generosity to aspiring authors has become, in fact, a legend: the "Only Uncle of the Gifted Young," [2] H. G. Wells called him as early as 1915 — a role which he played with immense credit until the very end of his life. And, for forty years, Ford was himself an active novelist, prolific, serious, and much admired. In the America and Paris of the twenties, his fiction indeed placed him among the reigning lions.

Yet, despite Ford's importance in the story of the modern novel, the niche to which he has been commonly assigned in contemporary literary history has not been that of a novelist. Instead he has been characterized as a brilliant literary editor and as a remarkable personality, Falstaffian and fabulous — his own best artistic creation. His works of fiction, the triumphs as well as the failures, have been on the whole neglected (or mentioned in passing as "interesting" experiments in technique), and he himself as novelist has often been scorned. Such an attitude, to be sure, is mistaken. But it is also understandable. For there are reasons, after all, for this neglect and this disdain, peripheral and accidental though they may be. For one thing, Ford wrote too much — in too many genres, and too quickly. And he repeated himself, particularly in his chatty, numerous memoirs, much too often. That the superb should have been obscured by the facile is not very surprising, therefore, or that his literary reputation should have been slated. Nor was his reputation assisted in his own lifetime by the "unwisdom," as Walter Allen has called it, with which he conducted his far too publicly exposed private life. To not a few sternly punctilious contemporaries, Ford was obviously a "bad hat"— unreliable in his facts, unstable in his behavior, and not always dependable in his money dealings. And to the literary estab-

lishment of his native country, he often appeared a palpable absurdity: pretentious and "Olympian," externally a conventional English
gentleman, but irritatingly "Continental" and "aesthetical" in his
views — and still worse for being so repeatedly, and gallic-mindedly,
disrespectful of the natural superiority of the British Character. In
short, Ford was a type (whether called Sir John or Sir Toby) plainly
objectionable to the severe, the unimaginative, and the humanly
humorless — of all nations, no doubt, but particularly of his own.
(Surely there is a kind of Malvolian obtuse comedy in those very
many earnest, righteous pages over the years, in books, magazines,
and newspapers, that have been devoted to correcting the "facts"
of Ford's numerous anecdotes — as though these delightful and
harmless stories were not being told simply because they *were* good
stories, and by a master raconteur who again and again declared that
he was not at all interested in facts but effects.)

Time, however, is restoring our perspective about the man and
his work. The unimportant has been sliding from view, the essential standing out more clearly; and we are growing better able to
see that a judgment which values Ford chiefly as a journalist and
personality is woefully inadequate. We are gradually realizing that
he is, at his finest, a distinguished novelist. More than that, we can
recognize that he merits an important place among the major writers of twentieth-century fiction, and that in this group he speaks
with a voice that is uniquely — beautifully and powerfully — his
own.

As a novelist Ford belonged (as he ceaselessly tells us) to the
French tradition of writing, the tradition of which Flaubert, teacher
of Maupassant, was the chief master, and whose important Anglo-
American descendants have been authors like James, Conrad, Joyce,
and Hemingway. It is the school which stresses craftsmanship — the
careful, suggestive, economic selection of incident and detail — and
which strives to approximate the aesthetic rigor and formal shapeli-
ness associated with poetry and the drama. And as a practitioner in
this tradition, Ford was a master, able to handle all of its exacting
demands freshly and with superb skill. What makes him unique as a

member of this school, however, is the kind of experience which he gives to us — the intensely emotional impact that distinguishes his best work. Almost alone among highly conscious artists of the novel, Ford has been passionately full-throated, generating and capturing an extraordinary depth of emotion and power. All the rewards that an aware, disciplined art can give, Ford has reaped: clarity and beauty of design, pace and intensification, economy of means and variety of effect, richness of texture and of surface. The aesthetic enjoyment of the reader, as a result, has been enormously enhanced, for he has been granted the heightened sense of pleasure, even of triumph, which comes from the fusion of the disparate, recalcitrant materials of a universe into order, balance, and proportion. Yet, at the same time that Ford was creating an art work of high formal beauty, he was also doing what neither James, Conrad, or even Flaubert (save in "Un Coeur Simple") could accomplish — either because of their temperament or their dominating allegiance to their aesthetic aims: which tended to make their actors more types and symbolic counters than vital, intensely living individuals. In his best work, in short, Ford engages unerringly and touches deeply our sense of pity and compassion for the human condition, absorbing us fully into the sufferings and intense sensibilities of his characters. In this power to seize his reader and wring his heart, Ford, indeed, is allied not so much to his masters as to quite different writers like Hardy and Dostoyevsky.

It is important to recognize, however, that this power of emotion in Ford's work has been achieved not despite but rather because of his allegiance to the French novel, whose principles, in fact, have only increased its intensity. Ford's subject matter and his technique are inseparable, each enhancing the other in an extraordinary fashion. "Anguish and Cat's Cradle" as image of Ford the novelist is therefore extremely fitting, for it crystallizes in one phrase the unique effect of his conjoined substance and form.

For "agony" is the emblem of Ford's spiritual universe. The word is, in fact, sounded again and again in his fiction, especially in *The Good Soldier* and *Some Do Not*. One source of this anguish was no doubt personal, springing from Ford's own stricken psyche. For as Ezra Pound has written of his friend's ultra-sensitive nature: "That Ford was almost an halluciné few of his intimates can doubt. He felt until it paralyzed his efficient action, he saw distinctly the Venus immortal crossing the tram tracks." [3] And the accuracy of this observation, particularly the closing image, any thoughtful reader of *The Good Soldier* will verify.

But this sense of pain in Ford's world also derives from a fairly objective vision of the decay, spiritual and material, of England in particular [4] and of the Western world in general. Himself emotionally committed to the values of a life he recognized to be dying — a life feudal, agrarian, local, scaled to human size — he looked with horror on the industrialized, giant, impersonal society which was emerging to take its place, and on the calculating, unrooted type of man he saw it producing. This theme of social decline was announced, indeed, almost at the outset of his career. This was in *The Inheritors* (1901), written with Conrad, in which Ford, its chief author, examined the cynical new attitude which the yellow press and men like Joseph Chamberlain had brought into British public life, the exploitive Boer War being one manifest symbol. This decay, the causes of which are by no means confined to a specific imperial group or governing class, he further detailed in such later novels as *An English Girl, Mr. Apollo, Ladies Whose Bright Eyes, The New Humpty-Dumpty,* and *Mr. Fleight.* In these books, Ford castigates the whole set of phenomena which characterize modern life as a result of the triumph of the bourgeois capitalistic industrial system: the profit motive, dishonest business and financial practices, the sensational popular press, ugly parliamentary politics, the tendency toward mediocre leveling, atheism, social climbing, industrialized urban life, and several varieties of socialism, Fabianism in particular.[5] In *The Good Soldier,* a book which dramatizes the emotional meaning of this change in the life of modern man, Ford's great theme, in fact, finds its quintessential rendering. And after the Great War of 1914–1918, whose devastation staggeringly dramatized this decline, the theme is even more pointedly treated in the Tietjens tetralogy and in the later post-1929 novels which reflect

the atmosphere of the world economic depression and the accelerating crisis of Western society.

The mark of the Fordian universe, its basic fact, is incompletion.
In his world, desire remains unfulfilled, thwarted doubly by the exterior conditions of life — its pointless vicissitudes, a blighting spiritual and social order, the insensitivity and cruelty of humankind —
and by the inability of his emotionally crippled figures to act and to
take. "We haven't learned wisdom," says one of Ford's characters
in A Call. "We've only learned how to behave. We cannot avoid
tragedies." More sadly still, there is not even the consolation of the
older tragedies: "In our day and in our class we don't allow ourselves easy things like daggers and poison bowls. . . . It's all more
difficult because it goes on and on." [6] Almost never in Ford is love
idyllic and tender. Relationships are always fragmented. If his men
and women love each other with some sweetness, they are separated
by circumstance. If they finally come together, one will be cruelly
dominant. Characteristically, the relationship will be one of unrest,
a failure in either or both of the partners — most often an aimless-
ness in the man and a devouring possessiveness in the woman. Passion, anguished and savage, lacerates them.

Ford's emotional stance toward his major theme of decay, as
with all writers, varied from book to book. Generally it was one of
pained helplessness, a pain masked frequently by irony, occasionally by humor. But his attitude was not always sadly acquiescent.
Though most often his protagonists are Hamlet figures, passive, ineffectual, there are notable exceptions. In his characterization of
Christopher Tietjens, for example (and, in a qualified way, in the
portrait of Edward Asburnham), Ford's stance takes on a heroic
cast, becoming a defiant reaffirmation of the worth and dignity of
those human values he intensely believed in: generosity and kindness, loyalty and responsible stewardship, the love of the creative
and agrarian arts. And, significantly, these instances of vivid conflict coincided with the occasions when Ford's own creative powers
were freest and most in function — when, in brief, his dexterity at
"cat's cradle" was highest.

The master metaphor of his form, "cat's cradle" was specifically, though subtly, used by Ford himself, in a scene of the *Fifth Queen* trilogy in which the old children's game is played by his chief characters. A player of the game, it will be recalled, interweaves a loop of string around the raised fingers of his hands, and a partner then carefully picks the string into a new formation about his own fingers; and so the cord is passed back and forth, with increasing tension, through a series of intricate patterns. Elsewhere, Ford used analogous images: in *A Call* it is lancers—a quadrille progressing through a fixed series of steps. Indeed, Ford's concern with formal patterning can be seen in his very first novel, written at eighteen, apparent in its title, *The Shifting of the Fire*, the glowing logs altering abruptly into a new configuration. So it is with the movement of Ford's novels. Their action advances not linearly but through a series of intricate, and surprising, turns. In this, of course, Ford's ends are particularly French, and modern. Writing of another school of novelists, that of Tolstoy and Dostoyevsky, Ford has acknowledged that they were story-tellers "with an unrivalled gift" [7] for rendering their scenes. But they chose those scenes, he added, without much consideration of whether they carry the story forward, or are of any use beyond the expression of passionate convictions. In the French school, on the other hand, "every incident, every word, every apparent digression, made towards the inevitable end. In that way a feeling of destiny was produced, a grim semblance of an implacable outside Providence." [8] A more formal statement by Ford of this gallic ideal of tight construction, which adds the important element of increasing tempo, is the following:

In writing a novel we agreed that every word set on paper—*every* word set on paper—must carry the story forward and that, as the story progressed, the story must be carried forward faster and faster and with more intensity. That is called *progression d'effet*, words for which there is no English equivalent. [9]

Such a novel, Ford argued, should consist "of one embroilment, one set of embarrassments, one human coil, one psychological progression," from which it gets its unity. And he added (very importantly for his own work) that the novel should proceed to one culmina-

tion which, generally in the last sentence or phrases, or the penultimate ones, reveals the psychological significance of the whole.[10]
("You will draw towards you the masterstring of that seeming
confusion, and the whole pattern of the carpet, the whole design
of the net-work will be apparent." [11]) After this may follow a coda
in which the tight pitch of the climax is released. The novel may
also have its caesura, or even several. "But these must be brought
about by temperamental pauses, markings of time when the treatment calls for them." [12] These pauses or digressions will give the
reader the opportunity to relax; but also, by tantalizing his attention with surprise, they will get him to wonder, "What the devil is
the fellow driving at?" The true fineness is to conceal the art of the
digressions — to make them seem like "real negligences, as they appear in the life we lead." [13] But such turnings-aside, Ford insisted,
should only be apparent: "not one single thread must ever escape
your purpose." [14]

It is these aesthetic principles and, still more to the point, his masterly application of them in his best work which have prompted
Caroline Gordon to say of Ford that he had "succeeded in doing
the thing that Poe said could not be done. He produced the long
work whose tensions are as nicely adjusted, whose tone is as sustained as that of the short tale or lyric poem." [15] High praise, surely
— and perfectly just. It is a kind of praise, indeed, which forces an
obvious, basic question: How has Ford accomplished this feat?
What are the means by which this "cat's cradle" effect of such high
artistic order has been won? The full appreciation of Ford's superb
and complex art can be meaningfully felt, of course, only through
close examination of the specific novel, for it involves his masterly
handling and modulation of many matters: of exposition, point of
view, character, narrative treatment and sequence, mood, style,
tone, rhythm, and the variety with which these are fitted together.
(And such elucidation will be one of the major tasks of this book,
notably in the sections on *The Good Soldier* and *Some Do Not* and
to a lesser degree on the *Fifth Queen* trilogy, *Mr. Apollo*, and *A
Call*.) But on none of these elements does Ford's achievement of

his intense narrative aims depend more than on the subtle and fascinating manner in which he unfolds his story.

In his earlier fiction the method consisted principally in withholding the full situation from the reader (and often from his major character) and only gradually exposing it. As Ford has written of the technique, which is essentially the method of the Henry James of *What Maisie Knew*, *The Turn of the Screw*, or *The Ambassadors*:

Supposing that your name is John, and that you have a friend called James, and for private reasons of his own James takes you into his billiard room and tries to shoot you with a rifle.

Now when that happens to you nothing in the outside world says to you, in so many words, "*That man is going to shoot me.*" What happens to you roughly is this. You are taken by your friend into a room. You perceive the greenish light thrown upwards from the billiard table. . . . Your friend talks. You answer. You are thinking of what he says; of what you are to answer. You perceive other objects; you perceive that some of the cues are not in the rack, and that the last game marked ended at 100 to 64. James says something else. You notice that his voice is rather high. You answer. You notice that you are saying to yourself, "I must keep my temper!" You also notice that the clock has stopped at 3.17 . . . So it goes on, the whole way through the incident — it is a mixture of things that appear insignificant and of real action. . . . To say that James took John into the billiard room would be statement for such a writer; to present the train of action would be art.[16]

The main dramatic tension in this example, it will be noted, rests in what is revealed as the situation unfolds through time. Characters, in their effort to find the key to unlock meaning, may recall past circumstances, but their persons and the incidents in which they take part are confined within the basic movement of an advancing present. Chronology is not broken. Later in his career, after 1914, Ford was to further complicate his story-telling by the adoption of the time-shift, a device which he has handled with probably more skill than any other practitioner, before or since. Ford's use of the time-shift varied considerably from novel to novel. In *The Good Soldier* it shifted from the focus of a disturbed and disordered narrator; in *Some Do Not*, from the point of view of the author. In still later novels, where it was joined with the current fashion of interior monologue, it shifted, though much less satisfactorily, on the principle of a random association of ideas. But in every case, Ford had for his aim the unfolding of his special cat's cradle narrative in an arresting, significant way. (For not one thread should ever be lost.)

Ford's view of his times, we have seen, was fundamentally unaccepting and critical. The whole body of his work makes that plain. Yet, paradoxically, the task which Ford set himself as a novelist (and which he urged on other writers) was the objective registering (*constatation*) of his age. His business, he said repeatedly, was to reflect, not to reflect on, his times. As Ford once put it, the novelist should be an exact scientist, never appearing, never buttonholing the reader, never moralizing. Nor should he twist his pictures of life — as do reformers like Wells, Galsworthy, or Shaw — to make it appear that "if the social state were what he desires it to be, all would be well with the world." [17] Whatever may be his private views — republican, Anglican, or autocratic — we should have no means of knowing them. Indeed, Ford went so far as to say "it is obviously best if you can contrive to be without views at all." [18] For they prejudice perception.

The artist content to register the life that we really live performs a service of immense value, Ford argued, since his work is concerned not with improving us, but with the truth, which is much more needed.[19] Under the conditions of modern life the necessity for a detached rendering of the world has become still more urgent. "So many small things crave for our attention that it has become almost impossible to see any pattern in the carpet." [20] Individuals have numerous casual contacts with their fellow men but much rarer intimacies. As a result, they have far less knowledge than before of how men really live. In a world grown highly complicated through limitless freedom of expression for all creeds and all moralities, it is the artist, concerned as he is with the values of life, who "can place before us how those creeds work out when applied to human contacts, and to what goal of human happiness those moralities will lead us." [21] By thoroughly exploring the meanings implicit within life's minute events —"by squeezing the guts out," as Conrad put it, of his human problem — the aloof novelist, examining society without preconceptions, may enable men to perceive more acutely the intricate predicaments that surround them.[22] That being done, readers may possibly draw their own lessons.[23]

The chief source of Ford's quarrel with traditional English novels —"nuvvles," he called them — was that they falsified life, with their external plots, simple psychology, and too easy morality. Instead of presenting men as they were, they dealt in heroes and villains, "those fabulous monsters." Such works amuse and entertain; they take us out of ourselves, "and when the hero bashes the villain one in the jaw we throw up our caps and shout 'hurray!' " But that, Ford adds, "has nothing to do — nothing on earth to do, with the world we live in." Regarded as conscious literature their value is "splendidly null." [24]

But if the novelist no longer allows himself to take sides with his characters, he very soon begins to see that such a thing as a hero does not exist —"a discovery that even Thackeray could make." "And, from there to seeing that it is not individuals that succeed or fail but enterprises or groups that do is a very small step to take. And then immediately there suggests itself the other fact that it is not the mere death and still less the mere marriage of an individual that brings to an end either a group or an enterprise." [25] His novel will not become, then, a rendering of the bashings of skulls, of plots, conspirings, piracies, of Wall Street panics, debauches, or the improbable rewards of virtue, nor the "arbitrary felicities of a central character." Instead, it will be a history of the "singular normalities" [26] of what Ford called an "affair"— a limited embroilment which takes its several characters at a certain period of their lives and leads them to the next. The novelist will proceed so because he (and everyone else) knows that that is what life really is — a matter of "affairs":

of minute hourly embarrassments; of sympathetic or unsympathetic personal contacts; of little-marked successes and failures, of queer jealousies, of muted terminations — a tenuous, fluttering, and engrossing fabric. And intangible! [27]

Ford's doctrine of detachment was, of course, an ideal which he himself did not attain in his actual practice, for a variety of reasons. There was in Ford's own, considerably journalistic spirit, for one thing, a good deal of the need to air "views." And to accommodate this impulse, while yet remaining within his critical code, he evolved (and on the evidence practiced) the theory that the author may create himself as a character of his book. "In his own pages he may stroll in and out amongst the figures, he may moralize upon their actions; he may, by his own actions, modify their psychological workings." The limit to this form of propagandizing will be interest, and the conscience of the novelist.

If he act indeed as a *deus ex machina* solving all problems set by the story, then the book must be regarded as a mere Utopia. But if the author, regarding himself as benevolent but meddlesome, fine yet malicious, generous but naturally unsound (or even supposing he psychologise himself as a villain, if he represent himself as marring fine destinies and making evil fortunes), then indeed this propagandist author will be giving us a rendering of modern life as exact as could be desired. He will be attempting to give us the world as he sees it — a world interesting to the measure of his personal value. He too will *constater*, not colour, the life of which he treats.[28]

Still more to the point, however, is the literal impossibility of such objectivity. "Mr. Conrad reveals himself as little in his books," Ford once wrote, "as does Shakespeare in his plays. Nevertheless no author, however rigid his technique of self-concealment, can conceal utterly his moral or material preferences — at least in his characters." [29] The comment applies no less to Ford's own work. By the very nature of selecting his materials, the artist will be composing a personal configuration which inevitably will express the structure of reality which he himself has perceived and responded to intellectually and emotionally — as any reader of such "aloof" writers as Flaubert, James, Conrad, Joyce, or Ford himself, must recognize.

Ford's emphasis on a philosophically detached *constatation* was undercut still further by two other doctrines. The first already has been hinted at, in his sentence: "He will be attempting to give us the world as he sees it — a world interesting to the measure of his personal value . . ." Ford's doctrine of the novelist as exact scientist is significantly different, therefore, from that set down by Zola in *Le Roman Expérimental*. Ford was well aware of the paradox of his position: that although an author seeks to avoid letting his personality appear, his whole work nevertheless will be "an expression of his personality." [30] Hence, Ford did not mean that the work of the artist should be a case history. "If you want to be a novelist," he wrote, "you must first be a poet and it is impossible to be a poet and lack human sympathies and generosity of outlook." [31] Indeed, a novel which does not express a personality, he felt, could have little worth. That is why, for all his dislike of *Tom Jones*, Fielding's novel was of greater value to him than *L'Assommoir*. "Since it is a more filtered work — since it is the product of the author's experience of life, whereas Zola's book is a product not of experience, but of tabulations —'Tom Jones' will probably have a more persistent vitality. It is a rendering of life; it is, such as it is, a picture of manners." [32]

Nor did Ford insist that the truth that the artist sees is the truth as it is absolutely. Whether his facts are right or wrong does not matter: the artist's business is to render rightly the appearance of things. "He is a sensitised instrument, recording to the measure of the light vouchsafed him what is — what *may* be — the Truth." [33] Whether he convinces his reader or arouses violent opposition is all one: "For the artist's views are of no importance whatever." The value of the artist lies not in facts but in his temperament. "The assembler of facts needs not temperament at all but industry. He does not suggest, he states, and save in the mind of professed thinkers, he arouses no thought at all. But the business of the artist is to awaken thought in the unthinking." As Ford saw it, the artist is the eternal mental prostitute standing in the market place, crying: "Come into contact with my thought, with my visions, with the sweet sounds that I cause to arise — with my personality." And, he observed, "the more men there are of his own type, the greater his sympathies, the greater [will be] the effect of his art upon the world." [34]

Thus, at bottom, Ford yielded to a mystery, life-long advocate of "technique" though he was. He could therefore say that Henry James decidedly possessed "his share of the talent which can't be defined," a talent which distinguishes a writer unmistakably from all others: "plenty of personality." James not only has, but *is*, a temperament. "You could no more confound him, say, with Théophile Gautier than you could confound Homer with Dante or with Quintus Horatius Flaccus." [35] Ford's understanding that the writer's personality will permeate his work, and draw or repel readers without regard to the craftsman's skill, can be seen again in another shrewd, self-appraising comment:

My friend on the New York *Times* calls me a master of the time-shift. He adds that a great many people dislike my books because I use that device. But he is mistaken. It is me they dislike, not the time-shift which is a thing that delights everybody. [36]

This recognition of the importance of personality in literature undoubtedly contributed greatly toward that tolerance of other artistic methods than his own which characterized Ford. Writing of Barrie and Shaw, for example, he observed that neither particularly rendered the life of his day.

Regarded philosophically, each of Mr Shaw's plays resolves itself into a variety entertainment in which character after character does his brilliant verbal "turn" and then retires into the background. It would be too extreme to say that this is the sole characteristic of Mr Barrie, for his chief, his distinguishing note, is the tenderness, the justness, of his sentimentality.

And sentimentality, he added, is as legitimate a medium as realism, pessimism, or cynicism. "If that be true to himself, if he be an artist of sufficient attraction, it will convince us of the reality of the story that he tells." And thus it is, Ford concluded, that

both Mr Shaw, who gives us real speeches producing an effective unreality, and Mr Barrie, who gives speeches in one evening more sentimental than any collection of real characters could utter in the course of a year—who convinces us, in fact, by very unreal means— both Mr Shaw and Mr Barrie do render some service to the Republic. The one quickens our emotions, the other our thoughts. [37]

It is this same Fordian tolerance, it should be added, which made him so valuable as a teacher. Technique was extremely important to him, and he constantly emphasized it, but not as an end in itself.

The significance of technique, he said, lay in its freeing power. It enabled those writers possessed of personality to discover the unique forms by which that personality, in its interaction with life, could most fully be expressed.

The other doctrine that qualified Ford's aim of an objective *constatation* was the necessity, which he often emphasized, that an author be interesting — that he please his reader. Above all, he insisted, the writer must not fail to capture and hold his reader's attention, for otherwise he will make no impression.

You will do this by methods of surprise, of fatigue, by passages of sweetness in your language, by passages suggesting the sudden and brutal shock of suicide. You will give him passages of dulness, so that your bright effects may seem more bright; you will alternate, you will dwell for a long time upon an intimate point; you will seek to exasperate so that you may the better enchant.[38]

Once the novelist has caught the reader's interest, he may inject into him what he wishes. "For you need not forget, when you write a novel, the gravity of your role as educator." "Only," he adds, "you must remember that in vain does the fowler set his net in the sight of the bird." [39]

The theory of *progression d'effet*, with its steady rise to climax, was in itself one method of holding the interest of the reader. And in his writings over the years, Ford set down still other hints: the vivid first appearance of major characters (usually by a revealing initial speech); the opening sentences of a tale in a tempo appropriate to its length; and a style which is continually interesting (the first, second, third, fourth, and fifth, business of style).[40] A good — an interesting — style, Ford wrote, will consist of "a constant succession of tiny unobservable surprises." These "slight crepitations of surprise, like the successive small explosions in a motor, keep the story running and lend to it actuality and life. They make it interesting at the third or fourth reading." [41] With such a stylistic ideal, of surprise crossed (as we shall see) with simplicity, it becomes easy to understand why Ford should have called Mark Twain "one of the greatest prose-writers the English language has produced." [42]

Yet despite these significant qualifications, the need for person-

ality and for being interesting, Ford's doctrine of *constatation* remained at the core of his intention. And from it certain narrative
principles followed. One, of course, was the ban on personal intrusion by the author, a commonplace of the Flaubert tradition. And
with a few minor exceptions, Ford's novels scrupulously obey this
tenet, at least within the text. His intrinsically discursive nature
found outlets for commentary, however, in various ways, such as
the dedicatory letters prefixed to ten of the novels and the one
epistolary epilogue; and in the titles given to the "parts" of his early
novels up to *The "Half Moon"* (1909).

Another, particularly Fordian, principle was the rejection of
authorial intrusion by way of an ornate and glittering style. The
charged prose of writers like Meredith, Pater, and Stevenson Ford
was always critical of, and this bias largely explains his early preference for the poetry of Christina Rossetti over that of her brother.
His own stylistic goal was to write as he said W. H. Hudson wrote:
"as simply as the grass grows." [43] Ford wanted to achieve a style so
simple and so naturally cadenced that it would be unnoticed.[44] The
rhetorical, the literary, the pompous, and the self-conscious were
to be excluded. Marching as he did under the banner of *le mot juste*,
Ford took pains to point out that this ideal did not mean "every
word a sparkler." [45] What it meant rather was that a passage of
good style "began with a fresh, usual word, and continued with
fresh, usual words to the end." [46]

With such an aim in mind it is not difficult to see why Ford rejected the involuted constructions of Henry James's final manner
and preferred his middle period — particularly *The Spoils of Poynton*, its stylistic culmination. As for Conrad's prose, that was a matter about which Ford was almost always silent, contenting himself
with urging his own views. Once, however, in *Return to Yesterday*, he did allow himself to hint an estimate. "Conrad produced
with agony and you saw how it was done," [47] he wrote, and noted
casually that his collaborator's English was "literary." [48] Such an
observation, in the light of Ford's ideal of language, was clearly not
praise.

As an avowed register of his times, Ford was obviously in the camp of the realists, but of the group which was less scientific and more poetic. The keystone of his intention lies in his statement that "the general effect of a novel must be the general effect that life makes on mankind." [49] The business of the novelist, as he put it, is "to produce an illusion of reality," [50] to "make each of his stories an experience." [51] (The reader should be kept entirely oblivious of the author's existence —"even of the fact that he is reading a book.") [52] And in order that a narration of events strike the hearer as an experience, the novelist must make them seem as nearly as possible as they would in nature itself. He ought not to give an annotated, rounded account of a set of circumstances — a chronicle formal and objectively corrected. Rather he should present "the record of the impression of a moment." [53] It is from this last conception that Ford's theory and practice earned from his contemporaries the name of "Impressionism."

At first dubious of such a label ("I don't know; I just write books . . ."), [54] Ford gave up resistance in time; and after 1914, when he published a long article on the subject, he often referred to himself as an impressionist — a member, as he saw it, of the same school of writers as Joseph Conrad, Henry James, Stephen Crane, Maupassant, and Flaubert. The inclusion of such names as James, Maupassant, and Flaubert should alert us, of course, to the fact that the Impressionism practiced by Ford in the ten years before 1914 is markedly different from that of novelists usually labeled Impressionists: authors writing after 1910 like D. H. Lawrence, Marcel Proust, Dorothy Richardson, Virginia Woolf. [55] It varies also, if less, from the work of such acknowledged Impressionists as Crane and Conrad, who wrote earlier.

By and large, the later writers differed from their predecessors in the importance they gave to the subjective. In an effort to render felt experience — what seemed to them the actual sensation of living — they scrapped much more of the abstracting, objective function. The change is a matter of emphasis and degree. Thus, for some, like Crane and Lawrence, the visual world tends to lack definition, its actuality distorted by imposed images which transfer our interest to the states of feeling of the protagonists. Crane's use of color splashes and startling metaphor in *The Red Badge of Courage* and *Maggie* (his description in "The Open Boat" of the waves as "barbarously abrupt" was praised endlessly by Ford), and Lawrence's passion for working through symbols are cases in point. Paul Morel in *Sons and Lovers* articulates Lawrence's impressionist aim. Explaining to Miriam why she prefers one of his sketches above the rest, Paul says: "It's more shimmery, as if I'd painted the shimmering protoplasm in the leaves and everywhere, and not the stiffness of the shape. . . . Only this shimmeriness is the real thing. The shape is a dead crust." (In such a passage can be seen how natural, once begun, is the subjective movement from visual intensity to the visionary, from a Flaubert through a Lawrence to a Virginia Woolf.) Other writers, like Dorothy Richardson, Virginia Woolf, Conrad Aiken, enter the character's mind, and limit themselves to rendering the unordered flow of mental associations that passes there, employing the technique known as stream of consciousness, or interior monologue. Proust, although he does not strictly use stream of consciousness, bases his entire method on the fact of the mind's involuntary wanderings. In most Impressionist work, conventional chronology does not count for much. Either time is considered of little real significance and is not emphasized, or it is broken, while the author shifts back and forth chronologically as the mental association determines the scene.

Concomitantly with this emphasis on the inner flow of life, the Impressionists tend to turn their backs on the tightly constructed novel developed by Flaubert and Turgenev and transmitted to writers like Maupassant and James and their followers. They reason that since life does not present itself to our apprehension as orderly, the novelist should not emphasize an artificial chain of cause and effect. However, since an author cannot jettison all aesthetic considerations, varying compromises with form become obligatory.

The Impressionism of the Ford who wrote before 1914, then, was relatively more objective. While he pursued the aim of rendering the impressions life conveys to the senses, he gave greater weight to "common-sense" objective modes of perception. In many ways, Ford's story-telling technique remained traditional. He did not employ interior monologue, partly because it was not yet developed, nor did he transfigure the external world into vibrating symbol. More important, chronology was unbroken.

The absence of the time-shift in Ford's writing prior to 1914 is on several counts surprising. For one thing, his own best work — *The Good Soldier* (1915) and the Tietjens series — employs distorted chronology brilliantly, and, indeed, the device is characteristic of all his novels, and several of his memoirs, published after 1914. Secondly, Ford, in his best-known chapter on technique, in *Joseph Conrad*, declares that the use of the time-shift had been developed by Conrad and himself:

It became very early evident to us that what was the matter with the Novel, and the British novel in particular, was that it went straight forward, whereas in your gradual making acquaintance-ship with your fellows you never do go straight forward. You meet an English gentleman at your golf club. He is beefy, full of health, the moral of the boy from an English Public School of the finest type. You discover, gradually, that he is hopelessly neurasthenic, dishonest in matters of small change, but unexpectedly self-sacrificing, a dreadful liar, but a most painfully careful student of lepidoptera and, finally, from the public prints, a bigamist who was once, under another name, hammered on the Stock Exchange. . . . Still, there he is, the beefy, full-fed fellow, moral of an English Public School product. To get such a man in fiction you could not begin at his beginning and work his life chronologically to the end. You must first get him in with a strong impression, and then work backwards and forwards over his past. . . . That theory at least we gradually evolved.[56]

That this assertion is true of Ford's collaborator at least, there can be no doubt: Conrad's violation of natural time-order is a contribution to the craft of the novel which has long been celebrated. In fairly commonplace forms — the simple flashback and the frame, used mainly for vivid exposition — it appears in his first published work, *Almayer's Folly*, and in several of his early short pieces. And in a more decided, more classic, way — in which the altering of time is the predominant condition of the presentation, and is intentionally provocative — it may be found, of course, in *Lord Jim*

(1900) and in later books: among them *Under Western Eyes* (1911) and *Chance* (1913). That Conrad's new systematic use of the time-shift was initiated not very long after the two men began their association (in October, 1898), and had launched their extensive, even endless discussions on the craft of the novel, is probably not, however, a chance.

Nevertheless, in Ford's own handling of the novel till 1914, he was much more Jamesian, time being managed as in the illustration of John, James, and the billiard room — the main dramatic tension lying in the revelation of meanings as the situation unfolds through time.

After 1914, Ford showed an increased focusing on the experience of the mind itself, with its backward and forward dartings. This new emphasis on the subjective, influenced in part at least by the literary trend of the times, can be seen in *The Good Soldier* of 1915. But it was already indicated in "On Impressionism" of the preceding year, where he presents an appeal for the rendering of superimposed emotions. It is perfectly possible, Ford wrote in that essay,

that a piece of Impressionism should give a sense of two, of three, of as many as you will, places, persons, emotions, all going on simultaneously in the emotions of the writer. It is, I mean, perfectly possible for a sensitised person, be he poet or prose writer, to have the sense, when he is in one room, that he is in another, or when he is speaking to one person he may be so intensely haunted by the memory or desire for another person that he may be absent-minded or distraught.

"Indeed," adds Ford, in a striking image,

I suppose that Impressionism exists to render those queer effects of real life that are like so many views seen through bright glass — through glass so bright that whilst you perceive through it a landscape or a backyard, you are aware that, on its surface, it reflects the face of the person behind you. For the whole of life is really like that; we are almost always in one place with our minds somewhere quite other.[57]

Hand in hand with this emphasis on the rendering of superimposed states of feeling went, of course, the time-shift itself. Ford experimented much with this technique after 1914 and employed it

differently in various novels, as we shall see. For the moment, however, we can gain an accurate sense of Ford's later Impressionism
by looking at a 1924 critical passage written to exemplify the
method of the school. In *Joseph Conrad*, he wrote:

Life does not say to you: In 1914 my next-door neighbour, Mr.
Slack, erected a greenhouse and painted it with Cox's green aluminum paint. . . . If you think about the matter you will remember,
in various unordered pictures, how one day Mr. Slack appeared in
his garden and contemplated the wall of his house. You will then try
to remember the year of that occurrence and you will fix it as August, 1914, because having had the foresight to bear the municipal
stock of the City of Liége you were able to afford a first-class season
ticket for the first time in your life. You will remember Mr. Slack —
then much thinner because it was before he found out where to buy
that cheap Burgundy of which he has since drunk an inordinate
quantity, though whisky you think would be much better for him!
Mr. Slack again came into his garden, this time with a pale, weaselly-
faced fellow, who touched his cap from time to time. Mr. Slack will
point to his house wall several times at different points, the weaselly
fellow touching his cap at each pointing. Some days after, coming
back from business, you will have observed against Mr. Slack's
wall. . . . At this point you will remember that you were then the
manager of the fresh-fish branch of Messrs. Catlin and Clovis in
Fenchurch Street. . . . What a change since then! Millicent had
not yet put her hair up. . . . You will remember how Millicent's
hair looked, rather pale and burnished in plaits. You will remember
how it now looks, henna'd; and you will see in one corner of your
mind's eye a little picture of Mr. Mills the vicar talking — oh, very
kindly — to Millicent after she has come back from Brighton. . . .
But perhaps you had better not risk that. You remember some of
the things said by means of which Millicent has made you cringe —
and her expression! . . . Cox's Aluminum Paint! . . . You remember the half-empty tin that Mr. Slack showed you — he had a
most undignified cold — with the name in a horseshoe over a blue
circle that contained a red lion asleep in front of a real-gold sun. . . .

And, if that is how the building of your neighbour's greenhouse
comes back to you, just imagine how it will be with your love affairs that are so much more complicated. . . .[58]

The contrast of this method of Impressionism with that of the
billiard-room passage, written in 1910, illustrates the extent of

change in Ford's theory. Where the focus of the earlier example went straight forward in space and time, this one ricochets erratically within the brain.

Although the analysis of Mr. Slack and his greenhouse is ostensibly supposed to clarify the nature of Conrad's Impressionism and the performance that earned the work of both collaborators that label, it is clear that the method involved — interior monologue essentially — was never that of Conrad nor, as we have seen, of the early Ford. Actually, Ford was explaining here his own current practice — the techniques he was then using in the Tietjens novels. Later in his last books, he was even to employ some of the flashing imagery that in modern writing ultimately derives from Crane.

Ford's novels after 1914 moved, therefore, much closer to pure Impressionism than can be found in his predecessors — with the possible exception of Crane, who worked much differently. But, in the last analysis, Ford probably should not be described as an Impressionist. What basically excludes him as such is his steady adherence to the ideal, learned from his Continental masters, of the tightly constructed novel. In that adherence he remained significantly traditional in his approach to the form.

Here, then, is the essential picture of Ford the novelist. In the following chapters the focus of our inquiry will turn to the specific works themselves, written over the course of more than thirty-five years. And, as we shall see, these books will tell a variously unfolding story. They will give us, for one thing, an expressive, fascinating picture of the evolving spiritual history of the first third of this century — since, true to his doctrine, Ford always sought to reflect his age in his novels. His own pessimistic attitude toward his times remained constant, it is true, but the atmosphere of his works very much changed. From decade to decade, in fact: from Edwardian to early Georgian, and from post-war twenties to depression thirties. But, of course, the most dramatic dividing was the war of 1914–1918.

These novels also tell the more personal, always interesting story of a writer engaged in finding his way — of his progress on the road to mastery, from callow apprentice to competent journeyman to resonant artist. For Ford this progress was to be slow and uncertain, as we shall see. One cause of this delay of full fruition, the economic, is extremely familiar to the literary life. Needing to write for his living Ford did not have the time to perform the careful labor required by a true work of art. Between 1907 and 1913, for example, he published no fewer than thirteen novels, not to mention eleven other books, voluminous articles for various periodicals, and his heavy work as editor of *The English Review*. (The delay in fulfillment is likely to seem more pronounced also because Ford's career as a writer had such a very youthful beginning.)

Probably most significant, however, was Ford's profound lack of self-confidence. "He was all too ready . . . to feel discouraged when things went wrong," Stella Bowen has written, "and he found so many reasons for feeling frightened." [59] When there was bad news, "the air would be so filled with pain that we could neither of us do any work at all." [60] And Miss Bowen adds: "He needed more assurance than anyone I have ever met." [61] Ford did not possess, in short, the force of character and will of a Conrad, who despite illness and hypochondria could push on with his work at high standards. (Indeed, Ford's experience of the strong personality of Conrad only seems to have increased his insecurity.) "Writing up to my own standards," Ford himself has commented, "is such an intolerable labour and such a thankless job . . ." [62] It is not surprising, therefore, that, so equipped, and powerfully buffeted by life as he was, Ford should lack that self-assurance which the artist needs to face the rigors of his task. Another handicap was his very facility with words, for too often it enabled Ford to avoid wrestling with difficult problems, and it led him once to say that he wrote better in French, since he then had to think more about the words he chose. It also explains the paradox of such a prolific writer's remarking of himself that he had always been lazy.

Yet, despite these handicaps, personal and economic, Ford's powers steadily grew. In his constant writing and conversation over the years, he was experimenting with many elements of structure and style. And when the various favorable circumstances came together, he was ready to draw on his researches to powerful and original advantage. The lesser novels will be worth our study, therefore, because they reveal the deepening command of a writer who from the first was peculiarly conscious of the problems of technique. Such an inquiry will also enable us to see the best work in firmer perspective.

THE HISTORICAL NOVELS

Ford was an instinctive romancer. His first published book — it appeared when he was still seventeen — was a fairy tale, called *The Brown Owl*. And before he was twenty-one, he had issued two others, even more charming. A fourth would follow later. And during his career he was to write no less than ten books of historical fiction, and to subtitle two of his other novels "A Romance"— though not without irony. His first historical novel was *Seraphina*, begun in 1896, but not to reach print until seven years later. By then it would be called — significantly enough — *Romance*, and have acquired an imposing co-author. It is with this joint enterprise that our story of Ford's historical fiction, and his novels in general, may most usefully begin.

Romance: Collaborating with Conrad

Written with Joseph Conrad — and the best of their three collaborations — *Romance* (1903) is the earliest of Ford's historical novels, and the least typical. "A rattling good story," [1] as David Garnett has called it, the book teems with physical action and exciting adventure — indeed, with more of it than in all of the rest of Ford's historical fiction combined. Pirates and smugglers, enraged mobs, and intensely romantic characters sweep through its pages; and violent deaths, Cuban caves and dungeons, wild sea storms, ship boardings, kidnappings and tense escapes, sword and pistol play, and love and jealousy, not to mention the climax of a piracy trial in the Old Bailey, are its basic elements. Its title was not selected idly. And the reader who discovers that in *Romance* Ford's partner took his most active role will not be surprised: the book is plainly much more Conradian than Fordian.

Begun before the two had met, the original novel was completed by at least November, 1898. For on the seventeenth of that month Conrad wrote to Ford that he would be "very very pleased to hear *Seraphina* read," and added that afterwards he would read it himself.[2] Ford's account of that reading is instructive. Conrad, he writes, had expected a work as popular as *Treasure Island* and as "written" as *Salammbô*—to which "a few touches of description, sea atmosphere, mists, riggings and the like"[3] would be all that was needed. But instead Ford had composed a strange *tour de force* in which a very old man meditated upon his youth and its romance. ("It was like the whisper of a nonagenarian. . . . Every sentence had a dying fall and every paragraph faded out."[4]) Conrad was deeply disappointed. "But why choose such a subject?" he cried — disgusted "at the criminal who could take hold of such a theme and not . . . extract from it every drop of blood and glamour"—"a Book turned into the dry bone of a technical feat."[5] Yet he was apparently unwilling to give up such promising material. For a later synopsis of *Seraphina*, signed by both, bears the comment that the story "shall be greatly advanced if not absolutely finished in July, 1899."[6] Work on *Romance*, however, was not actually begun, though there were many preliminary discussions, until the December of 1900 — after *The Inheritors*, written mainly by Ford, was all but completed.

At which point there followed a period of intense and protracted labor, which was to last for more than two years, and to involve numerous struggles between two writers who were sharply disparate in their temperaments. Ford's continual aim was to tone down: "ever on the watch to suppress the melodramatic incident and the sounding phrase."[7] Conrad, on the other hand, sought inclusion and highly dramatic effects. ("Give! Give!" he would cry,

Ford tells us. "You must invent. You have got to make that fellow"—their young English hero, John Kemp —"live perpetually under the shadow of the gallows.") In the original, Kemp merely left England as a seaman; in the synopsis, he recklessly joins some smugglers in a "tub-raising expedition," founders, and is picked up by an outward-bound ship; but in the finished book, he flees the country to escape imprisonment. Similarly, on the island of Jamaica: In the earlier versions, Kemp was still only a planter's apprentice —"insufficiently hangable." [8] But under his partner's prodding, Ford rummaged through the Jamaican newspapers of the time and discovered a faction which had wanted the island to be annexed by the United States. Immediately Conrad's political imagination became fired, and Kemp was promptly identified — mistakenly, to be sure — with that group.

This at once made our leading character handleable by Conrad. John Kemp merely kidnapped by pirates and misjudged by the judicial bench of our country was not so vastly attractive, but a John Kemp who was in addition a political refugee, a suspect of High Treason and victim of West India merchants. . . . That was squeezing the last drop out of the subject. . . . So, by that moment, we had worked John Kemp into a position that can have been occupied by very few unjustly accused heroes of romance. When he stood in the Old Bailey Dock he had the whole legal, the whole political, the whole naval forces of the Crown, the whole influence at once of the City of London and of the Kingdom of Spain determined to hang him.[9]

Conrad's impulse toward inclusion and heightened tension — quite clearly — was dominant.

But *Romance* is no more pure Conrad than pure Hueffer. Ford has written of the "third artist" who emerged from their work together, and Conrad has spoken of their ideal of "welded" collaboration.[10] And no doubt there is real meaning to these concepts. Yet the over-all impression the novel creates is one of disharmony. In vision, tone, and diction, and in narrative style, *Romance* is a mélange, the struggles between the two temperaments being not so much concealed in the final product as made evident.

Nor is this disparity very surprising. To begin with, the different sections of the book — of which there are five — were drafted more or less independently. The first two and the fifth Parts were conceived by Ford; whereas Conrad was mainly responsible for Part Three ("about 60 per cent," he has acknowledged) and entirely so for Part Four ("both in conception and writing," according to Ford). In the process, the novel became greatly altered from the version Conrad first listened to: names were changed, new characters introduced, old incidents reshaped, and entirely new sequences interpolated. And it is between these differently conceived parts that, naturally enough, the more obvious evidence of mixed purpose is found. To be sure, Ford has cautioned that this assignment of responsibility is accurate "if conception alone is concerned," and he has pointed out that a draft completed by one would be worked over by the other — and that all the parts except the fourth "are a singular mosaic of passages written alternately by one or other of the collaborators." [11] Yet, nevertheless, a deeply rooted incongruity between the separately written parts is unmistakable.

Probably the most striking variance is in the handling of the visual. Conrad's world is rendered with extreme physical clarity and vividness — an effect deriving chiefly from his handling of space. Conrad is particularly fond, for example, of composing a stage of fixed points upon which his actors perform — dramatically interrelating with each other and, even more, with such material objects as the sea, masts, cliffs, mist, or deck railings. It is, in fact, through their motion in juxtaposition with these points of reference, or in static poses which are elaborately detailed, that Conrad's characters take on much of their definition and vital energy. Chapter VIII of Part Four contains an especially brilliant example. Having spied two hostile pirates approaching, Kemp and his beloved Seraphina plunge into their sheltering cave.

The rocky ground under our feet had a gentle slope, then dipped so sharply as to surprise us; and the entrance, diminishing at our backs, shone at last no larger than the entrance of a mouse-hole. We made a few steps more, gropingly. The bead of light disappeared altogether when we sat down, and we remained there hand-in-hand and silent, like two frightened children placed at the center of the earth. There was not a sound, not a gleam. Seraphina bore the crush-

ing strain of this perfect and black stillness in an almost heroic immobility; but, as to me, it seemed to lie upon my limbs, to embarrass
my breathing like a numbness full of dread; and to shake that feeling off I jumped up repeatedly to look at that luminous bead, that
point of light no bigger than a pearl in the infinity of darkness. And
once, just as I was looking, it shut and opened at me slowly, like the
deliberate drooping and rising of the lid upon a white eyeball.

Someone had come in.

We watched side by side. Only one. Would he go out? The point
of light, like a white star setting in a coal-black firmament, remained
uneclipsed. Whoever had entered was in no haste to leave. Moreover, we had no means of telling what another obscuring of the
light might mean; a departure or another arrival. . . .[12]

Ford's physical world, on the other hand, is much more indistinct
and subjective. Through his fondness for unusual, slightly startling
imagery it takes on an aspect that is more intellectual than visual.
An excellent illustration is the climax of the trial scene in Part Five,
when Kemp addresses the court:

I remembered that in my cell I had reasoned out that I must be very
constrained; very lucid about the opening. . . . I *did* keep cool; I
was lucid; I spoke like that. I had my eyes fixed on the face of the
young girl upon the bench. I remember it so well. Her eyes were
fixed, fascinated, upon my hand. I tried to move it, and found that
it was stuck upon the spike on which I had jammed it. I moved it
carelessly away, and only felt a little pain, as if from a pin-prick;
but the blood was dripping on to the floor, pat, pat. Later on, a man
lit the candles on the judge's desk, and the court looked different.
There were deep shadows everywhere; and the illuminated face
of Lord Stowell looked grimmer, less kind, more ancient, more impossible to bring a ray of sympathy to. Down below, the barristers
of the prosecution leaned back with their arms all folded, and the
air of men resting in an interval of cutting down a large tree. The
barristers who were merely listeners looked at me from time to
time. I heard one say, "That man ought to have his hand bound up."
I was telling the story of my life, that was all I could do. . . .

I seemed to be back again in Cuba. Down below me the barristers
were talking. The King's Advocate pulled out a puce-colored ban-
dana, and waved it abroad preparatorily to blowing his nose. A
cloud of the perfume of a West Indian bean went up from it, sweet
and warm. I had smelt it last at Rio, the sensation was so strong that
I could not tell where I was. The candles made a yellow glow on

the judge's desk; but it seemed to be the blaze of light in the cell where Nichols and the Cuban had fenced. I thought I was back in Cuba again. The people in the court disappeared in the deepening shadows. At times I could not speak. Then I would begin again.[13]

Another difference is the extent to which the material is worked over and filled out. That Parts Three and Four comprise almost sixty per cent of the book points to a truth found in the reading — Conrad's imperative to develop his material is much the stronger. The description of the cave is a splendid example in brief compass, each sentence adding a new twist. The light at the cave opening is first a mouse-hole, then a luminous bead, a pearl in the infinity of darkness, a white eyeball, and finally an uneclipsed white star setting in a coal-black firmament. Having arrived at the conception, Conrad rings all the changes. Ford's elaboration of his material is much less thoroughgoing. Consequently his narrative moves much more rapidly; but his world is far less solid and real.

Nor is the disharmony felt only between the parts. As these two markedly different personalities labored alternately over a section, the prose at times became a strange amalgam. Particularly is this true of Parts One and Two. Dominated by the low-keyed, sometimes farcical Fordian manner, it betrays the more readily the intrusion of Conrad's forceful, distinctive note. The reason for this entry is evident enough. Conrad wanted to vivify a moment or an impression which seemed vague in Ford, as may be seen in the passage which opens Part Five (Conrad's insertions are italicized):

"Why have I been brought here, your worships?" *I asked with a great deal of firmness.*

There were two figures in black, the one beside, the other behind a large black table. I was placed in front of them between two soldiers, in the centre of a large, gaunt room, with bare, dirty walls, and the arms of Spain above the judge's seat.

"You are before the Juez de la Primiera Instancia," said the man in black beside the table. He wore a large and shadowy tricorn. "Be silent, and respect the procedure."

It was, without doubt, excellent advice. He whispered some words in the ear of the Judge of the First Instance. It was plain enough to me that the Judge was quite an inferior official, who merely decided whether there was any case against the accused; *he had, even to his clerk, an air of timidity, of doubt.*

I said: "But I insist on knowing. . . ."

The clerk said: "In good time . . ." And then, *in the same tone of disinterested official routine*, he spoke to the Lugareño, who, from beside the door, *rolled very frightened eyes* from the judges and the clerk to myself and the soldiers —"*Advance*." [14]

That Conrad's interpolations and changes often enhance the effectiveness of a particular scene cannot be doubted, but it is at a large cost. For not being in tune with the rest of the style, these added words, phrases, sentences, and paragraphs tend to give an effect of inflation, of the empty rhetorical beating of tom-toms. Heightening is done for heightening's sake. And the very competence of Conrad's diction, with its vigor and dramatic flair, has yet another unfortunate consequence. Erupting into Ford's much vaguer, less forceful prose ("large, gaunt room," "large and shadowy tricorn") it makes that prose over the length of pages seem still paler. The style being thus at odds and drawing attention to itself, the experience which that style transmits inevitably becomes blurred and slightly artificial, and the illusion of reality dims. Hence, the overwrought, and even turgid, effect of the opening page:

To yesterday and to-day I say my polite "vaya usted con dios." What are these days to me? *But that far-off day of my romance, when from between* the blue and white bales in Don Ramon's darkened storeroom, at Kingston, *I saw the door open before the figure* of an old man with the tired, long, white face, *that day I am not likely to forget. I remember* the chilly smell of the typical West Indian store, the *indescribable* smell of damp gloom, of locos, of pimento, of olive oil, of new sugar, of new rum; the glassy double sheen of Ramon's great spectacles, the piercing eyes in the mahogany face, *while the tap, tap, tap of a cane on the flags went on behind the inner door*; the click of the latch; the stream of light. *The door, petulantly thrust inwards, struck against some barrels. I remember the rattling of the bolts on that door, and* the tall figure *that appeared there*, snuff-box in hand. In that land of white clothes that precise, ancient Castilian in black was something to remember. The black cane that had made the tap, tap, tap dangled by a silken cord from the hand whose delicate blue-veined wrinkled wrist ran back into a foam of lawn ruffles. *The other hand paused in the act of conveying a pinch of snuff to the nostrils of the* hooked nose that had, on the skin stretched tight over the bridge, the polish of old ivory; the elbow pressing the black cocked hat against the side; the legs, one bent, the other bowing a little back — *this was the attitude of Seraphina's father.*[15]

By now, it should be clear that *Romance* is an art work in considerable disarray. And from the analysis also has emerged the distinct suggestion that the novel's superior talent is Conrad's — in the mounting and in the development of detail, and in the power to dispose his material dramatically. In addition, Conrad is far more able to communicate that dramatic force through his language. Ford's style in *Romance*, in the main, lacks energy. Its prose rhythms limp, in contrast to Conrad's punctuated phrase groups and rich coils of breathless sentences. Here is Ford, for example, describing Kemp in a knock down, drag out shipboard fight:

Twenty men flung themselves upon my body. I made no movement. The end had come. I hadn't the strength to shake off a fly, my heart was bursting my ribs. I lay on my back and managed to say, "Give me air." I thought I should die.[16]

So different, in fact, is the quality of achievement between the Conradian and Huefferian parts that each can be used to illustrate classic critical observations about the effectiveness of the first-person narrator — but on different sides. Ford's work demonstrates almost all the defects of the point of view. In the first two Parts and in much of the third, John Kemp is formless, without personality or perceptible shape. Having neither insides nor outsides, he does not exist; and as a result what Kemp describes also lacks definition. In Conrad's sections, on the other hand — and most particularly in Part Four — Kemp lives with a rich, pulsing vitality. So intense are his reactions to his environment and his various plights, and so defined are his responses to his world physically, that the reader feels his experience with remarkable directness.

Nor is Kemp's actuality in Conrad's hands weakened by the first-rate narrative in which he has in Part Four involved him. This "splendid" and "matchless" section — the adjectives are Ford's —

constitutes the high point of the novel, and is one of the greatest sequences of adventure-writing rising to poetry in Conrad. It, if not notably the rest of the book, is what will keep *Romance* as a novel alive.

In the creation of this work, then, Ford's was decidedly the lesser talent. But, having said this, we should make certain qualifying comments. It should be understood, to begin with, that in the world of *Romance* Ford was not in his appropriate element. As one moves down the lengthy canon of his novels, one is struck with how infrequently they contain scenes of physical action and suspense. Although Ford wrote a total of eight historical novels — a genre in which adventure is almost mandatory — he rarely presented physical struggles, and when he did, their management was normally oblique. And his other novels are almost entirely free of such material. It is thoroughly characteristic of Ford that his so-called war novels, those of the Tietjens cycle, have the very barest minimum of battle writing. Almost all of it is concentrated in *A Man Could Stand Up*, and is there indirect and without appeal to sensation.

For Conrad, on the other hand, the adventurous, exotic material of *Romance* was his true climate. From *Almayer's Folly* down the long roll of his work to *Suspense* the pages of his fiction are rich with romantically exciting action — to a degree of glowing success that surely few writers in world literature can equal. The crew clinging to the vertical deck of the *Narcissus*; the African savages propped in the overhanging trees and raining spears at the steamboat paddling up the Congo to Kurtz's trading station; the whole long Patna incident and Brown's desperate band besieged on their hill in *Lord Jim*; the silver-lighter episode in *Nostromo*; Razumov's terrified encounter with Haldane in *Under Western Eyes*; the tense closing scenes of threatened murder aboard ship in *Chance*; the excitement of sea stories like *Typhoon*, *Youth*, *The Secret Sharer*, and *The Shadow-Line* — these are a few highlights of Conrad's splendid talent for exciting adventure.

Ford's province as a novelist lies elsewhere. It is the study of society and the psychological interactions of its members — an area for which *Romance* gave little scope. To understand this, one has only to examine works like *The Benefactor*, *A Call*, *The Good Soldier*, and the Tietjens books, or any of the social satires. Ford's historical novels are mainly psychological in their interest. And it is significant that the Fifth Part of *Romance*, which is predominantly psychological, is the most effective of Ford's three sections.

Curiously enough, it is just this more traditional subject matter of the novelist, the interplay of society, that is almost entirely lacking in Conrad's work. His characters are nearly always uprooted, transient men; most usually they are set in alien contexts, largely in the East, on occasion in Africa, once in Central America, and another time in Russia and Geneva. Almost never are they integrated in the society around them, but stand in isolation, relating cosmically to some ideal. If ever they are part of a functioning community it is aboard a ship where the social order is clearly marked militarily. When his characters are set in England, as in *The Secret Agent* and *Chance*, the situation is little altered. Conrad's London in *The Secret Agent* is a magnificent imaginative creation — a benighted Utrillo — but, as has been pointed out, it is not the British capital. His London is the Modern City of the mind rather than a specific place. The figures who move through its stylized, brooding streets — the anarchists, the Professor, the Inspector, the Verlocs — take their larger than life-sized vitality from their political and ideological symbolism rather than their personal qualities. As for *Chance*, Conrad's London there is essentially a background — one more dramatic stage setting, but not fundamentally integral. Only rarely did Conrad try to do the social scene, and then with little success. His early story, "The Return" has been an embarrassment to Conrad as well as his critics. *The Sister* is unfinished. And *The Nature of a Crime*, his third collaboration with Ford, was given a quick death after two installments in *The English Review*. It is significant that Conrad's women seldom convince one of their reality, but are created in the vein of sentimentality or semi-Dickensian caricature. His conception of a woman is rarely as a human being, but as a symbol of loveliness, inspiration, or rest. And with such a presentation it is not surprising that they fail to relate with the other characters, and in particular with the men they are supposed to love. Indeed in Conrad very few relationships — the crucial stuff of the social novelist — are rendered more than superficially at all. Obviously they were not his forte. With his young partner, of course, it was to be quite otherwise.

But the inappropriateness for Ford's talents of the materials of *Romance* is not the whole story of his weaker performance. *The Inheritors*, his other collaboration with Conrad of the period, in which Ford was by far the chief contributor, focuses on the social scene and its treatment is fundamentally psychological. Yet it is not notably effective. Though on the whole it is of a piece and well written, it leaves a thin and faint impression, a study, as Ford later said ruefully, in silverpoint. Another qualifying factor therefore must be considered: Ford next to Conrad was at that time without question a callow, inexperienced youth both in years and in the kind of life he had led. In boyhood Conrad had been exiled with his parents to Russia because of his father's fight for Polish independence; as an adolescent in France he had joined the romantic conspiracy to restore Don Carlos to the Spanish throne; and for twenty years after that adventure he led a rich, exacting life on the sea, rising from grade to grade until he won his captain's certificate. It was a career thrusting upon him discipline and the character-forming responsibilities of command. In December, 1900, when the collaboration on *Romance* was begun, Conrad was forty-three, fifteen and a half years older than his partner. Ford's twenty-seven years, by contrast, were sheltered ones. Born with a literary silver spoon in his mouth, he had already published several volumes of various kinds and had frequently contributed to magazines. His personality, from all indications, was still undefined: he was, as he tells us, extremely late in coming to maturity. Yet when he was to reach the age his partner had been when they had worked together, Ford would have to his credit such impressive work as *A Call* and *The Good Soldier*. And he would be engaged in that experience apart from the literary milieu — World War I — which was to be his equivalent for the rich, toughening existence that had been Conrad's. The creative spans would be overlapping. Thus, at the time when Conrad, having put his best writing behind him, would be in a grave literary decline, Ford would be beginning to compose his largest work — the Tietjens series.

The three products of the collaboration of Ford and Conrad scarcely rank among the important achievements of either alone. Part Four of *Romance* adds luster to Conrad's record, but the rest of the novel is insufficiently rendered. *The Inheritors* is not only too thin, but also a dated *roman à clef*. And *The Nature of a Crime* is, saying nothing more, too slight. What, therefore, should be our estimate? Was the whole collaborative enterprise a fiasco and a mistake? Or was the enterprise worth while? The latter, without question.

The value of the partnership should not be looked for in its signed productions but rather in the salutary influence it had on the rest of the partners' work. To say that the younger man taught the older the art of the novel, as has been on occasion argued, is absurd; before Conrad joined with Ford he had already written *The Nigger of the "Narcissus."* What Ford did help Conrad with was his handling of English idiom, teaching him a more native usage and helping him to write more fluently than before. That he actually did have a favorable influence on Conrad's writing is clear enough from a comparison of the rhetorical, redundant prose of *Lord Jim* with the much cleaner, lighter style of *Nostromo*. Ford also provided Conrad with a sounding-board, a highly intelligent, testing consciousness, which must have been completely invaluable for him as he launched into the complexities of the creation of a *Nostromo* or *The Secret Agent*. That the two men spent countless hours discussing literary problems is an unquestioned fact well testified to by both.

As for Ford, the experience of the collaboration was crucial. "If I know anything of how to write," he has commented, meaning the technical side of writing, "almost the whole of that knowledge was acquired then." [17] He has also observed, in a letter to Herbert Read, that if it had not been for Conrad he would have been a mere continuation of Pre-Raphaeliteism. And elsewhere he wrote: "I owe a great deal to Conrad. But most of all I owe to him" the strong faith in the conception of the novel as a work of art —"that in our day and hour the writing of novels is the only pursuit worth while for a proper man. That was his strong faith and certainly it communicated itself to me." [18]

In the experience of collaborating with Conrad, therefore, Ford plunged deeply into the mysteries of his art. As a craftsman, he came out with enormously heightened competence. And as a consciousness he had been rubbed in daily contact with a personality of whose force he was in considerable awe. Ford was still a tentative person himself, but from the struggle he was taking on shape. And in the years after *Romance*, his powers as a novelist deepened. His next independent novel, *The Benefactor*, displays increased capacity. And steadily in his career he moved toward Conrad's greater sharpness of effect, not imitatively but adapted to his own special milieu. Gradually, too, his fictional world began to take on greater vividness, to generate more color, and to reach out more directly to the imagination of the reader.

The first area in which this greater color makes itself felt is in that genre of his novels which most demands it — the historical. In them, Ford begins to play with a richer palette, even as his modern novels remain essentially toned down. It is time then to turn to Ford's independent historical novels.

But before looking at these directly, we must examine their author's complex relationship to his native country. For "the theme of England" is central not only to the historical novels but also, as we shall see, to Ford's entire canon.

Ford and England

In one of Ford's literary memoirs of the thirties, he describes a conversation of his young manhood — he places it in 1898 — in which a fellow English author tried to explain why Ford did not like *Punch* or Charles Lamb. It was, the acquaintance said, because he was "not really English." At the time Ford protested vigorously. But he concedes that there must have remained afterwards in his subconscious a growing conviction "that I was not English" ("not merely 'not really English'" but "Not English at all"). And he adds: I never had much sense of nationality. Wherever there were creative thinkers was my country. A country without artists in words, in colours, in stone, in instrumental sounds — such a country would be forever an Enemy Nation. On the other hand every artist of whatever race was my fellow countryman — and the compatriot of every other artist. The world divided itself for me into those who were artists and those who were merely the stuff to fill graveyards.[19]

Although addressed to an American audience and made when he was sixty, this commentary is nevertheless fairly just. German on his father's side and in his name, with many ties of family in Germany, and oriented culturally under his grandfather's tutelage toward the French, Ford was cosmopolitan. His major literary friendships and admirations were all non-English — Conrad, Stephen Crane, Henry James, W. H. Hudson, Ezra Pound, to mention only those formed when he still made his home in his native land. In the years immediately before the war he was, to gain a divorce, even prepared to give up his British citizenship. And there was, of course, his editorship of the internationally-minded *transatlantic review.*

Yet, paradoxically, Ford's love for England ran extremely deep — so much so that it may be described without distortion as a unifying principle of his creative work. For down the years England and its affairs was, with a few late exceptions, his primary subject and, it might be said, his deepest passion. This emotion for his native country can be seen most directly in his long poem, "Footsloggers." In its opening line, the question is asked: "What is love of one's land?" And the soldier-speaker of the poem, riding on the 1:10 train to embark for France and the war, thinks:

> "In two days' time we enter the Unknown,
>   And this is what we die for!"
> And thro' the square
> Of glass
> At my elbow, as limpid as air,
> I watched our England pass . . .
> The great downs moving slowly,
> Far away,
> The farmsteads quiet and lowly,
> Passing away;
> The fields newly mown
> With the swathes of hay,

And the wheat just beginning to brown,
Whirling away . . .
And I thought:
"In two days' time we enter the Unknown,
But *this* is what we die for . . . As we ought . . ."
For it is for the sake of the wolds and the wealds
That we die,
And for the sake of the quiet fields,
And the path through the stockyard gate . . .
That these may be inviolate,
And know no tread save those of the herds and
    the hinds . . .

And the ending of the poem is the most explicit of all. "What is love of one's land?" it asks again:

Ah, we know very well
It is something that sleeps for a year, for a day,
For a month, something that keeps
Very hidden and quiet and still,
And then takes
The quiet heart like a wave,
The quiet brain like a spell,
The quiet will
Like a tornado, and that shakes
The whole being and soul . . .
Aye, the whole of the soul.[20]

Written during the Christmas season of 1917, "Footsloggers" is of course a war poem, drawing its strength out of an upwelling of patriotic emotion for an England embattled. Douglas Goldring is just enough when he comments that the war evoked in Ford "a simple 'schoolboy' patriotism not very far removed from Rupert Brooke's." [21] But this intensification was of a love which was always there — hidden and quiet, but not overly so. Only this basic feeling could explain the impulse, for example, which fairly early drew Ford to compose those three thoughtful, often brilliantly written studies of his homeland which were gathered together under the title of *England and the English: An Interpretation* (1907) —"The Soul of London" (1905), "The Heart of the Country" (1906), and "The Spirit of the People" (1907). And one need only peruse the editorials which he wrote for the aptly named *English Review* to realize how deeply Ford — who held the faith that "only from the arts can any safety for the future of the State be found" [22] — was concerned with the necessity of arousing a literary ferment in England. Ford's patriotic sensibility appears again in what he calls his "quite naive and perfectly genuine" [23] description of his feelings while watching George V's coronation in Westminster Abbey (1910), apparently composed immediately after the ceremony. Printed in the last chapter of *Zeppelin Nights*, the account has as hushed and reverent a tone as the work of the most enamored of poets-laureate. Ford's emotion for England, however, is most clearly revealed in action, by his conduct during the war. As Goldring observes, at his enlistment Ford was forty-two years of age and by no means of strong physique.

No pressure of any kind, whether of public opinion, or after 1916, of compulsion, could have been put upon him to volunteer for military service. There is no doubt that, with Masterman's aid, he could, had he wished to do so, have had a "safe" war and drawn considerably more than a subaltern's pay in some Government Department. The fact that he preferred the nobler course and deliberately chose to risk his life in fighting for his country, and for France, as a subaltern in a line regiment, was in simple terms, an act of unselfish patriotism. [24]

The closing chapters of *Zeppelin Nights*, written with Violet Hunt — indeed the whole purport of the book — well dramatize the force and character of his patriotic feelings, and his reasons for joining up. Ford's wartime propaganda books, *When Blood Is Their Argument: An Analysis of Prussian Culture* (1915) and *Between St. Dennis and St. George: A Sketch of Three Civilizations* (1915), are further evidence of his concern for his country. The point has even more weight when it is understood that, despite the somewhat sensational title of the first, these are volumes of propaganda in a good sense. The opinions and attitudes expressed in opposition to Prussian culture and in favor of the French are high-minded and perfectly consistent with Ford's thinking earlier and later — the products of his own deepest convictions on the values of life, not fakery trumped up for the occasion.

But the very fact that Ford could write these books out of intimate knowledge of the Germans and the French returns us to his cosmopolitan heritage, and to its significance. For if Ford deeply loved his native land, it was as one who did not fully possess it. That is perhaps why he was so fascinated by it — like so many literary (and non-literary) Americans who are unsure of the meaning of an untraditioned, poly-nationed, swiftly altering America, and of their stance toward it; and thus return to it consciously in a way unnecessary to one so in tune with his homeland that he may take it for granted. Ford's love affair with his country seems always to have been insecure. One might even say that all the love was on his side — that England in its traditional insularity did not in the process, or in the outcome, want him or his Continental notions about art and the literary life. And, in the end, neglected and reviled, driven out by the frosts of Sussex countrysides and London literary circles, Ford became an expatriate. But until then and for some time thereafter — most importantly of all thereafter — the exploration of England and the English existed as the crux of his work. Scarcely a novel draws its breath apart from this quiet, pervasive concern.

Those books discussed in Chapter III focus directly on the life of the England of his time in its political, social, cultural, religious, literary, and artistic aspects. Those treated in Chapter IV put the emphasis on character rather than the social scene, and yet the meaning of being an Englishman ever hovers, conditioning, in their atmosphere. And certainly Ford's great examination of the effect of the four and a half years of war on English life in the Tietjens cycle (and more limitedly in *The Marsden Case*), the subject of Chapter V, constitutes, as artist and register, the culmination of his abiding inquiry into the changing nature and status of his country.

And his historical novels? Are they also concerned with England? The question almost answers itself. For one need only reflect that the deepest impulse of the study of history and of the desire to recreate it is, as many writers have commented, a patriotic one. It was, for example, the tug of a love that Ford had for the land of his grandfather and the Browns that set him to gathering materials for a life of Henry VIII, and a particular affection for its southeast corner, where he dwelled many years, that led him to write the history of the Cinque Ports.

This same patriotism is at the source of the ten volumes of historical fiction with which his name is associated. And if by the very nature of their genre they are inferior to the best of his fiction with modern settings, they are also intimately related to them. Ford's sense, amateur as it was, of the greatness and vitality of England's past constantly informs his judgments in his novels which explore the contemporary English scene. Above all, it makes for the fundamental meaning of the embattled (and Armistice Day) England of the Tietjens books and the significance of the title he applied to it: "Parade's End."

The *Fifth Queen* Trilogy

For several years during the nineties Ford was engaged in extensive researches for a life of Henry VIII, a project stimulated by the recent publication of the state papers of that reign. But when he discovered that a more professionally qualified author had already contracted for such a work, he put aside his plans.[25] At the time Richard Garnett proposed that he turn the fruits of his studies into novels.[26] But the suggestion was not then taken up. In 1906, however, Ford published *The Fifth Queen*, the first book of a trilogy on the ill-fated Katharine Howard. And in the next years there followed *Privy Seal* (1907) and *The Fifth Queen Crowned* (1908).

With these books, Ford achieved his first critical success in the novel. London reviews were generally favorable, a comment on the first two volumes in the *Revue des Deux-Mondes* was particularly laudatory, and Conrad, when the third was published, wrote Galsworthy: "Ford's last *Fifth Queen* novel is amazing. The whole cycle is a noble conception — the swan song of Historical Romance."[27]

As historical fiction, the *Fifth Queen* trilogy is without doubt a performance of considerable brilliance — pictorially rich, complexly rendered, dramatic, ambitious, and serious. In it Ford displayed a capacity which justly earned such praise from his fellows. And certainly he demonstrated that his Tudor researches were turned to sound use, for the ultimate authority of the novels rests in their impressive illusion of authenticity.

In his choice of characters and incidents, Ford rejected the safer tradition of historical narrative, that which derives from Scott and which subordinates figures of history — kings, queens, ministers of state, and military heroes — and centers upon invented characters of lower rank. Instead, he essayed the more challenging task, concentrating after the Shakespearian example on the chiefs of the realm. The danger in such a method obviously is that the writer will not be up to making his kings regal, his queens queenly, or his statesmen statesmanlike, and that the dignity and elevation of the situation, being beyond his imaginative grasp, will be cheapened and ring hollow. Ford's greatest triumph in these books is that his historical personages walk through his pages with both impressive vividness and convincing force.

The period of Henry's career that Ford takes as his subject comprises the events of three years from the arrival of his fourth queen, Anne of Cleves, in December, 1539, to the execution of her successor, Katharine Howard. Politically these years marked the break-up of the King's brief alliance with the German Protestant states (formalized by the marriage with Anne) and a general return toward Roman Catholicism. At home, this shifting was marked by the fall of the potent Thomas Cromwell, Lord Privy Seal and King's chief minister, who had fostered the German tie; the diminished role of Cranmer, the papally unrecognized Archbishop of Canterbury; and the enhanced influence of the Catholic prelates and lords, led by Bishop Gardiner and the Duke of Norfolk, who was Katharine's uncle. Abroad, relations became, outwardly at least, more friendly with Catholic Spain and France. More personally, but intricately bound with the political, these years saw Henry's rejection of Anne on the grounds of physical repugnance (and her having served her political use), his revived spirits after his love marriage with Katharine, and his eventual discovery that his fifth queen had been neither chaste before her wedding nor faithful after.

The larger outline of these events the trilogy follows fairly closely, but there are in addition certain significant alterations of the facts as they have come down to us, primarily in the interpretation of Katharine, its central figure. In history, she seems to have been a young woman of small education and slight character. Her influence over Henry lay in her vivacity, charm, and beauty, and did not penetrate very far into graver affairs. Where it did, she was to a large extent the tool of Gardiner and Norfolk. As to her amatory career, it seems fairly well established that while she lived in Lincolnshire, as a neglected adolescent among the maids of her grandmother, the Duchess of Norfolk, she had probably had intimate relations with a musician named Manock and definitely had had them, on the basis of pre-contract, with a youth named Francis Dearham. The records indicate also that on coming to court she had fallen in love with her cousin, Sir Thomas Culpepper, a courtier from his youth, and that she continued her affair with him after she had married the King. They reveal, too, that as queen she attached Dearham, Manock, and one of her grandmother's maids to her household retinue.

In Ford's version Katharine's stature is greatly enhanced. She retains her beauty and femininity, but also becomes a woman of considerable intelligence, education, and impassioned will. Taking his lead from the scholar-queens of the period — Katharine Parr, Mary, and Elizabeth — Ford provides her with a firm grounding in classical learning, particularly in the Stoic teachings of Cicero and Seneca. As for her loose reputation, the matter is toned down with considerable skill: Manock and Dearham become hearsay figures and are not brought into the household, and the allegations about her relations with them are presented as made by suborned and tortured witnesses. The reader is given to understand also that the licentious revels practiced by her grandmother's maids occurred when Katharine was too young to have engaged in them. More important are the changes in Culpepper. Instead of being a courtier, her cousin becomes a quite uncourtly soldier from Lincolnshire, a rustic Hotspur of furious swordsmanship and passionate rages, jealously and unreflectingly attached to Katharine.

These changes in the conception of Katharine Howard are, however, not arbitrary. Structurally, they unite in her single figure the public issues of politics and religion, and the private love relationship. And they enabled Ford to dramatize far more effectively and powerfully the basic conflict of his work. This conflict is the fundamental one of the claims of God and Caesar — the struggle between the concept of a state existing under the greater sovereignty of the Deity and His Church, and that of a secularized nation in which the ultimate power lies in the ruler.

As his protagonist for the modern totalitarian state, Ford had readily available in history the impressive figure of Thomas Cromwell, the shrewd student of Machiavelli and champion of "kingcraft." Privy Seal is the creator and master of a world of iron and suspicion, buttressed by a vast network of spies held in force by rewards and threats. Though believed by the Protestants to be their champion, Cromwell views the religious question as one merely of power. "God," he says, "is very far away." [28] His steady object remains the establishment of the greater might and security of the king. "Before I came this was a distracted State," he tells Katharine. "Now no lord nor no bishop nor no Pope raises head against him here. And, God willing, in all the world no prince shall stand but by the grace of this King's Highness." [29] And, himself, Cromwell sees as perpetually beside the throne:

He would be there by right; he would be able to give all his mind to the directing of this world that he despised for its baseness, its jealousies, its insane brawls, its aimless selfishness, and its blind furies. Then there should be no more wars, as there should be no more revolts. There should be no more jealousies; for kingcraft, solid, austere, practical and inspired, should keep down all the people, all the priests, and all the nobles of the world.[30]

Since the historical Cromwell was executed before the full working out of the events of the trilogy, his Machiavellian purpose is carried on, in the last volume, by a disciple: one Lascelles, primarily a fictional character, into whose hands Cromwell ritualistically gives his annotated copy of *Il Principe*.

Such a forceful and dedicated figure as Cromwell required a

worthy adversary, and this Ford provided in his heroine. It is Katharine's high sense of virtue, intensified by her education, which
compels her, despite an essential womanly fearfulness, to seek to be
an influence for what she conceives the right — the restoration in
England of the Old Faith under the Pope, and the return to the
Church of the monastery lands seized and divided among the nobles. "Ye have made this King rich," she addresses Cromwell, "but
I will give to him again his power to sleep at night; ye have made
this realm subject to this King, but, by the help of God, I will make
it subject again to God. You have set up here a great state, but oh,
the children of God weep since ye came." And she continues: "It
is a contented people that makes a State great; it is the love of God
that maketh a people rich. . . . that State is aggrandised whence
there arise songs praising God for His blessings." [31] And to the King
himself, she appeals that he be above this evil world, for God, she
knows, made this world to be bettered.

   The figure over whose spirit these two antagonists — Cromwell-
Lascelles and Katharine Howard — struggle and seek domination is
the guileful, bull-like Henry, in whose self-doubting personality lies
the possibility of either direction. Heavy and grayed, wracked by
an ulcerated leg, disappointed in his new German queen, and appearing as one "about to charge the world with his forehead," [32] he
is, as the trilogy opens, a man possessed of many dissatisfactions and
fears. Once a scholar, he now dreads to read in Latin, for it reminds
him of the Mass; and his music-loving soul, vaguely guilty and ap-
prehensive, no longer is pacified by the lute. His throne itself he sees
tottering before the threats of rebellion within, and the combined
Catholic forces of Spain, France, and Scotland without. Suspicious,
beleaguered, weary and vacillating, he is a kind of personification
of his realm.

   In this troubled spirit, Henry is drawn toward Katharine. Her
beauty and learning speak to him of that center of rest he longs
for — an easeful world of pleasant talk, music, and women's love.
And gradually he finds himself swayed by her high feeling for England and her vision of a Golden Age, when it will become one of
the Islands of the Blest. More deeply, his guilty soul is moved by

her plea that he again turn to Rome. Much of the trilogy recounts the developing ascendancy of Katharine's point of view, and with it a shift toward a more joyful atmosphere in the kingdom and in Henry himself.

The central conflict of the *Fifth Queen* trilogy is clear-cut, but the world in which it works itself out is not. The milieu of the court that Katharine enters is cross-purposed and bewildering. As she eventually realizes, it is "a world of men who do one thing in order that something very different might happen a long time afterwards." [33] In it, powerful persons with strong wills move and maneuver, relentlessly driving to accomplish ends to which they are deeply committed — power and wealth, advantage and neck-saving, vengeance, love, justice, or some ideal of religious, political, or moral order — singly and in combination. It is a world of complexly structured tensions held momentarily in poise to reveal meaning and motive, and before our eyes, as one or another pressure in the system is adjusted, shifting into new configurations and exposures. Its perfect symbol is the children's game of cat's cradle, which Ford has Katharine play in a key scene in *Privy Seal*. Henry is a master at it; Katharine is much less good.

It is in the first book particularly that Ford renders the effect of a cat's-cradle world. In it, Katharine, for all her strivings to be a free agent, is essentially a pawn of higher policy, first that of Cromwell and finally that of the King himself. In the process of this experience her initial rudimentary understanding of the court situation, which had been framed in the blacks and whites of Protestants versus Catholics, becomes altered into something much more penetrating. The Catholic leaders, she discovers, are not holy, but suspicious, harsh, and scheming. Having themselves profited from the appropriation of the church lands, they are no more willing to give them up than the Protestants. And Cromwell, whom she had despised from a distance, she learns to respect, and fear more deeply. She learns gradually, too, that one's purpose may gain allies one does not wish — like the shrewd, villainous Throckmorton, Cromwell's chief spy, who is secretly plotting his master's fall.

In the second volume, *Privy Seal*, a less intricately drawn work, the duel between the two sides continues. Cromwell intrigues to destroy Katharine by inciting the king's jealousy of Culpepper, but at the same time he himself is tricked by faked intelligence. At the point of triumph, Cromwell is thus brought down, ironically accused of being a traitor to his king. But the doom of Cromwell does not close the novel with joy. Once again, as at the end of the first volume, a moral, and foreboding, abyss opens before Katharine at Henry's act, since she sees with frightening clarity that the King is well aware that the charges of treason are lies.

The third volume, *The Fifth Queen Crowned*, begins about fifteen months later. Katharine is now queen, and under her influence many changes in the realm, court, and King have taken place. There is an air of summer and relaxation — contrasting with the world of winter in which the first book opened. No longer does a sinister atmosphere of spies pervade. The people are more festive. The King, formerly gloomy, irritable, and tormented, is content, overflowing with playful wit, geniality, and fondness for his wife. The first scene, in fact, sees him dictating to Cranmer a letter to the Pope announcing his submission.

The section in which this picture is drawn is titled, "The Major Chord"— which it is of the entire trilogy. But within it are at work the forces that make the movement of the novel a long, slow, falling curve (passing through "The Threatened Rift" and "The Dwindling Melody" to "The End of the Song").

The chief rock upon which Katharine and her idealistic vessel founder is vested interest. Her determination to seek the restoration of the Church lands forces into combination against her almost all the leading powers of the realm; and through torture, threats, bribes, and the adept turning of chance to his purpose, Lascelles twists her girlhood past into a harlotry. Katharine's disaster lies also in her equivocal moral position (having come to her queenly influence by the route of divorce) and in her idealistic, even quixotic code as queen (which makes her unwilling to employ guile to cut any of the threads of the net which Lascelles is weaving about her). But the key to her fall lies in the character of the King himself, for intrigue and treachery and naked force are too deeply rooted in him. Appalled as Katharine may be when they flash out of him, her protests are helplessly overborne by a jollying, self-pleased, powerful monarch. ("If God in His Heaven would have me make a peace with Rome," he tells her, "wherefore will He not give victory over a parcel of Lutheran knaves and swine? Wherefore will He not deliver into my hands these beggarly Scots and these atheists of France?") [34]

The letter to the Pope is never sent. Cranmer lays the charges and evidence against Katharine before the King, and Lascelles, in a vivid impressionistic scene, takes Henry incognito to a meeting of his subjects — primarily Protestants — where he hears of the evil which has spread over the land because a wanton is on the throne.

The principles of Cromwell finally triumph. Yet, in the event, the King no more acts by them than by those of Katharine. Too selfish and unstable, too spiritually centerless and weak to yield himself to any, he is — for all his cunning and power — a man only to be acted upon. Pride-wounded and ashamed, unable to withstand the opinions of his councillors, or the criticism of his kingdom, Henry betrays his underlying trust of his queen and denounces her. Yet even then he wavers. Unwilling to consign Katharine to death, he wishes her to continue living with him as his concubine; but Katharine refuses, accepting her doom gladly. At the mercy of such a man, she cries, her life would be a thing of no surety. "I had rather be called a sinner, adjudged and dead and forgotten." And she reflects that the world of the court is no place for an ignorant, blind dreamer like herself, set in the belief that in the end right must win through. "I think now," she concludes, "that it never shall — or not for many ages — till our Saviour again come upon this earth with a great glory." [35]

Ford's presentation of his central figure is, without question, sympathetic. But it also has an ironic reserve which lends his narrative a still larger dimension — a standing apart from both herself and her vision. He is clearly aware, for example, of the deceptions that often lurk in the spirits of idealists like his central character who, in their high ambitions to achieve their glowing ends, accept the ideal-subverting necessity of compromising means.

"If I will be Queen," Katharine tells Anne of Cleves in their brilliant interview in *Privy Seal*, "it is that God may bless this realm
and King with the old faith again." And Anne's cool reply has added
ironic force in that she has withdrawn from contention, a neutral,
clear-eyed observer. "It is best known to yourself why you will be
Queen," she answers. "It is best known to God what faith he will
have in this your realm. I know not what faith he liketh best, nor
yet what side of a queen's functions most commendeth itself unto
you." [36] And earlier Ford had delineated the awakened power of
pride in Katharine: "She itched to be Queen — on the morrow or
next day; she desired to have the King for her own, to wear fair
gowns and a crown; to be beloved of the poor people and beloved
of the saints." [37] And still later, when she is Queen, it pleases her
"that now she swayed this land, and that soon she would alter its
face." [38]

To bring the King to her purpose, Katharine finds that she must
persuade the Princess Mary to be reconciled with him. The daughter of Henry and Katharine of Aragon, but officially proclaimed
bastard, Mary is a grim, cold young woman who intransigently
hates her father for his crimes against her mother and herself. The
extent of Katharine's readiness to compromise can be seen in her
urgent, kneeling appeal to Mary that she conduct herself graciously
with Henry, feign assent to a marriage to the Duke of Orleans, and
agree to wed the Spanish Emperor — proposals which Mary scorn-
fully denounces as a course of foul deception solely aimed at satisfying her father's monstrous vanities and passions. "And you will
cosset him in them — to save his hoggish dignity and buttress up his
heavy pride. All this you stand there and ask." And Katharine replies: "There is no other way." [39]

A more intimate self-deception, however, involves Katharine's
relationship with Culpepper and the King. As Ford presents these
two men, there seems no meaningful rivalry. Henry is too great and
compellingly complex, and Culpepper too wild, depthless, and ineffectual. That Katharine should be wearied of her cousin's im-
petuosity and be attracted to the brooding power of the King is not
strange. Yet, whenever she discovers that Culpepper is endangered,

Katharine reveals herself in word and gesture as deeply concerned, for in her country poverty he had protected her ("had sold three farms to buy her gowns"), and, in the warm June Lincolnshire nights, in the apple orchards, he had made love to her and received her pledges. Whether she was his lover in fact or not Ford leaves in an ambiguous shimmer which helps convey an essential power of relationship — a love in her with sources more deeply personal than that which she bears Henry.

Katharine's love for the King is at once of a higher and of a lesser order. Much of its force depends on her sense of her good influence over him. And much rests on what he stands for as a person, majestic and wearily weighted. The Greek writers had a myth, she observes, "that the two wings of Love were made of Awe and Pity." To which Katharine's attendant prophetically replies: "There is no man worth that guise of love."

Much of Ford's success in communicating his detached attitude toward his heroine depends on a skillful handling of point of view. The angle of vision is not limited to his chief actress but is that of an invisible, immediately present author — a method which in its freedom to range from character to character is clearly appropriate for rendering a cat's-cradle world of unclear knowledges and endless cross-purposes. Ford's principle in selecting his various focal characters is simple and effective: they want something, and their will advances the action. Some are minor actors, more or less foolishly willful, and hence valuable plot-movers — like Nicholas Udall, Poins, or Culpepper. Others are more central — deeply cunning men like Cromwell, Lascelles, or Throckmorton. Chiefly, of course, the focus is on Katharine, who is presented from all angles: from the view of the omniscient author; from within; from the perceptions and responses of other characters; and, dramatically, in action. The result is that Katharine is rendered with an impressive complexity and subtlety and endowed with a rounded, independent life. Most of the minor characters are presented, of course, in no other way but externally. Worth examining, however, is Ford's decision to treat some of his leading personages, such as Mary and the King, in the same manner — a method which is appropriate on several counts.

Ford shrewdly avoids the pitfall of trying the almost impossible —
a convincing treatment of the consciousness of an historical personality as complex as was Henry's.[40] And he gains a great narrative
advantage, for the simple reason that is splendidly symbolized in
Chapter II of *The Fifth Queen*, which opens with Cromwell standing in the stern of his barge, looking across the night and the winter
river. "The flare of the King's barge a quarter of a mile ahead
moved in a glowing patch of lights and their reflections as though
it were some portent creeping in a blaze across the sky. There was
nothing else visible in the world but the darkness and a dusky tinge
of red where a wave caught the flare of light further out." [41]
Through his absolute power as King, Henry is the fiery center of
the *Fifth Queen* world, its Destiny. It is he whom others — like
Katharine and Cromwell — must fear and placate, move and alter.
How he will act, what he will do, provide the fundamental interest,
just as whether or not Mary will be reconciled with him causes yet
another tension. The suspense lies in our not knowing the inner
thoughts of either. Indeed, when one reflects that Henry's character is such that he himself is not certain of what he wants, we can
see that the problem of composition created by entering his consciousness would be hopelessly unmanageable. For the story, after
all, is Katharine's — and the King is but tickle, unstable Fate.

But if Henry performs the role of Destiny, he remains a figure
who is all too human — the trilogy's most memorable character. His
remarkably rich and life-like literary portrait compares very well
with the celebrated pictorial ones by Holbein, from which the descriptive details clearly were drawn. Much of his success may again
be attributed to Ford's objective method. For as the turbulent personality of the King flashes out of his physical frame in explosive
speech or again is subdued in calmer words and gesture, Henry is
alive in the way that ultimately is most convincing — in action. And
so it is as well with the hard, imperious Mary. Their own vital movements vouch for their existence. Subjective presentation might only
blur their firmness of shape and definition and call into doubt the
life-giving strength of their unpredictability.

The characters in the *Fifth Queen* move in a world which, as already noted, is impressively solid and authentic. Part of this effect can be attributed to Ford's detached point of view and to the essentially objective, and hence objectifying, nature of his cat's-cradle system of conflicting wills. But there are other key elements making for the illusion. Ford has exercised a good deal of care with his settings, rendering them vividly and closely relating his people to them. Much attention is focused on the characters' colorful and richly ornamented garments, their massive stone apartments, bare-walled or covered by high tapestries; the peaceful gardens they sit in (playing cat's cradle); the Thames their swift-oared barges race upon; the doors they enter, the stools they sit on, the tables and desks they eat and write at. About many of Ford's settings there is an element of tapestry itself — a kind of slowed, slightly romanticized pictorial description in which flashes of color have a significant vivifying role.

A rich example is the opening of the chapter in *Privy Seal* in which Anne of Cleves receives Katharine Howard — the only chapter in the trilogy in which Henry's rejected fourth queen appears. The whole interview makes a brilliant scene, and is brilliantly begun:

The Queen sat in her painted gallery at Richmond, and all around her her maids sewed and span. The gallery was long; along the panels that faced the windows were angels painted in red and blue and gold, and in the three centre squares St. George, whose face was the face of the King's Highness, in one issued from a yellow city upon a green plain; in one with a cherry-coloured lance slew a green dragon from whose mouth issued orange-coloured flames, and in one carried away, that he might wed her in a rose-coloured tower on a hillside, a princess in a black gown with hair painted of real gold.

Whilst the maids sewed in silence the Queen sat still upon a stool. Light-skinned, not very stout, with a smooth oval face, she had laid her folded hands on the gold and pearl embroidery of her lap and gazed away in the distance, thinking. She sat so still that not even the lawn tips of her wide hood with its invisible, minute sewings of white, quivered. Her gown was of cloth of gold, but since her being in England she had learned to wear a train, and in its folds on the ground slept a small Italian greyhound. About her neck she had a partelet set with green jewels and with pearls. Her maids sewed; the spinning-wheels ate away the braided flax from the

spindles, and the sunlight poured down through the high windows.
She was a very fair woman then, and many that had seen her there
sit had marvelled of the King's disfavour for her; but she was accounted wondrous still, sitting thus by the hour with the little
hounds in the folds of her dress. Only her eyes with the half-closed
lids gave to her lost gaze the appearance of a humour and irony that
she never was heard to voice.[42]

In his handling of descriptions like this, Ford displays certain affinities with the methods of the pictorial tradition of nineteenth-
century poetry, represented by such names as Tennyson, Rossetti,
and William Morris, with its static, prettified, frequently lush descriptions. Ford's treatment, however, represents a modern purifi-
cation in the direction of greater restraint and sophistication. Where
in his Pre-Raphaelite forebears such pictures were often no more
than mannerisms, indulged in, particularly by Morris, for often un-
controllably dreary stretches, in Ford these descriptions of settings
and persons always serve an artistic end. In the chapter-opening
quoted, it is an essential means of dramatizing Anne for her highly
significant encounter with Katharine. And throughout the trilogy
such tapestry-like presentations are employed either to enhance a
dramatic situation, as in the labyrinthian corridors down which
Katharine flees in the closing pages of the *Fifth Queen*; or to set a
mood, as in the tranquil garden scene in *Privy Seal* in which Henry,
renewed by love and dressed in husbandman's green, awaits the report that Anne has freed him for Katharine, or again in the theatrically lighted, color-blotched council chamber at the end of *The
Fifth Queen Crowned* when Katharine confronts her enemies and
the King.

It should not be forgotten, however, that Ford's concern for pictorial detail is especially appropriate for the historical period he
was concerned with. The court of Henry VIII was extraordinarily
colorful and the documents of the age vividly transmit its love of
pageantry. Cavendish's description of the Field of the Cloth of
Gold and the rich adornment of his master, Wolsey's, processions is
one example, but less classic documents demonstrate the same fascination with colorful array and splendid fabric and garments. No-

where is the record of the period's love of richness better preserved, however, than in the great portraits that Holbein painted of English courtiers and citizenry. Since Ford's monograph on Holbein's painting was published a year before the first *Fifth Queen* book, it may well be argued that his studies for this, together with the earlier ones for his abandoned life of Henry, provided more real stimulus for the efflorescence of his description and color than did his Pre-Raphaelite background.

This reminder of Ford's extensive researches into the time leads us to a consideration of still another key achievement of the trilogy, one without which the success of any such novel is almost impossible — its illusion of historical authenticity. It has often been said that an essential condition for the creation of any good work in the genre is that its author's mind be factually and imaginatively saturated in the period long before he attempts to set a novel in it. He may have been fascinated with its history for its own sake, or have studied it for some non-fictional purpose. But however his interest may have been aroused, the historical novel he writes will be a kind of by-product. As Herbert Butterfield has written,

If a writer wishes to "work up" a period in order to set a story in it, he will feel history a fetter and every unexpected fact may hamper the story he intended to tell. But if he has steeped his mind in some past age, and has lived in that age, turning it over and over in his imagination, realising the conditions of affairs and the relationships of men and pondering over the implications of these and so recasting the life of the age for himself, then that particular age and these special conditions will suggest their own story, and the historical peculiarities of that age will give point to his novel and will become a power.

If his imaginative penetration of the age is full, he will no longer be working under limitations, but will have "captured new fields of experience and of circumstance" and have "conquered a new world for his art." [43]

The *Fifth Queen* novels, with their richness and intimacy of detail, seem to amply confirm the shrewdness of Butterfield's analysis. "I spent, I suppose, a great part of ten years in grubbing up facts about Henry VIII," Ford later wrote of his studies for his abandoned biography. "I worried about his parentage, his diseases, the size of his shoes, the price he gave for kitchen implements, his relation to his wives, his knowledge of music, his proficiency with the bow." [44] And although Ford's comment is likely to give a false picture of the kind of authenticity meant here — he does not present information on the size of Henry's shoes, for example, or the cost of his kitchenware (and is, indeed, condemning the worthlessness of mere fact) — his words do give an impression, which the books well support, of his absorption in the period. Certainly none of his five other novels in the genre, set in historical periods about which he was much less familiar, manages to establish and sustain this vital note of authenticity, and authority, as these do.

The means by which Ford creates this special atmosphere are various. The weight and aptness of the physical details which are selected and their careful assimilation into the action are, of course, fundamental, as is his concern, already discussed, with making the settings appear solid. Particularly effective are those special parochial touches which arrest the reader and clinch for him the illusion of mastered intimacy — such details as the guards' custom of striking the stone floors with their pikestaves as they approach with the king, and the whispering movement the sound makes through the palace.

Ford's most obvious technical resource in the books, however, is the style he has created for them. Words current in the Tudor period but now obsolete are frequently dropped into the prose and there is much use of the age's syntax and speech rhythms. "Sha't wear a hair shirt," Henry says with dominating tenderness to Katharine on the last page of *Privy Seal*.

"Sha't go in sackcloth. Sha't have enow to do praying for me and thee. But hast no need of prayers." He lulled her in his arms, swaying on his feet. "Hast a great tongue. Speakest many words. But art a very child. God send thee all the joy I purpose thee. And, an thou hast sins, weight me further down in hell therewith."

Remarkably appropriate and effective as a medium for transmitting the *Fifth Queen* world, Ford's style, however, is significantly different from that used in his novels with modern settings, its conscious use of archaisms and inversions representing a departure from his ideal of natural simplicity. The point should not be exaggerated, however, for the vast bulk of his archaic diction does not occur in his own voice as author. On occasions he will write such a sentence as: "Cromwell stepped to an aumbry, where there were a glass of wine, a manchet of bread, and a little salt." [45] But these instances are rare and on the whole confined to the names of objects and titles. The archaic diction is mostly to be found in the mouths of the characters, where it appropriately belongs. What chiefly distinguished Ford's style in the historical novels from that of the modern ones is their much greater elaboration of descriptive detail and color — the pictorial, tapestry-like manner earlier discussed.

Much also is to be admired in the structure of these novels. Ford's exposition, in its economy and tight progression, is managed with a fine art. An excellent example is provided by the opening division of the trilogy, which is made up of seven chapters. In One the general state of affairs in the realm is presented by way of the popular understanding of it: the King is scarcely mentioned; instead it is Cromwell who dominates this public world, its imagination and fears. Two moves immediately to Cromwell himself, standing under a burning cresset and riding his barge after the King's on the dark Thames — and exposes a new system of relationships: where below, Privy Seal terrorizes men's hearts, at the top of power he himself has cause to dread. It is through Cromwell's eyes that Henry's aversion to Anne is elaborated, and the various powerful court figures presented. Three further develops the religious conflict, dramatized in a scuffling fight at the palace walls, and ends with Culpepper leading a mule upon which rides a young woman. Four introduces the King and establishes the various tensions of the court relationships, and Five alternates between the political situation and the King's distracted interest in the woman on the mule, Katharine. Six pits the two chief adversaries of the book together for the first time, as Cromwell, on Henry's orders, conducts Katharine to Mary's house, where she is to be a waiting woman. And Seven sets the scene of Mary's apartment, relates Katharine to the other women attendants (who assume her to be a tool of Cromwell), and drives home to the reader the sense of the palace as a place thick with distrust and spies. Thus the world of the novel with all its rich levels and complex tensions has been superbly laid out for the voyager, examined in its public and private aspects, in its hierarchy of power and passions of belief, and in the intrigue-infested atmosphere indicated in the new Part that follows: "The House of Eyes." Noteworthy also is the skill with which Ford has knitted together the separate volumes, each complete in itself, so that they may be read as one long, continuous novel, through which the ordained tragedy unfolds.

The *Fifth Queen* trilogy is thus rich with merits of many kinds. And yet it also disappoints. The conception is noble, as Conrad said; but the reader who has concluded its nearly one thousand pages is left unsatisfied, and in the end untouched. What is amiss would seem to be that Ford was unable to flesh out with invention such a lengthy, demanding effort. His shortness of breath can be seen in both his structure and characters. Each volume, for example, has its flaws which soften the total intensity of the experience. The middle third of *The Fifth Queen* is thus much less economically mounted than the splendid opening part; and the defeat of Cromwell in *Privy Seal* is too clearly forecast, while the final unknotting of the struggle (Culpepper suddenly sobered) is too merely turnabout to be compelling. But the most serious weakness of deployment occurs in the final volume, in which Ford has failed to simplify his action adequately, and where we come to a basic inconsistency. Although he had earlier freely altered for his own purposes the historical personages of Katharine, Culpepper, and others, he here apparently felt it necessary to deal with the complicated material involving Manock, Dearham, Mary Lascelles, and other figures concerned with the historical Katharine. As a result, Lascelles' web-construction, for all Ford's resourcefulness, requires much too great a burden of explanation before the strands fall into place and significant action can begin.

Ford's minor characters represent another problem. Such plot-moving figures as Udall, Poins, and Culpepper effectively perform their work of advancing the action. Yet beyond this, they are for modern tastes inadequately created, drawn too much as "humors" characters without being sufficiently charming or funny in their own right. Compared with Ford's central figures they are fairly poor stuff. But even with his great ones Ford has here and there nodded. The initial momentum of Cromwell's strikingly vivid presentation in the opening book, instead of being reinforced, has to carry him through the second. Consequently, he loses stature, and his fall becomes for the reader much less the terrible, treacherous thing Katharine sees it to be. More significant a weakness is the handling, in *The Fifth Queen Crowned*, of his successor, who is not adequately differentiated, being conceived too much in stock terms as "the fox." Nor, unlike his mentor's, are Lascelles' intellectual motives ever articulated for us. Katharine's thematic antagonist consequently tends to be reduced to a theatrical villain — to the detriment of the tension of the closing pages.

Such weaknesses naturally diminish the luster of the *Fifth Queen* trilogy, but by themselves they do not explain its final disappointment. In the end, what seems to be the essential inadequacy is the way, in the third volume most particularly, Ford has managed his central character.

Katharine's portrait deteriorates with each book. In *The Fifth Queen* she is rendered imaginatively as a spirited girl of shrewd intelligence. In the second volume, this individualizing note begins slightly to fade; in the last she becomes a mere vehicle. Part of this decline can be attributed to Ford's relaxation of irony. No longer does his vision stand apart from Katharine's, adding a reverberation of meaning and the appearance of independent life. There is no Cromwell or Anne of Cleves in the final novel, for example, to challenge the authority of her attitudes. Nor is the sense conveyed that her ambition and compromises qualify her idealism and therefore humanize it. Where the historical Katharine cried out on the block: "I die a Queen, but I would rather die the wife of Culpepper," Ford transcribes these words but softens their poignant force by adding, "or of any other simple lout that loved me as he did, without regard, without thought, and without falter." [46] The passion for her cousin that Ford has hinted is never allowed to take its meaningful shape. Katharine, in the end, had to be a shining, delicate flower, too fine for such a world of malevolence and cupidity. And as she turns into a stock sentimental heroine — and her adversary into a mere villain — she, and the book, diminish in vitality and significance.

But sentimentality is but one element of this failure. Where earlier Katharine had a unique life of her own, she eventually loses it and becomes a pastiche. The effects in which she is involved in the last half of *The Fifth Queen Crowned* are second-hand, borrowed mostly from Shakespeare. Aiming at a grand climax, Ford in these pages has produced only derivative, empty work. The crucial episode[47] late at night, near the end of which the drunken Culpepper bursts into Katharine's quarters (and thus all but dooms her), is in its earlier parts directly modeled on the last-act scene in which Desdemona prepares for sleep just before Othello enters her chamber. Katharine herself assumes the qualities of the Moor's wife: gentle, considerate, sweetly thoughtful. There is the reflective conversation with the woman-in-waiting who helps her untire, the removal of jewels and rings, the slow unpinning of her coif, the calmness of person, the humming of a melancholy song ("When all the little hills are hid in snow, And all the small brown birds by frost are slain").[48] The atmosphere and trappings of pathos are there; what is lacking is the piercing poetry, the psychological depth, and, above all, the vivifying sense of newness.

As an entire creation, therefore, the *Fifth Queen* trilogy must be set down as a failure, a case of swimming out too far before the swimmer was ready.

Yet it was not, after all, a puny venture — and its attempt earns Ford much credit. Nor should we forget the superb skill of very much of the performance on the way. The entire edifice may not be solid, but it contains, as we have seen, many exquisite apartments.

The "Half Moon," The Portrait, The Young Lovell

The "Half Moon" (1909) takes as its subject Henry Hudson's voyage of 1609, during which he discovered the river that bears his name.[49] Subtitled "A Romance of the Old World and the New,"

the book is a kind of overture to America in which are announced
the themes of its passage through time and across space, an adventure already under way as the book closes.

In the novel the historical is crossed by the supernatural. And at
first glance the use of black magic in *The "Half Moon"* may seem
an easy indulgence in claptrap, especially if the reader happens to
know that Ford's brother, Oliver, had shortly before published a
study called *A Book of Witches*. Obviously, tried and tested materials were ready to hand. And certainly the book employs more
of the familiar machinery of suspense fiction than any of his other
independent novels: flights from the law, concealed treasure, strange
savages, hand-to-hand grapplings, a plot to mutiny on the high seas
— and the counter-intrigue which smashes it. Nevertheless, for all
these trappings, the supernatural material is essential to the book's
effect and meaning. For its ultimate function is to arouse in the
reader a feeling of the awe and the mystery of the inevitable.
Witchcraft, as well as the many signs and portents, helps to convey
the thrust of a destiny which cannot be disputed since in real time
past events are irrevocable. As in *Macbeth*, with its portentous
witches, author and reader know what must happen because it has
happened.

The epigraph of the novel reads: "Come: let us take ship and sail
unto that Avalon where there is no longer any ill." And one who
does take ship is Edward Colman, an industrious builder of merchant vessels. The Old World has grown weary, torn and wracked
by religious persecution and superstition. The great Tudor line is
spent, and the alien and foolish figure of James I sits on the throne,
sanctioning repressive laws. Forced to flee his native town of Rye,
Colman goes to Amsterdam and there joins the great English navi-
gator as interpreter to his all-Dutch crew. In America, the ship-
builder envisions a town rising on land in what is now Manhattan.
Through Colman, it is clear, Ford foreshadows the hard-working,
peace-wishing individual who will populate the New World.

The journey to the New World of the *Half Moon* and of Edward Colman is, however, a voyage assaulted by dark powers.
Their magician is Anne Jeal, a vauntingly proud woman, who is

infuriated at Colman's rejection of her, and who fiercely seeks by her witchcraft to bring him to his knees. Thus, against the vessel she rouses wild North Atlantic storms, and, by means of a waxen effigy, tortures her lover over the distances. In the end, in a moment of rage and jealousy, she thrusts a knife into the image, and gives Colman his mortal wound – a blow which has its naturalistic counterpart, its simultaneous acting out in destiny, in the slaying arrows of American Indians. The Indians, however, are but the instruments of Colman's death. The deeper cause is the crew of the *Half Moon* – typified by the superstitious, ominous sailor, Old Jan – who had wantonly fired into the Indians as they had first approached, bearing white flags and chanting songs. The full meaning of this act is worked out in the complexly moving final chapters of the novel.

Impressionistically, and poetically, under the sway of an elegiac emotion, Ford shifts back and forth across the Atlantic, creating a cluster of contending values, and a pregnant air of silence, size, and strangeness. And the final pages cap the section. For in the morning the Indians bring the bound Old Jan, gibbering and unintelligible, to the shore: their towering leader makes a long, sonorous, incomprehensible speech: their prisoner is freed: and they vanish into the forest. And Hudson, "mad with grief," cries out against the crew, saying that with their clemency the Indians were better Christians than all of them. "But they [the Dutch crew] could not understand one word in ten of what he said, and at last, signing them to up anchor, he went down into his cabin to be lonely with his grief. So they sailed away up that broad stream."

In these closing sentences is crystallized emotionally the final comment of the book – for the development of the New World will be burdened by the corrupted human condition, bringing the Old World with it, the Old Adam. Men of good will like Colman and Hudson will be unable to stop it. The voyage of the American adventure will be dominated by evil. Thus the hopeful epigraph becomes ironic, the ultimate source of the wail of grief that pervades the closing pages, the knowledge of loss and the failure of the ideal. There is the knowledge also of continuing alienation, the ancient human inability to bridge the chasm between person and person — a comment which Ford makes with great subtlety through the failure of language between English, Indian, and Dutch.

Not all of The "Half Moon," however, is as compelling as its concluding chapters. Still the novel remains a well-told piece, its exposition deftly absorbed into the action and its narrative effortlessly unfolded. If Ford's characters tend to be theatrically conceived, they are as such handled with impressive skill: varied in their poses and movements, sharply contrasted, and sufficiently rich to enable the book to rise to the power of its climax.

The other two novels are worth less attention. The Portrait (1910), set during the reign of William and Mary, is concerned with the wits and fops of the period. A comedy that is never too comic and which ends on a serious, even moralizing note, it is the story of an arrogant but worthy gentleman of vast fortune who is properly humbled for his own well-being. The plot is fairly absurd, the action turning on the protagonist's impulsive wager of twenty thousand pounds that he will find and marry the model in a painting that he has never seen. After various difficulties, as a consequence of which he becomes a ridiculous figure to London, Mr. Bettesworth learns that the woman who posed is actually the lady whom he loves. In the process he has deepened in understanding, having learned the truth that one must take one's laurels and wear them, not inquiring too closely what hand holds the knife which cuts them. For, as his wife-to-be tells him in the words that complete the book, "most great victories are like this, and most great victors, if you could search their hearts are much as you are; for it is nine parts fortune and one of merit, and so the world goes on."

Of all Ford's historical fiction, The Portrait is the least authentic, too sketchily worked up from relatively few sources. Levies are made on stock material from Restoration comedy: the exploited tailor, Mr. Boodle; the embezzling steward of the estate, Chuckel; the two foolish provincial justices; the improvident younger son. One character is modeled directly on Sir John Brute in Vanbrugh's The Provoked Wife — a debt amusingly acknowledged by Ford's statement that Vanbrugh modeled Brute on his character. To round out the atmosphere, Ford introduces Hogarthian scenes of prison squalor, a Jacobite invasion scare, and, anachronistically, a Methodist preacher and denunciations of Walpole. The historical paraphernalia is not organic, and the theme even less so. The book could have been set at any time. The fact is that *The Portrait* is a Fordian modern novel manqué — its theme, and its final resolution, having far more affinities with works like *The Benefactor* and *An English Girl*. Probably its chief interest is its introduction of an important character type of Ford's novels, the protagonist Mr. Bettesworth, who, in his isolating pride and vast learning, is an early, ungenial Christopher Tietjens.

The Young Lovell (1913) is set in the Border Country in the first year of the reign of Henry VII. In the opening pages, young Lovell meets a mysteriously beautiful woman riding on a white horse. Cast under her magic spell for three months, he wakes to find that his brother has seized his inheritance and is seeking to possess his betrothed. The main action concerns Lovell's attempt to regain his usurped rights and domains — the climax being the storming of a castle held by the wicked brother. Lovell is killed, and the final scene shows him in a life after death beside the beautiful woman, who is the goddess Venus. In short, the Tannhäuser theme.

The novel reveals certain of Ford's characteristic virtues: the striking physical descriptions of his personages, the archaic language, the high prides, and the complexly maneuvering, masterful politician. Its chief flaw: an excessive dependence on narration.

Ladies Whose Bright Eyes

Of his seven historical novels written before the war, *Ladies Whose Bright Eyes* (1911) is the only volume Ford later considered worthy of reprinting. During his lifetime it was one of his most popular books, being reissued in 1919, and again, revised, in 1935. A work greatly admired by the literary circles in which he moved, it caused him harder work, he tells us in his dedication, than he had given to any of his stories up to that time. And certainly of the present group it is the most polished and professional.

Ladies Whose Bright Eyes is also the only one of Ford's historical novels whose action is not wholly set in the past. For its protagonist bridges centuries — from the twentieth to the early fourteenth and back again. Through his use of the medieval world, Ford thus makes telling commentary on the modern. Such a method obviously has its affinities with Mark Twain's in *A Connecticut Yankee in King Arthur's Court*, and the similarity is no accident. For essentially the book is a reply to the American's picture of the Middle Ages.

As his hero Ford has chosen a figure who, in his highly developed sense of the practical, is not unlike Clemens's Yankee. Mr. Sorrell is an up-to-date businessman who, having gained control of the old-line family publishing house of Sorrell and Sons, has shifted it from unprofitable and dispensable books, such as literature, to solid-selling items for the masses: encyclopedias and salacious memoirs. As the book opens, Mr. Sorrell, returning to London aboard the boat train from Southampton, is somewhat uneasy at his possessing, as security for a loan, an ancient gold cross known as the Tamworth-Egerton crucifix. This cross is said to have been brought from Palestine during the year of the battle of Bannockburn by Sir Stanley Egerton, who died on reaching English soil; it was then carried to Tamworth by a converted Greek slave dressed in a linen shift. As Mr. Sorrell's train streaks at too great a speed across England, it wobbles violently and overturns. The ceiling crashes in upon him, and suddenly his temples ache severely.

The next thing Mr. Sorrell is conscious of is that he has been walking on a plain for a long time. At first believing that his garment is a hospital gown and that his head is bandaged, he gradually realizes that his body has been transformed into the head-dressed Greek slave's, and that the year is 1326. At the outset, Mr. Sorrell, like the Yankee, sees tremendous opportunities in the situation. "Why, good Lord, if it's the fourteenth century I can do anything. Just think of the things I can invent! Why, we can begin right bang off with flying machines; there's no need to go through any intermediary stages. . . . Why, we can terrorise every city in the world. We could burn Paris down in a night. They couldn't do anything — anything at all." [50]

But, in the end, Mr. Sorrell discovers that he cannot execute any of these plans. For he is ignorant:

"It is no use my saying that I can do nothing because I have not the materials — that is an idle excuse. We might fit out ships to go to the end of the world to get rubber; but even if we did that I do not know . . . from what tree rubber is procured. Or if I had the rubber should I know what to do with it. . . . Don't you understand, I have been so in the habit of having all these things done for me that I am useless as the grub in the honeycomb that the bees feed. . . . it is a condemnation of a whole civilisation." [51]

Thus Twain is inverted. By drawing the typical modern whose knowledge of his scientific and technical civilization is thoroughly superficial, Ford makes out of the identical notion of juxtaposed periods a point that is very different.

And as Mr. Sorrell makes this discovery, he also finds himself increasingly sympathetic to the Middle Ages, stirred by the various ideals of a chivalric social order: to succor the poor and those in distress, to draw one's sword only in high quarrels, to support the Church, to protect the sepulcher of the Lord Christ from the Saracens, to pray for the souls of all Christians alive or dead. And he is deeply satisfied at being made a knight and at being given a small castle with a few acres of land. He also falls in love with the Lady Dionissia, and plans to marry her.

But at the height of his happiness, Mr. Sorrell, again struck on the head, awakes back in the present, in a hospital room; and at this separation from all he has learned to cherish, he is desolate. For the modern world and his old role in it are now detestable to him. His bitterness softens, however, as he discovers the nurse who had tended him through his crisis, and who had fallen in love with him — a young woman named Dionissia Morant. Deeply versed in history, she had often read, it seems, old chronicles at his bedside. Gradually, under Dionissia's influence, Mr. Sorrell yields his intransigent disgust and comes to the conclusion that one century is just as good as another, and just as bad.

"We aren't so adventurous as we used to be, but we don't go in for so many lawsuits. We aren't so romantically dressed, but we have got electric light and better baths. . . . what we lose on the swings we gain on the roundabouts." [52]

One's work is to make a good job of what one's got in hand, romance being the flavor of any life at any time. Thus instead of giving up his publishing business, Mr. Sorrell will attempt to run it well, and he will do something for literature. Whether the fourteenth century is still there behind a sort of curtain or not, Dionissia tells him, does not matter. "There's you and there's me, and there's the sunlight. . . . We set out — we set out together, and we take our chances of what we find in each other." [53] Love, Dionissia tells him, is the real mystery, and the only mystery that matters.

Ladies Whose Bright Eyes is a novel of genuine charm. Its picture of the medieval world is crowded with appealing and intimately described details of its daily life: the garments worn, the interiors of the castles, fittings and furnishings, even the food. One highly effective scene is Mr. Sorrell's initial supper:

It was quite true that the first course consisted of fourteen dishes, the dishes themselves being mostly turned wood, though one was of gold and two of silver. The golden dish held a gilt structure of pastry, shaped like a castle, and from this the Dean and Mr. Sorrell and the two ladies were first plenteously served, having only the two plates of silver between the four of them. . . . Encouraged by the Lady Blanche — and, indeed, he was so hungry as to need little encouragement — Mr. Sorrell took with his fingers a piece of dark-looking meat. It was sweet, it was salt, it tasted overpoweringly of nutmegs and of cinnamon, and it was of the consistency of soft jelly.

Mr. Sorrell exclaimed: "Oh, my God!" and drank quickly from a cup of silver. But even the wine was spiced with cloves.

Later his hostess explains that the first dish of the first course was very excellent,

being compounded of the tongues of rabbits, hedgehogs, deer, geese, and wild boars, together with the breasts of partridges and the livers of pheasants. It contained, moreover, force-meat balls made of honey, cinnamon, and flour boiled in wine, and the sauce was made likewise of honey, nutmegs, cloves, garlic, and mint, and all these things had been stewed together so that there could not be found anywhere a dish more savoury.[54]

Even more delightful is the episode in which Mr. Sorrell washes in a special, highly civilized bath, the details of which, and of his dressing in new garments afterwards, are elaborated with loving care.

Great attention is also focused on medieval decorum, customs, and institutions. Ford recounts, for example, the methods employed by a masterful abbess to discipline her new community of lax nuns. He enters into the details of marriage pre-contracts, delineates the atmosphere of a castle in which the women are left with boys and old retainers while their men are away at the wars. And he gives considerable care to his settings: the downs and the plain, and Salisbury with its cathedral and spire.

Nor does Ford neglect the less attractive sides of medieval life. Among the first things Mr. Sorrell sees as he walks along Salisbury Plain are numerous bodies, with ravens perched on them, dangling from trees and gallows — thieves executed by the lords before going to the fray. He is also disturbed by the stench of decaying animal matter deposited by custom in the courtyard and removed only once a year — this practice side by side with great attention to personal cleanliness and hand-washing. The novel also brings out the tendency of the Middle Ages toward a naive favoring of ornament over function.

As for Ford's medieval characters, they are attractive and well-distinguished from one another. One of Ford's favorite devices, in fact, is to set off a pair of them into sharp contrast. Thus Lady Blanche is a furious firebrand, while her rival, Lady Dionissia, is quiet and tender. Similarly with the two lords away at the Scotch border: the Young Knight of Egerton is a flaming, irrepressible warrior of high valor, but a slave of his peasant-born, fickle mistress, Gertrude. His comrade, the Knight of Coucy, on the other hand, is a cunning, self-confident, amused personage on excellent terms with his Griselda. Other vivid characters are the abbess; the Dean of Salisbury Cathedral, who is less tantalized by the thought of Mr. Sorrell as a holy man, commonplacely allied with angels, than that he may be in league with the devil; and Little Jehan, the fifteen-year-old page, teased by Lady Blanche and her companions because he loves no women but his mother and the Virgin. There are also the Queen Mother, Lord Morton, and the Young King; and finally, the aged Sir Ygorace de Fordingbridge, the model of the chivalric code, and the judge of the great tournament which is the high point of the book.

The plot by which the novel moves toward this high point is managed with impressive skill. After Sorrell, and the reader, become adjusted to the historical situation, a conflict develops between the ladies Blanche and Dionissia over possession of the cross, and the pair agree to determine the issue by single combat. With this conflict established, Ford shifts to their husbands for an amusing section, and then treats the tournament itself — a highly effective episode developed through fifty pages, which ends with Lady Dionissia defeating her rival.

Of all Ford's historical novels, *Ladies Whose Bright Eyes* is, as was said earlier, his most professional. The details are rich, and the atmosphere is managed with considerable care. Few flat stretches mar it as they do each of the *Fifth Queen* books. And although the sub-plot of the two knights does not bear directly on the main action, it is very engagingly handled. The book is not, in whole or part, a pastiche, from Shakespeare or elsewhere, but is filtered throughout by way of Ford's own literary personality.

Yet, in the end, there must be certain reservations, and in developing these it will be useful to compare the novel with the book by Mark Twain that prompted it, and with which it shares a common plot device. The spirits of the two works are, on the whole, thoroughly dissimilar. *A Connecticut Yankee* in its method is basically a farce, full of jokes and slapstick situations, and written in a style and tone frankly those of a humorist. It raises little problem of fidelity to life. Where Ford carefully justifies Mr. Sorrell's knowledge of fourteenth-century Norman English, Twain is bothered by no such scruple, since in the world of farce anything is possible. Ford, on the other hand, by the nature of his approach was far more concerned with the problems of the "truth" of presentation, and since it is much the harder task, his accomplishment is the more to be valued. All in all, with its charming and civilized picture of the Middle Ages, Ford's book provides a good corrective, for those who need it, to the absurd picture of stupidity, superstition, and inhumanity presented in *A Connecticut Yankee*.

Aware of the problems of comparing such essentially dissimilar books, one may venture to say, too, that in many ways Ford's novel is the superior. The plot is much more integrated than Twain's generally episodic work. Its characters are rounder, and its passages of description and scene-painting subtler and deeper. Nor is Ford's style as uneven as Twain's, many of whose chapters fail to rise above the level of quick journalism.

Yet there can be little doubt that the American's is the greater book. *A Connecticut Yankee*, although a farce in method, is a more profound work than Ford's, both in its power and purpose, for in it Mark Twain rides a deeply felt indignation. With complex swiftness his humor is able to shift to biting satire, and to present (for example) scenes of wasted lives tyrannously and capriciously thrust into black dungeon-keeps, scenes which powerfully grip his reader. If he is unfair to the Middle Ages, he claims the satirist's privilege of exaggeration for his purpose. Twain explores and ridicules the past in the service of democracy and rationality and against reaction. He asks that all men stand up as such, that each of them be a man and cast aside the yokes of religious superstition and of awe for the millinery of nobility.

Twain's theme is thus well buttressed by sending the Yankee back to the time of King Arthur. What more effective way to cast ridicule on the attitudes of the old regime?

The same appropriateness can not as easily be assigned to the method of *Ladies Whose Bright Eyes*. If Ford's final point is that, on balance, one century is much the same as another and that romance is the flavor of any life at any time, there does not seem to be much relevance to his backward turn into history. If his aim is merely to provide a corrective to *Connecticut Yankee*, the imaginative and emotional force of the book can scarcely be strong or urgent. Had Ford gone all out to support the medieval as opposed to the modern world, argued for a simpler life and for community

on feudal lines rather than on commercial, industrialized, and atom-
istic ones — the materials for which conclusion are all present in the
book — the work would have had point. Had the novel closed with
the grieving note of loss that wracks the ending of The "Half
Moon"— Mr. Sorrell desolately trying to return to the fourteenth
century — it would have been, whatever one might say of it on
intellectual grounds, artistically whole. As it is, it is not integrated,
for its theme does not rise out of its form.

That the ending of the novel troubled Ford also is clear from
his revision of it in 1935. But before these changes are examined, a
few observations about the original may be of value. It is highly
probable that the ending owes much to the influence of Violet
Hunt, with whom Ford was then in love. Ford acknowledged in
his dedication that the idea of the novel was suggested by her, and
she herself has claimed that she also supplied the title. From internal evidence there seems good reason to believe that her role did
not end there. For Ford's rendering of the relationship between
Mr. Sorrell and Lady Dionissia is highly uncharacteristic. A meeting of true hearts, its sentimental flavor is epitomized in the following passage near the end of the book:

"It's this that I've come back from the dead for," he said. She held
him so tight that it was almost as if she shook him. She held her face
back from his lips.
"It's a beautiful world," she said. "Say that it's a beautiful world."
"It's beautiful," he said.
"Say it's as beautiful as the world ever was," she commanded im-
periously.
"It's as beautiful! It's as beautiful," he repeated.[55]

But love in Ford, apart from this novel and Romance, is (as was
earlier observed) almost never tender. Fragmented, incomplete, it
is characteristically anguished and lacerated. The implication is
clear therefore that Ford's depiction of such a love affair was influenced by Violet Hunt, just as he had been earlier influenced in
Romance by that other sentimentalist of the relation between the
sexes, Conrad. The ending of Ladies is also atypical. With a few
exceptions, Ford's novels are always set in a minor key. Melancholy,

sadness, loss, grief, pain, isolation, defeat, helplessness — these are the moods which close his books. That Mr. Sorrell's grief at returning to the twentieth century be unassuaged is not only the most proper ending in the logic of the novel, but also perfectly in keeping with the spirit of Ford's other work.

Whether this assumption of Violet Hunt's influence is correct or not, the fact remains that in 1935 Ford drastically altered the closing section. As it stands in the original, the ending is not only unintegrated but also dramatically diffuse and overly long. In the revision Ford made a decided improvement by reducing the section to one half its former length — from thirty to fifteen pages. Scrapped is the entire theme of the mystery of love, nor is there any long romantic scene about the beauty of things. The nurse Dionissia's instant love for Sorrell has no opportunity to appear improbable, since it is simply assumed. In the original it was Mr. Sorrell's plan to build a castle on the ruins of the one he had been granted in the fourteenth century; in the revision the land is to be taken over for an air station: as they both agree, "Nothing can stop these things." Instead of the recourse to the mystery of love as an answer to life, the emphasis is placed on the importance of beginning anew, and of faith. Even if we went back to the beginnings that existed in the fourteenth century, Dionissia says, "We'd have to go forward again. And only reach here." She tells him that he must never go back. And adds, in the closing words of the book: "What we have to do is to go forward — don't they say: over the graves?"

As a resolution to *Ladies Whose Bright Eyes*, the 1935 version, if not the most truly logical, is still superior to the original. It looks longingly back — humanly acceptable enough — but turns ahead out of the realistic knowledge that one can do no other. It is probably unfortunate, however, that the beginnings and the faith that Ford should select for Mr. Sorrell and Dionissia to look forward to lie in the Soviet Union — specifically in the Caucasus where, it is implied, Mr. Sorrell as a mining engineer will develop ore-crushing machinery. This resolution, it should be noted, Ford depicts with only a few swift references, and involves no ideological approval. It was simply what idealistic individuals in 1935 would have thought of as a fresh, new beginning, and Ford was merely echoing, though rather too distinctly for art, the fashion of a time.

These lapses in purpose and conception are not the only short-comings which beset the book. Despite the over-all superiority of *Ladies* to Ford's other historical novels, the *Fifth Queen* trilogy, when successful, is much more to be valued. The key element that sets the trilogy above Ford's later book is its freshness: in style, in narrative method, and in characters. About *Ladies* there is an air of decadence. Ford's distinctive historical style has settled into a manner, a little too slick, a little too detailed for lucidity. There is too great a tendency, for example, to describe medieval customs for their own sake, to linger over them rather than to use them to forward the action. One becomes conscious of word-painting, and the slowness of tempo which somewhat retards the book is an inevitable result of such embroidering. In contrast with such figures as Henry VIII, Cromwell, Katharine Howard, and Mary, the characters of *Ladies* lack excitement and tension, their outlines and inner spirits softer and more blurred.

That indeed is the basic lack in the later work, despite its high degree of craft and charm — a sense of artistic excitement. Interestingly enough, the lack of narrative energy seems also to have disturbed Ford, for in his 1935 revision, he made extensive changes both in the structure and the style of the book. These alterations deserve to be examined in some detail, for they shed much light, both on his pre-war historical technique and on the method he was generally using in his novels of the thirties. Certain of Ford's changes result from his decision to update the book to the time of new publication. Mr. Sorrell thus has fought with Allenby in Palestine; trench warfare and poison gas are referred to; and dated matters like Parnell and Irish Home Rule are dropped.

More to the present purpose, however, are Ford's alterations in narrative method. These all move in the direction of greater impact and away from the more subtle and oblique earlier manner. The 1911 version, for example, begins with Mr. Sorrell stepping out into the wildly swaying train corridor and does not attempt a rounded description of him until the second chapter. The revised version lifts this description and, with considerable alteration and condensation, sets it down at the head of the book:

Mr. Sorrell, just landed from New York after an almost too pleasant voyage, was accustomed to regard himself as the typical Homo Sapiens Europaeus. He was rising forty; he was rather fair, with fresh, brown hair; he was by profession a publisher and at the top of the tree; he had a vigorous physique, a drooping mustache and a pink, clear skin. He owed no soul a penny; he had done his duty in the war; he rose usually at eight, voted Conservative and had been given to understand that he might be honoured with a knighthood at a near date. So his eyes which were clear and blue were slightly threatening — as if with an expression of being ready militantly to assert at once his right and his rectitude. He stood just six feet.

He stepped out into the swaying corridor . . .

Ford also points up the links between the past and the present. In the original the reader's first realization that Mr. Sorrell is actually in a hospital does not come until late in his medieval experience — when, stretched on the grass and with sudden dread, he smells, in a stunning moment, the odor of chloroform. Until he wakes again in the modern world, no other allusion is made to his real state. The revision makes it much less tenuous. Into a pause during the tournament, Ford inserts three pages which return his hero in drugged reverie to the odor of chloroform and swiftly add to it the sight of a fever chart, the sound of a telephone bell, and Dionissia as nurse. The passage also acquires a lengthy reflection on the possibility of the co-existence of ages.

Another structural change worthy of mention is a shift in the sequence of chapters. In the original the first two chapters with Mr. Sorrell on the express are succeeded immediately by two more which trace his progress across the plain. The fifth chapter then moves to Stapleton Castle and Lady Blanche. In the revised version this fifth chapter is put immediately after the train crash — a change which improves the narrative in several ways: promptly placing the reader into the Middle Ages, greatly enhancing interest and sus-

pense, and even avoiding a certain monotony of effect (since the
sixth chapter has a development which is of necessity similar to the
shifted one).

Even more interesting are the drastic and extensive stylistic
changes. The nature of Ford's prose in his historical novels has already been glanced at in the section on the *Fifth Queen* books,
where the archaisms, descriptive detail, and color were pointed
out. Not discussed earlier, however, was its element of explanation,
a style which makes frequent syntactical use of connectives, and
causal and consequential constructions. In the *Fifth Queen* cycle,
this explanatory component is managed with decided restraint, being largely limited to the reasoning processes of the characters, both
in their reported thoughts and more frankly in their speeches to one
another. But with *The "Half Moon"* it enters directly into the tone.
The method has much in common with that used in the telling of
fairy tales which, being addressed to an audience of real or assumed
children, takes on with perfect naturalness the tone of explanation.
One of the interesting features of *The "Half Moon,"* in fact, is that
Ford applied to it techniques which seem to draw on his own experience of writing child's stories (like *The Brown Owl, The
Feather,* and *Christina's Fairy Book*). The basic materials of *The
"Half Moon"* — its serious reflections on America and its destiny, its
themes of alienation and of the onward adventure, its passionately
possessive woman — are, of course, fundamentally different. But its
means have certain affinities: the magical and the supernatural, an
atmosphere which is generalized, and remoteness in time. To these
the explanatory tone of the fairy tale adds a flavor which sustains
them, and helps in itself to create the special aura of an unfettered
world of romance. In *The "Half Moon,"* this fairy-tale note is carried still further by the frequent use of modifiers like "much,"
"very," "little" (to describe Colman's ship), and by the compilation
of lists — the fairy-tale, and childlike, naming of things:

There fell out from the parcel many rough things — a hammer of
stone, with two points bound with leather thongs to a leathern-
bound stick; a strip of hide with dark eagle feathers attached to it;
a little knife of green stone with a handle of painted wood, a necklet

of white beads, and a little rattle, made of a sort of osier-withing in basket-work, and a letter wrapped in a green cloth.[56]

One section of the novel even falls into the paratactic rhythm of sentences steadily joined by "and," in the manner of the child.

Although *Ladies* is not so explanatory as *The "Half Moon"* or the other casuals, nor draws anywhere as much on the child's-story tone of that book or of *The Young Lovell*, these elements, and particularly the former, are certainly characteristic enough. The alterations which Ford made in the 1935 version are all aimed at reducing this paraphernalia of explanatory syntax and detail.

The nature of Ford's changes is well displayed by a comparison of the following two passages:

. . . some high mounds of gorse. If he slipped behind these and knelt down he would be fairly out of sight till they had passed. He found a nearly circular hollow. It had the disadvantage that the spines of the gorse pricked him through his nightshirt, but when he knelt down he was certainly quite hidden from view. He could not any longer see the procession, but he supposed he would be able to hear it when it went past. He knelt, therefore, in some tranquillity. The sun poured its warm rays down into the motionless air; great bees buzzed sleepily above his head. The sound of the singing died away, and in his intense weariness Mr. Sorrell dropped asleep.

. . . .

He was always very dizzy and stupid upon awakening, so that when he was gently shaken he had not the least idea where he was. Then he saw the dirty face of the beggar peering at him through the bushes, whilst an old man in priest's robes was gently shaking his shoulder, and trying to remove from his finger the ring of the Egerton cross.[57]

This first is from the original. Here it is, revised, in 1935:

. . . some high mounds of gorse. He found a nearly circular hollow in one of the groups. When he knelt down he was there quite hidden. The spines of the gorse pricked him through his nightshirt but there was just a man's length of rabbit nibbled turf. He could not any longer see the procession and he lay down in some tranquillity. The sun poured its warm rays down into the motionless air. The place smelt of thyme; great bees buzzed sleepily just above his head. The sound of the singing died away. . . .

He was gently shaken. He did not know where he was. A dirty face was peering down on him; an old man in priest's robes was trying to remove from his finger the ring of the Egerton cross.[58]

In part these changes represent an impulse to return toward the cleaner, more objective prose of the *Fifth Queen* books, but the alterations are far more radical than that. Much more influential without doubt is the laconic example of Hemingway, in whose work the motives of characters tend to be revealed externally by what they say and do rather than by a report of their psychological processes.

For the reader, the existence of two forms of *Ladies* poses the practical dilemma of choosing versions. The ending of the revised form is clearly more effective in theme and treatment, the structural changes are in the main improvements, and certainly the style has greater impetus. Yet, for all that, the alterations of the 1935 version seem more wrong than right. What is objectionable is a pervasive quality, but probably it can best be indicated in the revamped prose. Executed by a man twenty-four years removed in personality and literary feeling from the original, in a style characteristic of his fictional method in the thirties, they are changes imposed from the outside, not organic. With its abrupt cadences, its external rendering of characters, and its elimination of embellishments in which the sensibility of the reader may rest, the novel loses its charm and grace. And its spirit becomes hard and unpleasant. There can scarcely be a clearer case of the truth that atmosphere is not a mere matter of setting, but is integrally related to style. The explosive, detached prose of the revision is entirely unsuited to an historical recreation whose vein is primarily pictorial and romantic. The same criticism, when extended from style to the over-all treatment, applies to such alterations as the book's new opening (the typical Homo Sapiens Europaeus, etc.), and the sharpening of the link between the past and the present. These changes away from subtlety violate the spirit of the work, pulverizing its delicate fabric with a sledge-hammer presentation.

On the whole, then, the reader is wisest to choose the original. In the process he can allow for Ford's own criticisms expressed in the revision, and knowing that *Ladies* is not the first novel of worth which has closed unsatisfactorily, he is also able, in part at least, to discount the final chapters as a concession to public expectations. What remains may not be high art, but it is a work of considerable flavor and distinction. And in its own terms it suffices very well.

Ladies Whose Bright Eyes was followed two years later by *The Young Lovell*. After that, Ford was not to write another historical novel until 1928, when *A Little Less Than Gods* appeared, a silence of fifteen years. His fictional manner was so altered by that time, however, that it seems sounder to treat it later, in Chapter VI. One other work of historical fiction with which Ford's name is associated should, however, be touched on: *Zeppelin Nights* (1915). Written with Violet Hunt, the book is not a novel, but a series of sketches moving chronologically through English history. These are framed in the conversations of a group of British intellectuals gathered together on a London roof during the early days of the war, as they wait out the nightly visits of the German zeppelins — much, the authors remark, as the Florentines in the *Decameron* waited out the plague. In the book, however, each of the stories is read by the writer Serapion Hunter, a thinly disguised Ford. In all, the historical sketches number twenty-four, of which from internal evidence the first twenty are by Ford. Many of these are written with a care of style and detail scarcely to be equaled among his historical writing. They conclude with a twenty-fifth reading, already referred to, on the coronation of George V in Westminster Abbey. (The frame is probably more Violet Hunt than Ford.)

The fundamental purpose of the book is to set the contemporary jeopardy of England against the stirring memory of its past, and of the past of western civilization. The book concludes with the discovery, after the reading of the coronation piece, that the over-aged Serapion has enlisted to fight for his country.

Of special interest for the purposes of this chapter are certain comments about the nature of historical fiction made in the frame portions. One member of the audience, who probably stands for Ezra Pound, argues that Serapion's language is too archaic, that such tales would be better told completely in modern phrases, including now and then slang and Americanisms. With this position Serapion is inclined to agree, up to a point. "One ought, he was of opinion, to be able to get together a vocabulary that was entirely modern and that yet did not contain any words that would jar with historic conceptions. You ought to be able to do without slang and without archaisms; but it was difficult." [59] (Certainly, these sketches are much freer of archaic vocabulary than Ford's earlier historical writing.)

Even more interesting is an observation made directly in the name of Ford as author. All historic fictions, the comment runs, are "merely *tours de force* and, as such, negligible in the realms of high art." [60] This same evaluation of the genre Ford also made later in *Joseph Conrad*: "a historical novel even at the best is nothing more than a *tour de force*, a fake more or less genuine in inspiration and workmanship, but none the less a fake. Even 'Salammbo' is that." [61] A writer's justification for engaging in the practice of historic fiction, Ford says, is "as a recreation" [62] or "just for practice in writing." [63]

Ford's argument that historical fiction is negligible in the realms of high art is not further elaborated; but it is difficult to quarrel with his verdict. In one sense, all novels are historical. But there is a crucial difference between those set in times contemporary, or almost so, with the lives of their authors, and those placed in periods which are remote, as in all of Ford's historical novels. The difference is that in the contemporary work the writer is able to draw unconsciously on his immediate experience of life, in all its thickness. Whether he wills or not, the special reality of his times will have hurled him into complex interchange with it and have compelled him to fathom something of its shape. If he is penetrating enough, he will come to and wrestle with the deepest issues of his age, often without being fully aware of their centrality. But for the historical novelist, in the usual sense of the term, the experience which he presents can only be conscious and inevitably thin, lacking a living knottiness. The intellect will have to construct with effort and, in the end, futilely what the "contemporary" writer naturally breathes. And even should the historical novelist put modern characters with modern sensibilities back into older times, as Ford later said he had done, the case is not seriously altered. In such an instance the characters may well have greater life than those created by the more archaeologically-minded novelist, yet even then the circumstances and conditions in which they move, if they are depicted in any great detail, as in *Salammbô* or Ford's novels, must inevitably work against the vitality of the characters. For these are not the circumstances and conditions that modern sensibilities must act on and struggle with. There is fundamentally something of an exercise about it all, a feat of main strength, a tour de force.

Of course, there are many great works, particularly in the tragic drama, set in times distant from their authors', but then the historical background is only general, not particularized. What is actually treated is not a historical period but remoteness itself, a remoteness which frees the characters to become more heroic, and thus more tragic, in stature. All great tragic works, whether they be by Sophocles, Shakespeare, or Racine, have always been, whatever their setting, intensely contemporary.

For these reasons, therefore, we must accept Ford's own evaluation of his historical novels as being barred from the first rank of high art. But short of that level, we may freely admire much. There are many splendid, imaginative pages in them. They create a convincing atmosphere very skillfully, and are full of charm and grace. And none of them is cheap in its appeal. All are works which, falling short of the deepest seriousness, yet remain serious and thoughtful in what they say. And in them many of his major themes and characteristic situations got their first trying out.

Finally, they reveal a preoccupation with the past of his native country, which, as we have seen earlier, becomes a yardstick for testing contemporary life. That this is Ford's impulse becomes increasingly clear in the later books in which the modern scene plays a prominent part — *Ladies Whose Bright Eyes* and *Zeppelin Nights*. From the vantage point of history Ford examines the values of the modern world.

In the next chapter, we shall examine those of his novels which focus directly on the contemporary English social scene.

NOVELS OF SOCIAL SATIRE

REGISTERING the life of one's day — this to Ford was a basic task of the novelist. At bottom, his rationale was social. By making such a *constatation*, the novelist would be displaying for his readers just how they and their society were actually conducting themselves — an extremely salutary accomplishment. In the works we now turn to — *The Inheritors* (1901), *An English Girl* (1907), *Mr. Apollo* (1908), *The Simple Life Limited* (1911), *The New Humpty-Dumpty* (1912), and *Mr. Fleight* (1913) — this aim is particularly clear. Each holds Ford's reflecting glass up to the age in which he lived. And their focus, appropriately, is not on a few richly delineated, probingly explored, characters, but on society itself — an entity made up of many different types.

Judged by exacting literary standards, these novels are not of high or enduring literary value, with possibly one exception, to which we will come later. *The New Humpty-Dumpty* and *Mr. Fleight* have been called by Ford's friend, Edgar Jepson, "the best presentations of polite and cultured London at the end of the Edwardian age." [1] And undoubtedly Ford's treatment of the contemporary scene gave these books at their appearance a certain success and lively aptness. Yet, as their specific world vanishes from sight, they are bound to prove perishable. Most also are weakened by haste and by a resulting thinness, in texture and in motivation. (*The Simple Life Limited* and *The New Humpty-Dumpty* did not even appear in Ford's own name, but under the pseudonym "Daniel Chaucer.") So that in the main the group is more the work of the journalist than the artist.

Nevertheless, the books do have their importances. They contain frequent pages of excellent writing, and several well-drawn, significant characters; and one of them, *Mr. Apollo*, is possessed of considerable distinction. Ultimately minor, it yet is, as such, a work of art of genuine feeling and value. Of special interest also are *The Simple Life Limited* and *Mr. Fleight*. And each of the six has in addition a number of attractively amusing episodes, freakishly comic at times, and often very funny. Most importantly, the sextet comprises a valuable guide to their author's picture of the world in which he found himself, as we shall now see.

Ford's Attitudes toward His Society

Ford's basic view of his times was articulated early in his career — in *The Inheritors* (1901), which, though written with Conrad, was essentially the younger man's in the conception and the writing. "The Inheritors" are those relentless individuals — called Dimensionists, since they exist on the plane of the Fourth Dimension — who will supersede the old order: they are "a race clear-sighted, eminently practical, incredible; with no ideals, prejudices, or remorse; with no feeling for art and no reverence for life; free from any ethical tradition; callous to pain, weakness, suffering, and death, as if they had been invulnerable and immortal." [2] In short, they are the men who are making the modern age, with its frauds, cheats, exploitations of humanity and cold-blooded maneuverings. And their objective, which they accomplish, is to discredit the old virtues, honors, and faiths, and the probity and altruism of the tried, valued, and trusted.

Although *The Inheritors* suffers in its indictment (as in what it values) from being too general, the subsequent volumes amplify its basic vision with instances. Ford's perception of social decay, indeed, is his largest and most pervasive theme, and applies not only to the novels of the present group but to much of his other fiction as well. It is a significant part of books like *The Benefactor*, *The "Half Moon,"* and *Ladies Whose Bright Eyes* (allowing for its conventional ending), and extends also to his work after the war, to both the Tietjens cycle and the last, post-Depression novels in which the continuing crisis of modern times is the central subject.

To call these novels satires does not mean, of course, that they are obviously such, as may be inferred from Ford's theory. The satiric tone is adopted only occasionally, and it is not Ford's method to set up targets to be exposed as the climax and point of a scene, as in Swift or Thackeray. The criticism is keyed much lower. The world he sees is registered, and characters who in other novels might be clearly defined as villains are provided with plausible justification for their behavior and attitudes. His indignation is not thrust upon the reader and, more often than not, can be discerned only through nuances and revealing juxtapositions. Ford is not an angry satirist, but a sad one, and the rage that he feels does not explode but smolders. These novels demand, therefore, that the reader's moral sense play over the materials presented and form its own judgments, for the trace lines are loosely held. With such a method interpretation may vary widely, and the possibility of ambiguity increases in Ford's work as his technique and perception grow more subtle and objective. The later *Mr. Fleight* and *The New Humpty-Dumpty*, for example, are far less obvious in their points than the earlier *The Inheritors* and *An English Girl*. Nevertheless, Ford's moral position and fundamental attack, particularly on the larger questions, can scarcely be missed. They emerge in the careful reading of the particular novel, become clearer from work to work, and are fixed more firmly by a variety of comments which appear in his non-fictional writings.

The objects of Ford's satire are diverse, and include the most prominent, and entrenched, institutions of the modern age. His lash flicks the profit motive, and crooked financial and business practices. It strikes out against parliamentary politics; the popular press; democracy; and socialism, both Fabian and the more sentimental types. And it scores as well a host of other targets, such as muscular

Christianity, atheism, social climbers, the official intelligentsia, and industrialized urban life.

In the following pages, Ford's attacks will be detailed from scenes and episodes in the novels. Taken together, they constitute a full arraignment of the twentieth-century world, and by implication they provide a better understanding of what he himself stood for.

Ford's disapproving attitude toward the contemporary business civilization already has been glimpsed in *Ladies Whose Bright Eyes*, and probably is best summed up in his book on James, where he wrote of business that "It is a matter of dirty little affairs incompetently handled by men of the lowest class of intelligence."[3] In the present group, his blows fall heaviest in *An English Girl*, which recounts the futile attempts of young Don Collar Kelleg, inheritor of the world's largest fortune, to redress the wrongs committed by his tycoon father. In particular he is disturbed by the betrayal of a certain Kratzenstein, from whom was stolen the Montana mine which had launched the great fortune. But when Don offers to make reparation, Kratzenstein — proclaiming himself an independent and self-respecting citizen — indignantly rejects the offer as charity. His reasoning sums up the business ethic: old Kelleg had after all executed "a perfectly legitimate stroke of business."[4] And Kratzenstein immediately proposes a deal by which Don could rig the market.

Parliamentary politics receives its main onslaught in *Mr. Fleight*, at the head of which is ironically set the following inscription, from the *Herefordshire Weekly Chronicle*:

In no faltering tones the candidate proclaimed the virtues of the constitution of our country, the twin pillars of its shining façade being the unspotted purity of the British Parliamentary machine, and the inviolability of the British hearth.

The plot of the book, which concerns the campaign to elect Mr. Fleight to Parliament, is cleverly calculated to dull the sheen. For in its working out is revealed a thicket of political chicanery, with Mr. Fleight's immense fortune, founded on soap, as the foremost political fact. "If you're going to go up at all fast as a climber," his mentor explains to Mr. Fleight, "it's going to cost you £150,000 a year for sheer bribery":

"The party funds will cost you about £40,000 every two or three years — every time there is a general election, at least. You will have to run a daily paper in order to boom yourself with the general public, and you can't lose less than £60,000 a year on that. You will have to run a serious monthly or weekly to advertise you to a thinking people — another £5,000. You will have to have a constituency with a solid 2,000 majority, and that will cost you about £2 per vote per annum — say £7,000. You will have to have an expensive wife for the social side of things; her establishment charges will run you into at least £12,000 if you do the thing at all decently." [5]

Both political parties, of course, vie to have Mr. Fleight as their candidate. But when the government learns that, being an honest man, he would probably break party discipline, they drop him. The opposition, on the other hand, can afford a certain irregularity, for the time being.

Ford also depicts the underhand campaign maneuverings of the politicians, and the selfish, shallow motivations that govern the electorate. The chances of Mr. Fleight's opponent are being rehearsed: "There's Mr. Gregory. . . . He's a stick, isn't he? What have they put him up for? Just money? I thought so. He's cotton; our man's soap. There's nothing to choose between those two commodities." [6] Ford also cites the vilification heaped up on the candidates. Mr. Fleight is a Jew, and his opposition has got out placards depicting him "as a gentleman with a nose about two feet long stirring up a soap vat labelled 'Filthy Lucre,' and the inscription is 'Englishmen vote for Englishmen and not for Jew sweaters.'" [7] On the other hand, Mr. Fleight's supporters want to proclaim that his opponent keeps pigs in his drawing room — a notion not uncharacteristic of Ford's freakish invention. And only through the intercession of Mr. Fleight himself is the nonsensical tale dropped as ammunition.

But the modern institution Ford's criticism lashes most persistently is popular journalism, on both sides of the Atlantic. Each of the six novels contains scenes which variously dramatize the flashy inaccuracy of the cheap press, its dependence upon sensation, and its invasion of privacy. Attacked also is the cynical use by its backers of the press's strategic position to manipulate public events for financial gain, as in *The Inheritors*. Still more disheartening is its corruption of gifted and honest personalities through the allurements of its power and affluence, as occurs to the protagonist of the same novel. The Northcliffeian press lord in *Mr. Apollo* is particularly shrewd in spotting a clever talent whose writing will boom circulation:

He seemed to take a stable-boy at random, out of the streets; to develop one of these tremendous furores for him; to set him to describe the singing of a prima-donna, the effects of a revival meeting, or a new watering-place in the Riviera — without the least rhyme or reason in the choice. And the things got done. There could not be any doubt of that. The stable-boy described the top notes of the diva as "each an electric pin-prick." And the public tumbled over itself to read the middle pages of the paper.[8]

Democracy also comes under Ford's censure, for its rejection of traditions, its drive toward leveling, and its short-sighted goals. The post office clerk in *Mr. Fleight*, with his eager democratic bias, is a type of this. When Mr. Fleight, badly beaten by thugs, enters the building to make a phone call, the clerk is highly indignant. "Look here," he officiously cries, "if you're suffering from a mortal disease you've no right to use the telephone box! It's forbidden by the Act."[9] But, then, deciding that Mr. Fleight is actually Cannoneer Toms, the champion bantamweight of the world, just returned from a tough fight in Chicago, the clerk is all solicitous, and is ready to serve him in any way: something he would not do, he declares, for the Prime Minister himself. For — as the democratic vicar, the Reverend Pennyfather Blowater, had said to him only the other day —

"Jumnor, what is the whole country interested in? What takes the mind of everybody — all the world over? What has fascinated the attention of Maeterlinck, the great poet? Or supposing that you wanted to start a paper that you wanted to make money by, what would it have to be about? Boxing!" "Now," said the Reverend Blowater, "it's no good shutting our eyes to things that are a great public manifestation. This is one of the aspirations of the democracy, and the aspirations of the democracy are always right. The trouble of the age is that it's too much of a machine age; it's too grey, too unromantic. Now what do we see in a professional prize-fighter? Heroism, romance, the democracy asserting itself. What is needed for the career of such a man? Sobriety, temperance, determination, physical fitness, dash — all democratic virtues. Consider the career of such a man." [10]

Far more biting, however, is Ford's satire in *Mr. Apollo*. To the title character, yet another clergyman, this time the Reverend Mr. Todd, is boastfully showing the city of London —"the biggest the world has ever seen"— and the houses of the working people among whom he has his ministry. After a time, Mr. Apollo, in his clear, passionless voice, asks: What are the aspirations of all these people? And what becomes of them and their aspirations? At these odd queries, a faint weariness falls upon the missionary: "They — they fill graveyards," he replies. The scene goes on to drive home Ford's point. Troubled by his answer, the minister pauses to "recover" "his breezy and comforting common sense":

How could he have answered with such an extraordinary — with such an obviously improper phrase? "Well," he thought to himself, "it was the odd questions which called for odd answers." If he had asked — as he ought to have — what was the population of the city; what proportion of that population were of the criminal class; how many belonged to the Established Church; what were the rents of the shops; or what even was the average income of the inhabitants of this parish of the middling poor? But their aspirations! And what became of them!

The questions were disagreeable almost; they were certainly quite disagreeable. . . . They were almost, as it were, contemptuous — these questions. It was as if this stranger, this mere foreigner — for after all he *was* a foreigner — had suggested that this city did not justify its existence. It was like a sneer at the largest city the world had ever seen.[11]

As for the nobility, few are not ignoble. Many have aligned themselves with the forces of economic speculation and with the popular press: among them, the Duc de Mersch, chief promoter and exploiter of *The Inheritors*; and the Grand Duke Nicholas of Russia in *The New Humpty-Dumpty*, who supports a monarchist counter-revolution against the republican government of a country resembling Portugal solely to make a coup on the market. An avid collector of obscene and pornographic literature (with pictures), he cares not a whit for the venture's kingly ideal. Similarly, the intensely vain Queen Mother in the same book, being primarily interested in receiving deference, much prefers exile in her comfortable London quarters to the burdens of regal duty at home. In *The Simple Life Limited*, Lady Croydon increases the rents on her tenants to make her husband more comfortable, and variously exploits her rank and position. When a public subscription is raised, she has herself put down for twenty pounds, but pays nothing. For her name will stimulate other contributions, she explains, well pleased with her generosity.

The idle upperclass commoner is also a Fordian target in the person of the Blimpish, trivial-spirited Eugene Durham in *Mr. Apollo*. Such individuals, says the title character, are like gods in that they make no effort and fulfill no functions in the human republic: "fed from unseen sources; their means of life are assured, and by no effort of their own; they are without fears and without doubts." But being mortal and not gods, they are susceptible to decay; the absence of a need for effort brings about in them capricious, unstable passions. Having everything that he needs, such a man "will set his heart upon things of little purpose," exhausting his passions of hope and despair on such an unimportant fact as the settling of birds on his roof or windows.[12]

Still sharper, certainly much more thorough, are the barbs Ford aims at socialism — and, in particular, the types that it produces, or perhaps attracts. His fullest presentation of the subject is in *The Simple Life Limited*, a novel which focuses on the activities of a small cooperative community, after the style of William Morris. In defiance of the modern spirit and of the established order of things, the members of the colony, socialists of the picturesque and medieval variety, seek to live the "Simple Life," to be a self-sustaining community and an example to the world. Before the book is long underway, however, the colonists are seen to be an absurd, pitiful, ineffectual band acting on a cluster of discomforting, half-baked prejudices and notions. They disapprove of bicycles, for instance, because they are machines manufactured by other machines, and were not used in the Middle Ages. When a modern device is installed to enable their chimneys to draw properly, the colonists raise strenuous protests and cause its removal; as a result, their rooms are always filled with smoke and their walls darkened by soot. They ban cooking as unnatural and live on a diet mostly of nuts, cheese, sour milk, and whole-meal biscuits. Meat, of course, is taboo. And instead of evil alcohol, the colonists have revived the drinking of mead (a modest little Fordian joke). For clothing, they wear only fabric made by the community — a coarse gray material shaped into garments which make the wearer look like a convict ("We feel that we are hideous but it is in a good cause"),[13] and which fail to keep out the rain. Because of the heavy downpours, some Simple Lifers degenerate so far as to purchase waterproofs.

It is true that they compounded with their consciences by acquiring, instead of anything so vulgar as mere macintosh, fishermen's coats of shiny yellow varnished canvas with sou'westers to match. These they considered were more legitimate since they were authentic costumes, since they were certainly not conventional and since, equally certainly, they lent a touch of colour to the countryside.[14]

When one young Simple Life couple marry, they defy conventions by adopting the girl's family name, an act for which, naturally, they have excellent theoretical reasons, his being "Gubb" and hers "Bransdon": "Fine-sounding names would be perpetuated, ugly or grotesque ones would disappear and to that extent the world would be reckoned more beautiful." Then, too, since she is the daughter of the noted poet and leader of the community there is satisfaction for the young man in being associated, even in such fashion, with great men. When a member of a Tory family explains that the adoption of the family name of the wife is nothing new, and goes far back in English tradition ("the Duke of Northumberland's name, if one of his ancestors hadn't imitated you, would have been Smithson, not Percy"), the boy replies: "Oh, that's mere snobbishness. *We* acted on principle."[15] Similarly, when one of the supporters of the movement appears at the colony wearing a check cap which he had unthinkingly purchased in an emergency, the Lifers feel it necessary to hold a meeting to consider its implications. Afterwards, a delegate approaches him and tactfully explains the pain and consternation caused by his using such a head-covering. Their objection, of course, is simply on principle. "The wearing of it was only a beginning. But to what dreadful ends of conventionality might such beginnings not tend? Mr. Parmont might end, that is to say, in wearing brown boots or returning the Squire's call." [16]

"The Simple Life!" one of the observers of the colony scoffs. "It's the most accursed, the most complicated tangle there ever was in the world." [17] Though intended to develop harmony among its members, the community is in fact torn by jealousy and bickering. When one of the female members claims herself to be the "life and soul" of the colony, another sets herself to obstruct her in every way. And between them the colony splits into bitter factions. Relations with the English peasantry are hardly any better, for the Lifers reveal themselves as callous toward the rights of the country people and are exasperated by their shell-backed recalcitrance to progress. In return, the peasantry resent them deeply.

The leader and inspiration of the colonists is one Simon Bransdon, famous poet and novelist, a lazy and slovenly man who looks like a sea anemone, and who is celebrated for such sayings as: "Whoso eateth of his fellow creature, though it be but a chicken, wrings the angels' bosoms" and "Sovereigns, corsets and leather boots, these shall bring upon our cities the fate of Sodom and Gomorrah." [18] (The American editions have "dollars" instead of "sovereigns.")

If Simon Bransdon is the inspiration of the community, the power behind the throne, however, is Horatio Gubb: "a parasitic gentleman, who fattened entirely upon the associations and upon the ideas of such distinguished people as would permit him to enter their houses." [19] A close disciple and friend of the late William Morris, undistinguished (unhappily) in bearing and manner, and a solicitor by profession, Mr. Gubb has moved in on the illustrious Bransdon. Mr. Gubb is a promoter, in short, a man who, if incapable of swaying multitudes himself, is nevertheless untiring and highly practical. "What he desired, though he had never put it in words to himself, was to be the actual organiser, the dictator of a properous 'going' concern along lines of a sufficient idealism to gain for himself a certain sphere of influence." [20] And he sets about the task of exploiting both the poet and the Simple Life, compelling the colonists to hold dances around maypoles, and to appear in yet other ways attractively picturesque.

One of the most devastating scenes is the "visit" which Gubb arranges to display the great Bransdon at work.[21] Bursting in to warn Simon that Lady Croydon is coming, he asks: "Will you weave or will you dictate?" Working at the loom, he says, looks more simple, but dictation is really more impressive. "Of course you prefer me to dictate," replies Bransdon. "It lets you show off your devotion!" Ignoring this rebellion, Gubb persists: "If you haven't got anything fresh in your head to dictate, you could do 'Riders to the Hills' or 'The Waste Places of the Sea' over again. . . . It's just to show people a typical example of how we live." And at last consenting, the poet begins to chant, "I will hie me to the waste places of the sea. To the weary, waste places of the sea where ever the wind wails weary from the north —" With the greatest of gentleness the latch of the door is lifted, and the visitors peer in, in rapt silence. "Oh, Ulalume lost! Girl of the grey eyes and the milk-white feet: no more beside the lone rath nor upon the lorn hillside shall thy silver hand beckon me to pursuit — Unseen of thee shall all the little foxes play by the Corrighan Ghu: the doves of Eimir shall call unto thee and they shall not hear thee. Nevermore, oh girl of the snowy forehead and shell-like breasts, nevermore shall thy grey gown rival the tender mists of Oysium — Lo, I have begotten me to the waste places of the sea. Black and bitter is my bed. Black and bitter is my companionless bed. . . ." The door closes "with a movement of the slowest and most reverential." "And when the catch of the latch was once more securely in the hoop, Mr. Bransdon, retaining his high and hollow note of voice, changed his chanting to the syllable: 'Ow! Ow! Ow! Ow! Ow!' "

More significant, however, is Mr. Gubb's gradually developing conviction that the colony can be made to pay, and pay very well. The wedding of an idealistic social community to the profit motive is one of Ford's deftest strokes of satire. Mr. Gubb is no other than a sound, industrious entrepreneur, a small capitalist, and the community is transformed into a company called The Simple Life Limited. After a year's workings, the enterprise pays a dividend of eight and a half per cent, the profits coming from Mr. Gubb's shrewd management, an amiable backer, and, to be sure, the slave-like labors of the unfortunate socialist members of the colony. Ironically, Gubb is fêted for his achievement by the surrounding nobility and gentry, while his fellow Simple Lifers are not invited. Out of his success in managing the socialist community follows an offer from a wealthy syndicate to direct an important realty development, and Gubb's fame and fortune are made.

Similarly, Simon Bransdon ends by throwing over the colony and becoming a popular playwright. Marvelously, his health and spirits improve and his chronic laziness vanishes. His daughter Ophelia, one of the most rabid of the colonists, when applauded for her beauty by a music-hall operator, decides to become an actress and finally marries the impresario. By the end, the whole community has become infected with the attitudes of the social order which it had so intensely criticized. When their buildings are vindictively set afire by a maniacal and depraved Russian refugee, the destruction seems the appropriate finish to the enterprise.

"They're making the whole movement into a laughing-stock," a socialist footman in the novel says of the colonists, whom he refers to as "those amateurs." [22] But if Ford shows himself as ready to poke fun at the ineffectual amateurs of the Simple Life, he is much more serious and concerned about socialists purposeful enough to be called professionals.

The most favorable presentation of a doctrinal Socialist in Ford's gallery is Miss Stobhall in *The Simple Life Limited*. A haranguer and agitator, she is also shrewd and clear-sighted, at least about Bransdon, Gubb, and the colony. Detesting individualism, her greatest sorrow is that she has not been able to make Hamnet Gubb, Horatio's son, see its evils. "An Individualist is everything that's bad. It's a person that believes in competition and doesn't recognize that it's his duty to consider himself as part of the State." [23] "I've tried everything. I've read Karl Marx to him night after night, I've had over all the Fabian tracts, and I've read one to him every night with comments for the last six months." [24] ("Oh, poor devil!" one of her hearers declares.)

Much less attractive are such figures as Ophelia Bransdon and Mrs. Lee (the two warring ladies of the colony), and Countess Macdonald and Mr. Pett of *The New Humpty-Dumpty*. It is with these socialists — doctrinaire and narrowly oriented toward science and economics — that Ford's satire and disapproval cut deepest. These are the really dangerous people whose intellectual energy is sparked by hate and the vivid sense of their deprivations, and whose intense, often hysterical drive is aimed at winning power. Ophelia Bransdon seems to sum up their position: "In the cause of spreading light," she says, "cruelty is a merit. We shall have to take many hard blows. We shall have to be stoned, perhaps, but we mean to hit back. For that reason we have determined to get our blows in first." [25] To such personalities doctrine is more important than humanity. It is no accident that the shrill, determined Mrs. Lee is the great champion of the destructive Russian. So much is her perception swallowed by the abstraction of downtrodden Russian revolutionaries that she can no longer examine the individual. The irony is that not only is the man a criminal type, but also a double agent, whose work for the Czar has betrayed hundreds of revolutionaries. The perfectibilist, the point would seem to be, is blind to the dark forest that stands in the hearts of men.

As for the intelligentsia at large, their vices vary little from those described among the socialists. Some are passionately doctrinaire, like Augusta Macphail, the journalist of *Mr. Fleight*, or the Dumas enthusiast in *The New Humpty-Dumpty*. There are pompous pretenders, like Callan, the novelist in *The Inheritors*, or literary butterflies lacking in dedication, like the gossipy dilettantish poet, Cluny Macpherson, in *Mr. Fleight*. Others, more clearly venal, are chiefly eyeing the main chance, like Pollhampton, the publisher in *The Inheritors*, Arthur Bracondale in *Mr. Apollo*, and again Augusta Macphail. Still others are confirmed hacks ready to write whatever line is demanded by their employers, like Soane, the editorial writer in *The Inheritors*, or to deliver favorable write-ups for services rendered, like the London dramatic critics described in *The Simple Life Limited* (those "sodden critics" always prepared to gang up on whatever first-rate authors might come "butting into" the theater). A telling shot at the pettiness and lack of idealism in literary circles who have hooked a rich backer is made by Ford when Cluny Macpherson announces Mr. Fleight's support of a new magazine and his willingness to lose five thousand a year on it:

Think of that! It meant five thousand a year thrown complete into the laps of those present. It might mean anything from a hundred and fifty a year for every one of them. . . . There wouldn't, as he expressed it, be any crank of them all who would not be able to make her voice heard. "Isn't it glorious? isn't it fun?" [26]

"Timon and Falstaff," the poet Robert Lowell has described Ford Madox Ford in a poem [27] honoring him — a peculiar and yet appropriate juxtaposition. Many writers have verified the picture of Ford the man as Falstaff, a role that particularly finds its ascendancy in his memoirs. But in the novels here under study, he is clearly in his Timon mood. In the mass, human nature, together with the institutions it constructs and devotes itself to, is for Ford an ugly spectacle. The world that he unfolds in these novels embodies the burden of two of his favorite aphorisms: "That will give you a proud idea of man," and "Man is a wolf to man."

But the picture that Ford presents, if drawn in dark shades, is not completely black, nor a mere negative expression. If it is plain that Ford's attitude is opposed to the bulk of the trends of the modern age, what he stands for is also apparent both by implication from his criticisms and through the example of those of his characters who are attractive. The values that Ford abides by are traditional: generosity and kindness, loyalty and steadfast devotion, the dignity and the integrity of the arts within a society, the deep responsibility of superiors to those they rule, and the subordinate position of women as sustainers to their men, who in turn honor and protect them. The ideal individual for Ford is the classic Christian gentleman — the man of goodness and true gentility whose primary wish is that of helping those in need.

These values, in part or whole, are expressed in the books through various figures. The integrity of the arts is upheld in the person of Lea, the publisher's reader in *The Inheritors*, who fosters promising literary talent only to sadly watch it sell its gift on the popular market; and in the painter Jenkins in the same book who has lived a hard and uncomfortable life, and who fiercely resents being patronized, but who has not abandoned his work. Another attractive character is the aggressively democratic cockney science teacher, Carver, in *Mr. Apollo*. Although intemperate and polemical in his argument, and to that extent unlovely, he is a man of depth and generosity. As Ford puts it, his personality contained "a real humility when he came into contact with any man whom he imagined to have come nearer expressing the truths of science or of life, or who exhibited fortitude, bravery, endurance, or strength." [28] The proper role for women, sensitive and understanding and loyal, may be seen in the persons of Eleanor Greville in *An English Girl*, Mrs. Todd and Frances Milne in *Mr. Apollo*, and Wilhelmina Macphail in *Mr. Fleight*.

The Christian gentleman is presented in various states of purity. To a lesser extent, the type may be found in the landowner, Gerald Luscombe, of *The Simple Life Limited*, who is concerned for the welfare of his peasant tenants and who for a while supports the Simple Life project, and in the generous and tolerant impresario of show business, George Everard, in the same book. On a small scale it can be seen in the kindly butler Mr. Creedy, also in the same book, who gives the four children of Mrs. Lee apple halves he has broken for them, and who softly urges them that it is not nice for children to say shocking things about their parents. Still more significant representations of the ideal may be found in the figures of Mr. Churchill, the Foreign Minister in *The Inheritors*, Don Collar Kelleg in *An English Girl*, Mr. Apollo himself (particularly as a critic of its lack), Hamnet Gubb in *The Simple Life Limited*, the Duke of Kintyre in *The New Humpty-Dumpty*, Mr. Fleight, the Jew, in the book named after him, and, most fully, in Count Macdonald of *The New Humpty-Dumpty*.

As for the proper polity for mankind, Ford's position is highly idiosyncratic. No doubt most of his attitudes are those traditionally associated with Toryism, with its aristocratic and feudal ideal of society and its conception of the gentleman. And Ford frequently called himself a Tory. The plot of *The New Humpty-Dumpty*, as has been seen, involves the attempt made in the country of Galizia to restore the monarchy that had been abolished by the republicans. Although this counter-revolution is guided by Count Macdonald, who helps to instill in the young king the noble ideals of kingship, it actually was born in the acute, intense brain of the intellectual cockney, Mr. Pett. Beginning as an anarchist, Mr. Pett had proceeded to the stage of being a socialist when he had a startling and revolutionary experience. While he was riding on a bus with Macdonald, an accident occurred in which an injured lower-class girl was accused by the police of shamming. With the poor man's fear of the law, Mr. Pett did nothing; but Macdonald descended from the bus top, presented his card to the policeman, defended the girl, and added half a sovereign to guarantee medical expenses. To Mr. Pett, accustomed to accepting police brutalities, the action was the bravest he had ever seen, but for Macdonald it was no more than duty: he had behaved in the tradition of a gentleman of good breeding and lineage. What impressed Mr. Pett most was that Macdonald had done the right thing automatically. As Mrs. Pett explains:

"It struck Herbert on the top of that bus that if you've already got a stratum of society that does its duty automatically and efficiently, we Socialists were on the wrong track. We were trying to pull down when we ought to have been trying to lift up. What struck Herbert was that *he* ought to have been trained to act as Macdonald acted, not that Macdonald ought to have been levelled down to act like Herbert, or rather not act at all. . . . It struck him that humanity had spent millions of pounds and millions of lives to train him to be the chivalrous and self-sacrificing creature that he is. Then what was the good of our spending just about as many efforts to undo what humanity has unconsciously been doing for ages? . . . . 'if a system of society can breed an animal as finely adapted to the needs of society as Macdonald is, then that type of society is what we want to preserve, not to destroy.' " [29]

For a novel with such a political framework, *The New Humpty-*

Dumpty is, however, surprisingly unpolitical in its texture. Scarcely any more serious charge is leveled at the republicans than that they accept bribes and are as dull as Methodists. As for Toryism, its virtues are left in generalities. Ford frequently said that he was never much interested in practical politics [30] and the truth of that statement is demonstrated, once one gets beyond the surface, in his fiction, which shows little real insight into its purposes, methods, and psychology. Ford's Toryism was basically sentimental. Toryism as actually practiced, or for that matter any political system, was repugnant to him.* The character in these novels who comes closest to Ford's own position toward the social order is surely Hamnet Gubb of *The Simple Life Limited*.

Hamnet, it will be recalled, is the young man the socialist Miss Stobhall had unavailingly sought to reclaim from the perils of individualism. Hamnet will agree that every word the Fabians ever uttered is "perfectly true and perfectly valid as applying to a state of Society such as ours is." But he says that it simply doesn't interest *him*. He's an Individualist, Miss Stobhall mourns, and not even of a reasoned kind. "He doesn't believe that competition is beneficent: he doesn't care about it: he doesn't care about freedom for the In-

---

* In a delightfully satiric passage he once wrote that for a writer to be a nonsensical Tory has its advantages:

Thus [Dr. Johnson] was a nonsensical Tory: and every man of letters should be a nonsensical Tory — to keep him out of mischief. . . . it is a matter of expediency. Shelley has pointed out that he styled himself atheist not because he was an Atheist but to avoid theological discussions. So, it is a good thing to call yourself a Tory to avoid the imbecilities of politicians. It works two ways: the Tory party — which is invariably the Stupid Party — never employs writers of any talent to support it, so you will be saved the temptation to waste your time in the corruption of your Times. If you announce yourself as belonging to one or other parties of the Left you will eventually succumb to the temptation of prostituting your pen; you will be execrated by all belonging to every other party of the Left; you will be swept into every imaginable type of Society, Caucus, Department, and devil-dodging, until at last you write your article to prove that Flaubert cannot write. Sometime after that the devil flies away with you. Moreover Tories are inarticulate so that you will waste no time over talking with your own side; whilst by the Left, a Tory is regarded as such an incarnation of evil that they too will leave him alone — as the Churchmen of his day did to Shelley. Tories besides can walk about in any sort of old rags and talk of the lower classes; the Left have always to wear starched collars and black coats or their confrères will not respect them. These are very solid advantages. (*transatlantic review*, I, 323–324.)

dividual as long as he's left alone." [31] In the end, it is Hamnet who points the moral of the book. The torch has been spitefully put to the community and in the bleak aftermath policemen, firemen, doctors, and colonists blackly mill around.

Hamnet pulled his wideawake down over his brows. . . . In the background the steam rose sluggishly; high over head, a momentarily visible speck, the lark let its all-penetrating song shower down upon their heads.

"That," Hamnet Gubb exclaimed, and with his hand he indicated the sombre, ugly group of human beings, "that is the Simple Life!" [32]

In the world of these novels, however, the values Ford holds and the characters who live by them seem obscured in the shadows cast by a ruling corruption. Many that have been named — Lea, Jenkins, Creedy, Carver, most of the female characters — are minor figures who insignificantly affect the action. Hamnet Gubb is basically a commentator, leaving the scene early in the novel, and, except briefly, not returning until near the end to fix the moral. As for the characters who play a more central part, these seem curiously ineffective. They go down to defeat because, like Churchill, they do not understand the times. Impaired in their wills, they are unable to know their minds or be decisive, like Don Kelleg, or they passively put themselves into the management of other men, as does Count Macdonald with Mr. Pett, or Mr. Fleight with Mr. Blood. As a group all but the less central and more generalized Churchill fail to attain dignity. The causes for which they stand, or the roles which they play, frequently seem trivial or slightly ridiculous. Often it is both. Part of Count Macdonald's duty to the Grand Duke, for example, is to hunt for the pornographic literature he craves. There is something farcical, too, in the fact that the Count's full name is Sergius Mihailovich Macdonald, that he is a Russian, and that his ancestor who had come to Russia at the time of Peter the Great claimed to be the legitimate king of Scotland. (Shades of Cunningham-Graham!) Then, too, an absurd and ultimately futile air hangs over the whole expedition to Galizia, so that in the end when Macdonald is assassinated one cannot feel that any high or worthy ideal dignifies his death. His quixotic idealism lacks the grandeur and conviction that would redeem it.

Angels tend to blend imperceptibly into fools in these novels. One is reminded of Thackeray. It is as though Ford were saying that in such a world of universal self-seeking and pettiness, those who hold the traditional ideals of humanity can only be twisted and exaggerated, lacking in genuine force and often enough futile and ridiculous.

The Inheritors

Ford's evaluation of *The Inheritors* in later years was stringent. In *Joseph Conrad* he variously calls it a "thin collaboration with no plot in particular," [33] "a queer, thin book which the writer has always regarded with an intense dislike . . . having nothing to do with literature," [34] and a "farrago of nonsense." [35] With special aversion he speaks of its "tremendously sentimental last scene." [36] As to the pervading style of the book, if it is not as dreadful as in its final passage, "it is bad enough":

a medley of prose conceived in the spirit of Christina Rossetti with imitations of the late Henry James; inspired by the sentimentality of a pre-Raphaelite actor in love scenes — precisely by Sir Johnston Forbes Robertson dyspeptically playing Romeo to Mrs. Patrick Campbell's Juliet; cadenced like Flaubert and full of little half-lines dragged in from the writer's own verses of that day.[37]

Ford's specific criticisms are undeniably acute and accurate, certainly when *The Inheritors* is considered from the high standards of an author who had just completed *Some Do Not*, with its masterly structure, characterization, and style. Yet one cannot but judge that these strictures, at least in tone, are over-severe. Technically and conceptually, the novel displays many attractive qualities, and the mark of a considerable talent is obvious. Of the six books in this chapter, *The Inheritors* impresses one as having had lavished upon it the greatest literary polish, a polish it probably owes to the influence of Conrad. In conception the novel is Ford's and he, as Conrad said, held the pen; but it is obvious that the younger man profited greatly from the highly professional ap-

proach of his collaborator. Where the book is weak – in its thinness and sentimental lapses – the fault can readily be attributed to
the youth of its principal author.

The theme of the book, the supplanting of an old order of value
by a new one of remorseless efficiency, has been already mentioned.
The embodiment of this superseding order is an ethereal, goddesslike, never-named female who casually meets and chats on the road
with the young protagonist of the book, a cultivated but impecu-
nious novelist of old family named Arthur Etchingham-Granger.
To him she announces that she has come from the plane of the
Fourth Dimension in order to manipulate into being certain public
events. Specifically, her aim is to throw into disrepute the Foreign
Minister, Churchill, a man of uprightness and probity, and to give
undisputed political dominance to the Chancellor of the Exchequer,
Gurnard, himself a Dimensionist. The luminous female also explains
that although Etchingham-Granger will oppose for a time the cause
she represents, he, too, will become one of them. The young man
does not believe her talk, considering her words a playful element
in a delightful flirtation. But at their separation, the first stage in the
betrayal of his standards begins. He turns into Callan's house, where
he is offered a job on *The Hour*. Gradually there evolve the means
by which the Dimensionist's purpose will be brought about. In an
effort to get into touch with the spirit of his times, Churchill associates himself with characters of a very different stamp – Fox, the
yellow-press editor, and the Duc de Mersch, the imperialistic ruth-
less promoter in Greenland of the System for the Regeneration of
the Arctic Regions. As may be expected, these various personages
had their actual prototypes, as Ford explains in the Conrad book:
Churchill stood for Balfour, Gurnard for Joseph Chamberlain who
had made the Boer War, Fox for Lord Northcliffe, and the Duc de
Mersch for Leopold II, King of the Belgians ("the foul beast who
had created the Congo Free State in order to grease the wheels of
his harems with the blood of murdered negroes").[38]

The novel recounts the successive steps by which the prophecy
of the goddess Dimensionist, who sets herself up in the role of
Granger's sister, is brought into being. The climactic moment oc-

curs when Granger, a passive instrument, prints an article exposing the inhuman exploitation of the Greenland scheme. With its publication, Fox and de Mersch are ruined; Churchill, who has generously befriended the young man, is discredited; and, of course, Gurnard, who marries Granger's "sister," reigns on top.

The principal ingredient which gives to *The Inheritors* its measure of distinction is Ford's conception and skilled handling of his young writer. Etchingham-Granger serves several key fictional purposes. As first-person narrator, his cultivated and subtle sensibility gives the style a literate, lively flavor, and the irony with which he presents himself and others adds a pleasing tonic dryness. But Granger's importance is still deeper. To some extent his role in the novel is that of observer, for the basic situation is the public onset of the Inheritors, which he describes. But the drama, and the book's greatest interest, are finally not public but private. The narrator himself is the central figure. At various crucial stages Granger has the power to interpose and alter the appointed course of events, but always he fails to act. Either he does not perceive the issue at hand or he justifies himself by rationalizing, as when he allows the article to appear. The fascination of the book is our witnessing, with the knowledge that Granger scoffs at, his moral failure to respond in harmony with his own values. Step by step, his personal force and dignity leak out. The discrediting of probity takes place not only publicly in the outer world of politics, but within Granger as well. At his protest that he acted as he did because he loved the woman of the Dimensionists, she mocks him. This illusion is why he has lost his ease, she says, and adds that he still deceives himself. It is not the thought of the harm he has done to others that wracks him. "It is because you broke; because you were false to your standards at a supreme moment; because you have discovered that your honour will not help you to stand a strain. . . . It is yourself that you bemoan. That is your tragedy, that you can never go again to Churchill with the old look in your eyes, that you can never go to any one for fear of contempt. . . . Oh, I know you, I know you." [39] And Granger concedes that she does.

Ford remarked that *The Inheritors* had "no plot in particular," and surely it contains little action, a circumstance which tends to follow from its central actor's characteristic failure to act. No doubt this condition is a flaw. Yet it also is part of a larger element that deserves praise — the novel's rather impressive rendering of the movement of Fate (for that after all is the real name of the Dimensionist). Principally this effect is arranged through the double vantage point from which the events are observed — an aspect already touched on. The reader, seeing with a larger vision than Granger, understands the consequences of acts which he is blind to. The effect is further sharpened by the novel's closely constructed exposition. The opening dialogue between Granger and the Dimensionist occurs in the first chapter, and is a kind of overture to the play itself, the curtain going up when they separate and he enters Callan's house. Through the first half of the novel, there is a steady formal progression, which effectively supports the dominant sense of a tightening fate.

The deftness with which Ford handles Granger is displayed as well in his presentation of several of the minor characters. Lea, who is modeled on Edward Garnett, is particularly fine; though he appears in only one brief chapter, he leaves a trace of his preoccupied and dry-witted rectitude trailing after him through the book. When told by Granger of a secret society of Fourth Dimensionists who are to inherit the earth, Lea replies while returning to his reading, "Oh, I wish them joy." [40] Churchill also gives off an attractive aura of benevolence and ability; and Callan's portrait is maliciously cut with mild acid.

But, of course, *The Inheritors* is no masterpiece. It indulges too much in youthful sentimentality. To Ford's own citations in support of this point may be added the trite scene in which the goddesslike Dimensionist confesses to the young man that for a brief moment, out of feeling for him, she had thought of giving up her relentless purpose. Then, too, Granger's persistent refusal, in the face of potent evidence, to believe her assertions is a device too obvious to be relied on, as it is, throughout the entire book. As much as this obtuseness helps to establish technically the sense of Fate and of moral failure, it contradicts Granger's general acuity and sets up in the reader a somewhat disillusioning awareness of plot machinery. And if some minor characters are skillfully and freshly managed, others are too vaguely drawn, such as the Dimensionist and Gurnard, or too conventionally handled, as de Mersch. Finally it is obvious that the level on which Ford has conceived the problem is not psychologically penetrating enough to be truly significant. Ultimately, *The Inheritors* suffers from the romantic vague.

An English Girl

Ford's first real public success as a writer came in 1905, with a book of impressions on the English capital, called *The Soul of London*. The volume was followed by a study of rural England, *The Heart of the Country* (1906), and by another of the British character, *The Spirit of the People* (1907). *An English Girl* (1907) — written "as a variation on a book of essays to give the effect of a tour in the United States" [41] — is an obvious attempt to repeat this success in fictional form. It is also patterned, as Ford said, upon James' "international" novels, and involves much representation of the American character through contrast with the English and the Continental.

The shape of the narrative is that of a circle. It opens in England with the news that an expatriate American, Don Collar Kelleg, has become the "richest citizen in the world." It then moves across the Atlantic to New York, where the idealistic and aesthetic young man is promptly repelled at the materialism of the United States. His fiancée, Eleanor Greville, on the other hand — the "English girl" of the title (through whom the action is mostly seen) — soon surmounts her initial dismay at the brashness of Americans and learns to enjoy them. Eventually defeated by the Trust, young Don returns with the Grevilles to an England with which he feels in tune. And Eleanor, once home, again quickens to her native land, its scale and its pace, and its steadying traditions — ultimately agreeing with Don's half-brother, an Italian count, that Americans are to be taken no more seriously than children. The point of view is further dramatized at the close of the novel when the constantly wavering Don Kelleg again returns to the States, in a departure which he knows must mean a final rift with Eleanor — who, for her part, quietly allows him to go.

As a novel, *An English Girl* is among the weakest of the present group. It has, of course, certain attractions — notably the impressionistic accounts (now period pieces) of a ship's arrival in New York harbor, of the atmosphere of midtown Manhattan, and of a steamer trip to Coney Island. Eleanor's father is a lively and witty creation, and there are certain spirited comic scenes in America. But, as a whole, the novel is an aesthetic jumble. By turns fictionalized travel tour, farce, social satire, and psychological novel of character — with each manner at cross purposes with the others and with the whole — the novel leaves the unmistakable impression of hasty, make-shift carpentry. Its beginning has all the trappings of light comedy, with its newly created "richest citizen in the world," its external presentation of personalities, and its sprightly dialogue. Its end is serious and weighty, earnestly reflecting on the nature of the American type, and unconvincingly treating the split between young Kelleg and Eleanor with the tone of near tragedy.

The Simple Life Limited and *The New Humpty-Dumpty*

About *The Simple Life Limited* and *The New Humpty-Dumpty* — both published under the pseudonym "Daniel Chaucer"— not very much needs to be added to earlier discussion. Of the six novels, *The Simple Life* has the greatest particularity of detail. Not only are the colonists diversely ridiculed in a fashion that has the ring of authenticity, but Ford's characterizations also rely heavily on a thick texture of biographical detail, a method unusual for him. The lengthy explanatory backgrounds provided for Simon Bransdon, Horatio Gubb, Gerald Luscombe, and George Everard, in particular, are so carefully and effectively sketched in that a reader senses definite models. However this may be for individuals, it certainly is true that Ford was acquainted with the types he represents in the novel. In the late nineties, as he explains, under the influence of William Morris, he had himself tried to live a comparable sort of simple life in the country. His tone suggests that he judged the episode one of the follies of youth.

Such intimate knowledge of the subject matter of *The Simple Life* contributes greatly to its liveliness and charm. And this effectiveness is further supported by considerable technical craft. Thus Ford's shifting of point of view from character to character adroitly advances his action, opens new views of his subject, and enables him to sustain fairly lightly the weight of detail. The management of time is also deft. The action moves in waves as the colony grows and alters, and all the devices associated with Ford's impressionistic method — striking opening, exposition, and development — are skillfully employed at each new beginning.

Unfortunately this pace and freshness are not maintained throughout. Ford delivers himself of his best satiric buckshot in the first half, and after that the movement slackens. Instead of being worked out by dramatic means, too much of the novel becomes muffled through mediating figures who are inordinately expected to advance it as well. It is as though Ford grew weary of the task — most of the fun being over anyway — and had rapidly dashed the rest off, without imaginatively selecting his incidents. Inevitably, the book is much too long.

If the latter parts of *The Simple Life Limited* give the appearance of haste and of fatigue, these qualities pervade almost all of *The New Humpty-Dumpty* — which, symptomatically, is the lengthiest (432 pages) of Ford's novels. In it is scarcely any art. Its characters, of whom there are far too many, are drawn sketchily — without conviction or life. Scenes are rare. Page after page of expository writing, in short, must substitute for a living reality. An individual mind has played over the materials, but at a very low power, and uncreatively.

The most fruitful approach to *The New Humpty-Dumpty*, therefore, is almost surely not to examine it as a novel — as such its worth is slight — but as a combination of imaginative diary and workshop book. It is very much as though Ford were using the book as one might employ a journal, as a means of putting his emotional difficulties on paper to gain distance and so rid himself of them.

The relation between Count Macdonald and his wife is the most striking example of the inartistic importation of biographical material into the novel. The malignancy with which the Countess persecutes her husband, seeking to wreck his plans and to ruin him, and even resolving at the end to hurl vitriol in his face, is incredible. No motivation provided in the book explains a passion so vindictive and fierce. Her refusal to grant the Count a divorce so that he might marry Lady Aldington sheds light, however, on Ford's fantasy. Here, slightly altered, is his own difficulty with his wife, who had refused to release him to marry Violet Hunt. Similarly, Macdonald's plan to obtain from the Czar a ukase dissolving the marriage is not very different from Ford's own efforts to free himself by means of a German divorce.

But *Humpty-Dumpty* is not merely a fictionalized diary. The novel also proved to be a kind of workshop in which Ford was evolving new characters, or, perhaps more accurately, beginning to transform old ones. The type of the fiercely possessive woman had already appeared as Anne Jeal in *The "Half Moon,"* and as Katya Lascarides in *A Call.* With Countess Macdonald she is to become, in addition, the unloved wife who will not divorce.

Even more significant is the emergence of Count Macdonald, for his evolution signals an important shift in Ford's attitude toward his male protagonists. Ford's leading characters, as we have seen, are typically men marked by indecision and passivity — intensely as they feel, they are unable to act. In the earlier novels these characters are placed in a light of disfavor, the reader's sympathy usually being enlisted on the side of the women whom the men should, but do not, make their own. With the creation of Count Macdonald, however, the conception is transformed: new values are now accented, and an altered pattern of virtues and faults begins to stand out. Where before the character was a disapproved of, because indecisive, weakling, he now becomes a figure of enormous talents and knowledge who holds himself aloof and superior to the fray. Not above extending aid to those engaged in the struggle for place, he himself smiles on, indulgently. A hint of the type has already been seen in the protagonist of *The Portrait*, but Mr. Bettesworth lacks the attribute of non-involvement. He is simply arrogant and overbearingly proud. This is not, of course, to say that the type being described here is without arrogance. Indeed, Mr. Blood of *Mr. Fleight*, who is drawn on the Count Macdonald model, is in his brutal superiority a direct descendant of Mr. Bettesworth, as we shall see. Count Macdonald will, of course, evolve eventually into Christopher Tietjens — the figure in whom Ford has made the type memorable.

Beyond these observations, little more needs to be said about *The New Humpty-Dumpty* except to note Ford's delineation of Mr. Pett, the only creation in the novel who comes near to success. A kind of comic, even farcical, relative of Turgenev's Bazarov — intense, brilliant, swept in his emotions by envy and by a vaunting ego which perpetually injures itself, yet ultimately just — Mr. Pett's is a characterization which, if not always consistent or deeply examined, is endowed nevertheless with a genuinely fitful, complex life.

Mr. Fleight

It will be recalled that one condition of Ford's conception of the novelist is that whatever may be its author's private views, his reader should have no means of knowing them. Yet in most of the novels of social satire Ford is, as already suggested, not truly objective. His method may be indirect and subtle, but an attentive reader of works like *The Inheritors, An English Girl, The Simple Life Limited*, and *Mr. Apollo* cannot be long in doubt of where Ford stands. *Mr. Fleight*, however, poses a more difficult problem of interpretation. That Ford is castigating parliamentary politics is plain enough, the point clinched ironically without mistake by its title-page epigraphs. What requires more subtlety is defining Ford's attitude toward the other important subject of the novel: the Jew, and his role in modern society — specifically, toward its Jewish title character, Mr. Fleight, whose real name is Aaron Rothweil.

In his non-fictional writings Ford several times remarked that he did not like Jews.[42] And in his novels appear brief references indicating distaste, particularly if the Jew is a rich financier or businessman ("Of the Rand," for instance) and knighted. An example can be seen in *The Inheritors* when the narrator is greeted "Hullo, Granger" by a fellow journalist who is a Jew — a man "effusive and familiar, as the rest of his kind": "I was used to regarding myself as fallen from a high estate," the narrator observes, "but I was not yet so humble in spirit as to relish being called Granger by a stranger of his stamp. I tried to freeze him politely." [43]

A similar attitude of anti-Semitic class superiority colors the presentation of Mr. Fleight, whose mother was Scottish (Fleight being her name) and whose father was a Jew from Frankfort. Thus when Aaron decides to introduce himself to Mr. Blood, that true-born Englishman of doubly appropriate name is aghast, and exclaims:

"Good God!" in tones of such disgust that he appeared on the point of being sick. . . . "Aaron Rothweil Fleight!" Mr. Blood speculated as disagreeably as he could. "What sort of name is that for a human being? Half Scotch, half Hebrew! That's what it is. . . . And with that record you come to me? To me!" [44]

The distaste expressed by Augusta Macphail, who has been reared in a far more anti-Semitic Germany, is correspondingly sharper.

Ford's presentation of his title figure is unflattering in other ways. Undistinguished in appearance, he is pathetic and listless, indecisive, somewhat foolish, and vain. More unattractive still is the political manager, Mr. Garstein, who handles his party's crookeder tasks and who looks, according to the author, like an obese hog merchant. "The appearance of the Jew in our society means that the Jew is an unrivalled soldier of fortune," declares Reginald, Mr. Blood's brother. "He isn't part of our country; he hasn't got our morality, but he's extraordinarily able as a ruler. So our side takes him up and uses him. It doesn't matter to him which side he's on, because he can't begin to understand our problems or our ethics or our morality or our way of looking at things." [45]

In main contrast to Mr. Fleight is Mr. Blood, the "intelligence" of the novel, who has certain affinities of attitude with Ford and who resembles, in many ways, Christopher Tietjens. Omniscient and aloof, a wealthy landowner with vast knowledges and diverse abilities, and a man who has refused the brilliant public career which was universally expected of him, he is an anachronism: the fox-hunting squire, the typical English gentleman — of Napoleon's time. Mr. Blood looks on the modern world with horror; yet he is perpetually drawn to it in fascination, like a man whose tongue must repeatedly test a chronic toothache. We first see him, in fact, on Derby Day, seated at the window of one of his clubs, tallying the horses and the motor cars. For him the Englishman of the day is typified by the polyglot Londoner, who being the "product of restaurants and bucket shops and lacking marked national inheritance," is "nothing at all." Detestable to him is "the dirty comedy of life" unrolling before one's eyes, with all its struggling, cadging, and grabbing. "And doesn't it make you think that the whole thing is a disgusting affair," he cries out, "that life is more foul than it ever conceivably was, and that God has gone to sleep? If He hadn't He'd wash the whole unclean lot of us with one tidal wave into the Atlantic." His task, he sees, is to "crush it all up into a short period so as to make the affair all the more an object lesson — or, rather all the more of a joke, because I don't care whether anybody learns anything from it or not." [46]

Yet, as the novel develops, it is seen that, from the standpoint of humanity, Mr. Fleight is the most attractive and the most sympathetic character in the book, and Mr. Blood among the least. In the beginning, Mr. Fleight, having decided, vaguely, that he wanted "to do something," had approached Mr. Blood to put himself in his hands. His complaint is that, despite his immense wealth and great factories, he is a nobody. "Society being what it is, I feel that I ought to be Prime Minister, or a Privy Councillor at least." [47] And recovered from his shock, Mr. Blood decides that Aaron is perfectly right, and agrees to promote his rise. The role he then casts himself in is that of a God manipulating puppets. Hating a cynical age, he plays the game in revenge with the deepest of cynicism, as in his advice on the vast sums a climber must spend. Asserting that as a Jew Mr. Fleight needs a large showy blonde to set himself off, he contrives to wed him to Augusta Macphail, a woman without a heart who marries him for his money and high social prospects. This despite Mr. Blood's knowledge that, before all, what Aaron craves is affection, domesticity, and a motherly woman. He understands also that even for Augusta the marriage will be a torture — hating Aaron as she does for being a Jew, and yet afraid for her reputation to satisfy any of her desires apart from him. Only a man whose life is based on such foundations of torment, Mr. Blood comments sardonically, will be driven, in this age, to advance to the top of the heap.[48]

In marked contrast to Mr. Blood is his pupil. Mr. Fleight's desire for place is largely aimless. Lonely, modest, an orphan in search of family, he early discovers his distaste for climbing. What he would really like is to run a small shop. A sentimentalist by nature, he is chivalrous toward opponents and women, and is swept into his pain blindly by his passion for Augusta. The gentle Wilhelmina seems to be speaking for the author when she replies to Reginald's remarks about the Jew's inability to understand English ways: "But I can't help saying that although Mr. Fleight is a Jew, it's impossible to believe you when you say that he's a wicked man. I don't believe he's capable of a mean action, and I don't believe he ever did anything wrong in his life." And Aaron Fleight's role in the novel is significantly highlighted by the exchange that follows. For as answer to Wilhelmina, Reginald quotes Flaubert: "And since he was very strong, hardy, courageous and cunning in matters of war, he obtained very soon the command of a battalion." "It's perfectly true," Reginald adds, "I shouldn't in the least wonder if he isn't pretty soon leading us against the Sultan of Trebizond." "I don't quite know what that means," Wilhelmina replies, ending the chapter, "but I expect it means pretty well the same as what I mean." [49]

Reginald's quotation [50] is from "The Legend of St. Julian the Hospitaler." Occurring in the first paragraph of the second part of that magnificent conte, the words describe the saint himself, who in the cause of justice and charity has served with his mighty sword many famous monarchs in the Western and nearby Eastern world. And the quotation carries the full suggestion of the terrifying final scene of the tale. Having slain his mother and father through error, St. Julian in remorse and penance becomes a monk, wandering the earth. At last he reaches a treacherous ford, where he remains so

that he may assist wayfarers. Many of those he helps abuse and re-
vile him, but he accepts everything without complaining. One
night, a hideous leper, cold and weary, arrives at the ford, and compels every service, even at last requiring St. Julian to warm him by
nakedly embracing his naked body. When the saint complies, the
leper is revealed as the Lord Jesus Christ and in his clasp bears
St. Julian directly upward, into heaven.

Since Flaubert's name is introduced specifically, Ford wished the
legend of St. Julian undoubtedly to be applied to Mr. Fleight; but
the point is plain enough simply within the dialogue itself. The Jew
is the sacrificial, Christ-figure of the modern world, its doer and suf-
ferer and redeemer, who is also its outsider. It could be argued even
that Mr. Blood is both creator and flail, a cruel Jehovah of the Gnos-
tics. Indeed, only in terms of such a myth can Mr. Fleight's willingness to continue in his mentor's project be adequately explained.

If Mr. Fleight is a St. Julian, however, it is as a modern saint, one
about whom there is little romance and much pathos. Aaron is no
medieval hero; indeed he lives in a world in which there are no heroes. When hoodlums beat him for being a Jew, he accepts the blows
without offering a resistance that could only be useless, and about
him gathers considerable dignity. Yet this dignity is swiftly violated
soon afterwards when, upon seeing his bruised countenance in the
mirror, he reveals himself to be absurdly vain. At the great party he
throws for London — one which is immensely successful — Aaron
himself never witnesses what everyone agrees is the attraction of
the evening, the Russian ballet. Instead, he is comforting a young
girl who is unhappy. And in the moment of his political triumph,
when his seat in Commons is assured and he is being hailed (the
reader knows the irony of it) as the luckiest man in London, it is
clear that the glory will be Augusta's.

Nor is Mr. Blood, after all, a Jehovah. His needs are human
enough. Probably his most revealing moment occurs when Augusta
speculates on the possibility that he may one day quarrel with Mr.
Fleight. But this prospect Mr. Blood rejects completely, his reason
(shrewdly articulated by Augusta) being that Mr. Fleight, together
with herself and the greater part of the world, is so far below him

that it would be utterly impossible. To Augusta's cry that such behavior is detestable and odious, Mr. Blood responds amiably: "But, my dear, it's the way one keeps oneself alive. If I didn't think myself superior to Mr. Fleight I should take to drink, just as you, if you didn't think you had better hair and a finer figure than Wilhelmina, would be so humiliated that you wouldn't ever be any good in the world. Great heavens! if the crossing sweeper at the bottom of the road with the medals of three campaigns on his breast, didn't think himself superior to the ragged tramp he sees picking up a cigarette end, he'd die, too. This life isn't good enough for us to live it if we didn't cherish our illusions." [51]

These words no doubt also express Ford's own self-understanding and need. His social position was far more exposed than Mr. Blood's. In fact, vis-à-vis society, Ford was himself more of a Fleight. Like the Jew of his novel, he was estranged in his native land: half-German, French in spirit, an artist in a society that did not highly value the artistic life. It is perhaps understandable, then, that Ford, thus precariously placed in his society, should feel the more urgently the necessity of being superior. What is admirable in *Mr. Fleight* is the objectivity with which, in his cat's-cradle mind, he has dramatized this emotional ambivalence without perverting his moral understanding.[52]

Mr. Apollo

Chronologically, *Mr. Apollo* (1908) belongs after *An English Girl*. But because among the novels so far examined it stands apart in its intensity of feeling, excitement of vision, and narrative skill, it has been reserved for discussion last. Its subject is religion in the modern world — or more specifically belief in God and the supernatural — and its bias is toward belief and the need for belief. About the novel — in its intensity, particularly — there is an unmistakable quality of the personal, which suggests that the source of the book lies in Ford's own experience, as though he, like his Alfred Milne, had been an atheist driven toward the acceptance of God. And, biographically, this is almost surely true. Both his grandfather and father were free-thinkers, and it should be noted that his main characters in *The Shifting of the Fire* proclaim their atheism without any sense of disapprobation. But in the time that passed between those youthful influences and *Mr. Apollo*, one may infer in Ford much intimate meditation on the question, in all its intellectual reverberations. If Ford's turning toward Roman Catholicism, after the death of his father, was for motives not notably sincere, his urge for the consolation of the Deity must have quickened almost surely in the years that followed, as he struggled with the various psychological difficulties which on a number of occasions sent him futilely to the Continent for cures.[53] Certainly there is in *Mr. Apollo*, as in *The Simple Life Limited*, a thickness of texture — in character, scene, and argument — that has the ring of prolonged personal reflection and acquaintance. The book, however, is not disguised autobiography. Alfred Milne is not the author, and the part he plays, although a key one for the novel's ultimate point, is not central. Ford's vision is public and objectified, and it is in it, the larger product of the private meditation, that his feelings and imagination are involved.

In dramatizing this vision of belief, Ford adopted a startling, and expressive, literary contrivance. Selecting the Divine Godhead as his central character, he conceives Him as descending to earth to learn about mortal beings and the world they live in. The technical and thematic advantages of this device are considerable. In a classic role of social satire — the curious foreign stranger — the Godhead can thus ask with perfect naturalness ordinarily unasked questions about the lives and purposes of the characters. And we, as readers, can overhear their ordinarily unformed, revelatory replies. At the same time, being the Divinity, He articulates the ideal, through His actions and observations, by which the human figures are measured.

As the title indicates, the Godhead of the novel is Phoebus Apollo. Unlike the more customary treatment of the Greek gods in modern works, however, Ford's handling is decidedly not comic. In dignity and religious weight, his Apollo is almost as august as the Christian God, a conception that is justified in large measure by ancient mythology. To the Greeks Apollo was the most lofty and significant of their deities, and around him gathered many different powers. He was the god of the sun, of song and music, and of prophecy, the god who delighted in the foundation of towns and the establishment of civil constitutions, and the wrathful god who punished and, if propitiated, afforded help and protected against evil. And in delineating him, Ford draws upon these various attributes, along with such legends as that of Baucis and Philemon. (The god's classic sexual engagements are carefully muted.) As a deity, Mr. Apollo is naturally portrayed as a wonder-worker: he can read the minds of characters, illuminate the night, cause the pianola to play by itself, convert tea with cream into pellucid nectar, not to name for the moment more dreadful powers. Pictured as an aristocratic figure around whom a radiant light moves, he is variously called Mr. or Prince Apollo.

The selection of Apollo to represent the Godhead was, on Ford's part, a choice of considerable tact. It avoids the uneasiness, and perhaps inevitable vagueness, associated with serious literary attempts to render the Christian God. And the deity he does select is the most impressive spiritually of a great culture whose highly valued achievements permeate the awareness of his readers.

In the pursuance of his inquiry, Mr. Apollo visits three varied London groups, and thus enables Ford to make a wide range of social commentary. That Mr. Apollo is the Divine Godhead the human figures do not fully comprehend, but about him all discern special worth and powers. The major fascination of the novel lies in the Godhead's first confrontation with the human characters, and in the state of spirit in which his visit leaves them — since, as He says, "it is a natural law that no man may entertain a divinity and be as he was before." [54]

The most intense of these confrontations is with the Reverend Mr. Todd, the Protestant minister, and with his wife. A power-hungry, ego-strained, "muscular Christian," Mr. Todd is no loving shepherd, but a man whose clerical position is chiefly a means for swelling himself up. His religion is, as we have seen, shallow and materialistic. He is besides, and the fault is grievous, an inhospitable host. Starting out to buy cakes for his guest, for example, he elects not to purchase them, preferring instead to impress the Prince with his poverty — and to pocket two shillings of his wife's housekeeping money. Quite different is the Godhead's effect on Mrs. Todd. Normally anxious before her husband and his clever, self-centered friends, she suddenly finds herself moving with a forgotten, assured lightness: "For this stranger would accept the tea and jam as symbols of a desire to serve." [55] Pleased with her generosity, the Prince plans to reward her. As for her husband — he has soon vanished, to become, it is implied, the eighth bay tree in a garden of seven.

More public in meaning is the confrontation with Lord Aldington, the press genius, who, partly out of fear of his own approaching death, asks Mr. Apollo to write an article for the newspaper announcing who He is. The report will be placarded on hoardings throughout the country, Aldington promises, with the words, "A God in London." [56] The Prince agrees. "I am the God Apollo!" he proclaims. "I am God! I am immortal! I am omniscient! I am omnipotent! I was, and I shall be." [57] But the article never appears. In its place runs a story the press lord had earlier been intending to boom, on the mind-reading performances of two entertainers. The final glimpse of Aldington shows him, breathless and frightened, trying to find Mr. Apollo, anxious to explain: it was not because he did not believe that he had not published His words, but because it was not the time, or the method. "To publish it boldly would be to lose the paper millions of readers," he cries, and he urges that the Prince should understand that the ground needed preparing, that the mind-reading article was a way of familiarizing people with the Unseen. In desperation, the press lord offers half a million pounds, for temples to be built, out of his private purse. "I believe in him. But I can't damage the circulation of the paper. He could see for himself that would not do good to any cause." [58]

The situation is splendidly adapted to make its stinging point. With mind-reading or table-rapping, psychic phenomena which are humanly trivial, the public can dabble. But with a full Godhead, in whom the highest of values is embodied, there is neither profit nor capacity. This is the populace — with the press lord as an instrument "for registering the wind"— the people with the hearts and brains of children and young boys, "avid," as Mr. Apollo observes, "after those things which are futile, temporary, innocent, and fugitive." [59]

Of the Prince's encounters, the most richly drawn and interesting, however, are those with the atheist, Mr. Clarges, and with Alfred and Frances Milne.

Throwing his head back with little whistles, snorting with impatience, and with an appearance of hawk-like suspicion, Mr. Clarges marches under the banner of a man who will not be gulled. Indeed, the greater part of his life has been spent in writing to the newspapers "virulent, but usually accurate, attacks on the political or legal jobs perpetrated by whatever government happened to be in power." [60] Particularly infuriating to him is the trend toward an uncertainty in scientific knowledge and an open-mindedness about psychic phenomena. Mr. Clarges' own generation, he says, had backbones. "When we said that there was no God, we said that there was *no* God."

"We did not say only that there was no Jahwe. We said that there was no Brahma, no Vishnu, no Mithras, no God of the Sun, whatever his name was. . . . We denied it all; we denied the divine principle. We did not have a vague, floating, pantheistic deity at the back of our heads. We said there was no Hades, no Elysium. . . . We said that there was no immortal principle; we said that evolution accounted for all things upon a natural basis. . . . We were definite. . . . We *knew* . . ."

When one of the intellectuals at the Milnes' draws a distinction between Nature and the Godhead, the one following discoverable laws, the other those which cannot be even dimly discerned, Mr. Clarges cries out: "Yes; there you have it — the old priestly doctrine: 'God's ways are not your ways, nor his thoughts your thoughts.'" And when the voice of Mr. Apollo asks whether he would controvert that, the old atheist angrily cries that there *is* no God. Who are you? he calls to the Prince. "Some parson, I dare say, from your voice. An Oxford High Church product. Well, my dear sir, your cause is by no means a lost cause. . . . You'll come back. These people will bring you back." They've reached psychic phenomena and ghosts, but they'll get back to the temples and incense and mummery. "I had a dream one night. . . . The damnable way we are becoming retrograde has worried me so much that no wonder I dream. I dreamt I was in a desert with Huxley and Tyndall. And we saw a great globe of fire come towards us. And it was the Godhead. And Tyndall fell down on his face and cried out, 'Holy, Holy, Holy: Lord God Almighty.' And Huxley said, 'Mind! I never said there wasn't a God, I only said I did not know.' "

"And *you?*" the voice of Mr. Apollo asks.

"I'm not one to boast," the old man snarls at him, "even of my dreams." For what Mr. Clarges had done was to cry, "Shall I have been denying God for forty years to eat my words now?" and to take up a stone and cast it at the great light.[61]

During each encounter with the Prince, Mr. Clarges' temper steadily rises, and at its end he takes refuge in flight. Brave but superannuated, he is like a gnome buried in the caverns of the earth (as Frances Milne sees him), so obsolete as to appear legendary, laboring "in a dead cause, to prove that by no manner of means could mystery exist." [62]

And it is from the pole of atheism championed by Mr. Clarges to that of belief in God, embodied in Mr. Apollo, that the Milnes move during the course of the novel. This couple, about whom Ford's feeling is more deeply sympathetic than any other of his characters in the social satires, are people who are caught in the strain and weariness of constricted lives. Disaster to family fortune has early forced them to become teachers in the national schools, and to live on a meager salary, each year seeing the hopeful prospect of their being masters of a pleasant-aired country school grow dimmer. As young, thoughtful students both had been confident that Darwin and Huxley "had blown the Deity to rags." But when Alfred Milne first appears in the novel, he is recognizing that he has undergone a subtle change, one his wife already has passed through, a sense that there are, after all, phenomena in the world which he cannot explain along purely natural lines: "the immense wastage of the children that he saw daily; the pressure, the vicissitudes of his close-packed life." [63] In the face of the mere infinite number of things in the world, Alfred Milne is no longer a militant, full-blooded atheist but has become a weary, gentle agnostic.

From the first the Milnes are immensely drawn to Mr. Apollo, and Frances invites the Prince to stay with them for three weeks. Yet in both there persists an unwillingness to acknowledge him as God. Alfred Milne meanwhile grows increasingly despondent and weary at life. That he is a good teacher, in his way an "influence," that he has friends, and has kept and added to them, are all true. "Only," as his wife reflects, "what are mere numbers to a weary man?"

Life was a thing so gradual and so slow; it was like gliding down a stream. She was just strong enough to stand it; he not quite strong enough, unless, as it were, there came some sign from the bank of the stream. . . . A little before she would have considered it against her principles to look for a sign. Now, moved by this sudden pang . . . she would have prayed. But to whom? What she most loved in the world was in danger — for need of the proof that he was lovable.[64]

The climactic moment for Alfred Milne occurs when Mr. Apollo tells him that he has written the article proclaiming his Godhead. The schoolteacher is appalled, by the vulgarity of the proposal — and then by its acceptance. Even more he is distressed by the literalness of the claim. With anguish, he cries out that he cannot aid such impostures. And, as he flees the Prince, he looks back to see, in a cone of illumination falling from above, an old woman pirouetting on the pavement and the God gazing with attentive pleasure at her beautiful creations.[65]

In the weeks that follow, Alfred Milne falls into a fever and delirium, and Frances senses that her husband will die. A doctor prescribes light, air, and quiet. But when the window of their flat is opened, smoke and soot pour in, and from the street below come cries, barks, and screams. The closing of the window brings a dead silence and a deadly heat. "Oh God!" Frances calls out at last, wearied herself: "If he does not come now it will be too late." But Mr. Apollo does come; and asks what blessing she will have of Him. "That you will stay with us for ever," Frances replies, "and that we may be your servants till we die." The Prince commends her wisdom in having asked what was best and easiest to have, and He adds,

And of this thing be certain — that to a God it is nothing if his worshippers be few or many or none at all, since it is not from the fumes of altars that the Gods grow fat nor through the beliefs of worshippers that Gods exist. But it is by the worshipping of Gods that men attain to happiness.

And Alfred Milne, who before had been fitfully dreaming of his guest, and who once in his fevered slumber had cried out, "I believe! I believe!" lies smiling in his sleep. And there is, as the novel ends, "only the sound of a happy voice on the stairs." [66]

Although Ford was Roman Catholic in faith, his novels, like those of his fellow religionist Conrad, usually present a world that is almost exclusively secular. Religious materials, if more common in his fiction than his collaborator's, are still infrequent, and incidental. A work like *Mr. Apollo*, in which religion is the central subject, is therefore a unique product from Ford's pen. And from it we may gain a certain insight into his religious attitudes, particularly toward Roman Catholicism.

Ford's presentation of his adopted faith in the novel is sympathetic, defined both by individual characters and specific discussion. Twentieth-century Protestantism is seen as inadequate. The most wicked figure is a Protestant clergyman; and the Milnes, raised on a vague Unitarian doctrine, were thus made ripe to lose their faith when they went to Cambridge and confronted the new scientific ideas. Of particular pertinence is the lengthy debate on the Church that takes place at the Milnes' circle, the general effect of which is to temper unfair and violent objections. When a Roman Catholic remarks that the doctrine of the Church is an unfolding one, like an unclosing rose which contains any number of petals in its bud, the anti-Catholic liberal Carver impatiently objects and denounces the image as simply a lie. "Whenever the Church puts out a new doctrine, that is a new petal," he mocks. "If they say the Pope's infallible to-day, which they didn't yesterday, that is one new petal. If they say he isn't again in fifty years, that would be another. . . . It's petals, petals, petals all the way." [67] But at this moment Mr. Apollo chooses to give the science teacher the power to speak the whole truth, not part of it, and without polemic. And Carver launches into a conscientious analysis, in which he concedes that he was speaking in the vulgar sense, that the doctrines are not lies if one grants the premises, and that the image of the rose has its truth. Yet, interestingly enough, Carver, who is a basically attractive character, is allowed by Ford to retain his fundamental objections to the Church, an institution which stands for everything he opposes. "She assimilates truths in the end, but she always holds them back for as long as she can," Carver says. "And we want to get on." Its claims to authority he similarly rejects. Significantly also, the Prince reprimands Carver not for his opposition to the Church but rather for his polemical and "unlovely" manner. As to whether the Church or Carver is in the right, the Prince is unconcerned — since "it should be evident to you that to a divine nature the beliefs of man must be a subject of indifference." [68]

Thus, the total effect which the scene and the book leave is one of sympathy to Roman Catholicism, but not of enthusiasm. Belief is the essential matter; the particular tenets of doctrine are not of first importance. Alfred Milne comes to the Godhead, not the Church of Rome. And when we examine Ford's conception of the Deity, this attitude is not surprising. The choice of Apollo to figure Him was not merely a matter of artistic tact; it had a deeper significance as well: for in the novel it is plain that the Godhead is conceived as being expressed in different forms in different religions, but as everywhere the same. As the Prince explains, the universe, being infinite, has room for a multitude of Gods —"for so many, that though the God of each man were a different God, yet for each man there would be a God attuned to him." [69] ("If your God came to you," the Prince adds, to Mr. Clarges, "you would be ready to receive him, for fighting men have fighting Gods.") Thus, in *Mr. Apollo* the Godhead is not merely the Roman Catholic God; and the Prince is quite clear that he himself is but one manifestation.

This point established, it is time to examine more fully the Deity Ford has created. As the Godhead, Apollo can scarcely be called sentimental. Like the Old Testament God, his retributions are often terrible and swift, as at the beginning when he suddenly strikes dead a London constable who has disobediently looked into his face. More wrathful still is his punishment of Mr. Todd, an act made more fierce in its sequence when Mrs. Todd paradoxically appeals for her husband's return. If God were good to us, she says, he would give women children that were always babies, for when they grow it is all sorrow. And Mr. Apollo grants her wish. If the clergyman will speak one contrite, selfless word in ten, he will be restored. But: "I have done nothing to be ashamed of, mark that!" is Mr. Todd's utterance, followed by a crashing fall to the ground. "After a little," the chapter concludes horribly, "his fingers moved convulsively, like an unweaned child's, out and in to the palms of his hands." [70] Mrs. Todd has been given her request. All her life she will tend her husband's helpless, infantile form.

Mr. Apollo's most fearful deed, however, occurs at the end, when to provide light and air for the oppressed Milnes he destroys the houses and the people in the area around their flat. In part, this act is intended symbolically, a figurative cleansing that floods light into both. But it also is meant literally. "And is it not justice?" [71] Mr. Apollo asks. For these people had been inhospitable and had hurled insults and obscenities at passers-by. The purport of the action, however, is not bound to this explanation, or to the immediate neighborhood alone. It extends beyond it, synecdochically, to the entire metropolis itself, which is depicted throughout with a quiet intensity as a dreary and unconsoling place — a wasteland. [72] The Godhead's act of destruction, with its echo of Sodom and Gomorrah, is thus as well a curse and a judgment on the entire bleak, industrial, inhuman, and godless modern city.

In his depiction of Mr. Apollo as the Deity, Ford is not rigorously consistent. Although He is always conceived as beyond good and evil, He appears earlier in the book as a Deity vitally concerned with just, ethical behavior — that mortals revere God, certainly; but also that they be generous, be hospitable, love truth, be affectionate. Yet, at the end, the Prince's ethical interest seems to be dimmed to insignificance while his awful majesty and power are emphasized.

That Lord Aldington is a sensation-monger, and a distorter of the truth, makes him no more condemnable, in Mr. Apollo's eyes, than Alfred Milne, with his absolute integrity and admirable ideals.[73] In the eyes of an ancient omniscience both are mere children who are concerned with impermanent things. All that Mr. Apollo requires is that their prayers be of equal earnestness. Ethical distinctions are thus leveled away. Pelagius fades out, and Ford's conception in the book of the relation of God and man becomes the strictest of Christian orthodoxy and almost as morally bleak as Augustine's. Yet, without question, much of the intensity of the novel derives from the very fact that it draws upon the sublimity of this Orthodoxy. Its awful vision has obviously touched and released Ford's imagination, much as a similar turning to Orthodoxy vitalizes Eliot's *Murder in the Cathedral* above his other dramatic work.

One of the more appealing aspects of *Mr. Apollo* is that it is completely free of the tone of the pious tract. No shrillness or raising of the voice forces the reader to think as the author does. Although the novel has a clear point of view, it does not preach it. In fact, within the terms it sets itself, the book is particularly objective and large-minded. The atheist Clarges, for example, is treated with considerable sympathy, even admiration. If as chief antagonist to Mr. Apollo, he can scarcely, in the nature of the case, be equal, he is anything but feeble, and his debates with the Godhead are among the liveliest and most exciting sections of the book. Nor does the novel obscure the fact that the appeal of God for its characters is based primarily on human weakness, with its incapacitating and anguished inadequacies before the strains of life. Ford makes no pretense that it is the religion of the vigorous. Indeed the dominant mood of the book is almost elegiac in its grieving sadness and sympathy for mortal failings. Creative exaltation is not offered, but quiet consolation and peace. Because it does not tamper with the evidence, the novel is as fascinating to the sceptic as to the believer.

The effectiveness of *Mr. Apollo* is not limited, however, to its intrinsically exciting dialectic. It is also remarkably well told. It arouses interest almost immediately through its surprising conception and suspensefully maintains it throughout. For all its variety

—"its exhaustion of aspects"—it is tightly constructed, rapid in movement, and well integrated artistically. And it is written in a style which often is not merely admirably competent but superb.

In catching the interest of the reader, Ford can rely in large measure on the fantastic elements of his story — its wondrous events and miracles. But even more basic is the contrasting of the various characters with the central figure (as we have seen), and the art with which he gradually unfolds Mr. Apollo himself. Who he is, his purpose in coming, his attitude toward men and their world, and his ethical and religious meaning, are learned by the reader but slowly. (At one point, indeed, the deity comments that, though omniscient by nature, a god must have the capacity for experience. "All knowledge is contained in him, yet the vicissitudes of fate and of mortality are, for him, as for you, inexhaustible.")[74] Only in the last few pages is Mr. Apollo's complete portrait drawn and his significance clear. As a feat of developing both narrative and a characterization, and yet of supporting tension to the end, it is extremely subtle.

Of the novels so far examined, *Mr. Apollo* also best exemplifies the doctrine of *progression d'effet*. Shifting its point of view to fill in a background, to forward action smoothly, and to prepare further action, the novel moves from scene to scene in a tightly knit structure. To illustrate this skill of Ford's in brief space is not easy; but perhaps the handling of the last four chapters, in which the tempo moves with extreme rapidity, will serve to demonstrate something of it.

The first of these chapters focuses on Mrs. Todd and develops her anxiety at her husband's absence; and at the end occurs her appeal for his return, and his terrible transformation. But as yet Mr. Apollo's part in the episode is unknown. The next chapter shifts to Lord Aldington, and as the scene continues, the Prince tells of having heard Mrs. Todd's prayer, and of his answer. The unbelieving publisher phones the Todds, and with astonishment hears the fact verified. With this, he is ready to boom Mr. Apollo. One intense action is thus made to precipitate another; nor is it the end of the chain. The Prince is asked to write the article, but this request Ford does not present at first hand. Instead, it is revealed through a conversation between Mr. Apollo and Alfred Milne, which is the substance of the following chapter. Ford is thus able to present the high points of an episode which, handled directly, would have slowed the action and been extremely difficult to make convincing. At the same time, the disclosure of Mr. Apollo's literal claim to Godhead immediately brings on Alfred's rejection, and the climactic moment of the book. The same economy and swift obliqueness mark the next, and last, chapter, which occurs several weeks later and centers on Mrs. Milne. Once more the press lord is presented indirectly, as through her memory we learn of his almost hysterical visit in search of the Prince. Through her also we understand the final condition and implied restoration of her husband. Directly and obliquely, the novel thus drives toward its close. Through such swift compression, the poetic intensity of experience which distinguishes *Mr. Apollo* is finely supported.

That *Mr. Apollo* is a genuine work of literary art — piercing, varied, tightly composed, and leaving a vivid emotional impression — cannot seriously be disputed. It is as such, however, as earlier observed, a work which requires the modification of "minor." For, measured by the highest standards, the book is not without certain shortcomings, accidental and intrinsic, which ask for such qualification.

Some of the weaknesses are those of carelessness or haste. Neither too common nor crucial, they are nevertheless there to shake a reader's security. One chapter opens, for example, with a reference to a conversation which closed the previous one, but disturbingly misnames a speaker.[75] Of greater significance are lapses in tone, and certain limits in the characterizations. The portrait of the press lord, for instance, is vivified by little more than a vaguely defined fear of illness and death. Compared with the other chief characters, he is much less actual, with the result that the last third of the novel is materially weakened. Nor is this vagueness dispelled by the indirectness of our view of him in the closing chapters. These move swiftly, as we have seen, even powerfully, but they also lack a richness and solidity which a more immediate rendering could have made possible. Reservations may be felt also about the Reverend Todd. As a man who stirs his own pain within him, he creates a sharp and breathing impression; yet his portrait is clearly too black to be convincing on deeper levels. Even the figures in the novel who are most thoroughly rendered — the Milnes and Mr. Clarges — are yet not presented roundly or in action enough for the reader to be drawn deeply into their lives. Firm, but not full, each at bottom is too single in his agony and desire. The swift obliquity of treatment in the novel often enough, one might even suggest, is craft's masking cunning, which in the end cannot conceal what the spirit has not quite delved. As a result, the book must remain essentially a novel of ideas, exciting in itself, but of a lesser order than if its characters had been full-scale.

One further, decisive limitation of *Mr. Apollo* must be considered: its conception as a fantasy. By introducing the Godhead, Ford gained certain clear advantages, as we have seen. He could strike off social observations not possible in any other way, and he had a ready means for making his narrative lively and interesting. Yet the device also has the defect of its quality, which in this case is to rule the novel out of true importance, since the terms in which it unfolds itself are not those of life. Manifestly in the book there is a God: to disbelieve is blind, willful, and absurd. But actual experience is not so clear-cut. Even devout believers must accept the necessity for faith apart from any unmistakable Sign. The terms of our real religious existence are not those of miracles and wonder-workings and direct argument with the Lord. As an "affair," as Ford himself might admit, remembering his description of what life is really like, it is ultimately a falsification. And like his historical novels, a tour de force. On completing it, the reader will have understood better than before the strong need for God felt by many. But in the total experience and with the book's basic theme of belief, he himself, whether devout or sceptic, is not likely to become involved, shaken, or altered. In his deeper places, he will be left almost surely as before.

But having drawn these boundaries, we may now rest and enjoy, allowing *Mr. Apollo* to be what it is — a work, within its limits, rich in imagination and beauty, excitement, and artistic skill — and one of Ford's finest two novels before *The Good Soldier*.

Of the present group of works probably the main shortcoming is that they are lacking in the attribute which is most prized in the novel — the creation of full-scale characters into whom one's sympathies and imagination may readily pass. Its characters tend to be insufficiently probed and developed, more vehicles than roundly living. In the novels discussed in the following chapter, the emphasis, as we shall see, will be quite the other way.

NOVELS OF SMALL CIRCLES

Unlike the social satires, the works in this chapter carefully limit their dramatis personnae. Their focus is not so much on the public scene as on the private, tightly interacting, intensities of a few characters — or "small circles," as Ford described them.[1] Beyond any so far examined, these books (with the unimportant exception of *The Panel*) are novels of character. They also include Ford's most ambitious, artistically challenging work up to the war. *A Call* (1910) is a performance of considerable brilliance. And *The Good Soldier* (1915) is almost surely Ford's greatest novel — an unmistakable masterpiece of twentieth-century fiction.

The Benefactor

"I have always been mad about writing." So Ford wrote of himself in 1927 — and in 1910, and in 1938. For his "madness" was lifelong. And to the numerous young men and women, in a variety of decades, who sought out his teachings on how to write, Ford's answer was undeviating: submit oneself to a tireless, intense study of the writings of the masters. For by so doing, the would-be writer would be learning something of the means by which the great authors had achieved their complex and surpassing effects. The aim was not imitation, Ford said, but rather a freeing of powers, a liberation. Its purpose was to capacitate the young writer to evolve his own method — the one which would be best for him and for what he had to say. The intelligent author models himself on the masters, in short, so that, by his knowledge and his command of technique, he may become one himself.

In this advice, Ford was drawing, of course, on his own experience. He himself had gone to the school of Flaubert and Maupassant. And the work of Henry James had particularly absorbed his attention. In fact, two of his earliest novels were patterned on James: *The Benefactor* (1905) and *An English Girl* (1906). The second, as we have seen, is a negligible and hasty production. The other, however, is a more artful and serious study in the mode of the Master.

Described by Ford himself as a Jamesian pastiche,[2] *The Benefactor* reveals its model in numerous ways, most obviously in its use of italics and quotation marks. One character assumes a pose, for example, with the air of "trying it on,"[3] another discovers what she is "in for,"[4] while a third "wanted a lift" in his career. Ford has also levied upon the Jamesian vocabulary and imagery. A family is described as conscientious and lovable: "That's their note,"[5] a character observes. And the protagonist, when abandoned by a disciple, is said to be "possessed by a graveyard full of tombstones of that kind, glimmering at him in the flashlight of Hailes's departure."[6] The influence of James is again apparent in the setting and characters. There is the great family house, which embodies the traditions and worth of its possessor, and which is gradually stripped and finally lost — the counterpart of the spiritual deprivation which is at the heart of the book. Finally, there is the master's special heroine — a cultivated woman of thirty named Clara Brede, whose life has been cabined by endless duty. Sensitive and intense, loving art, yet morally acute, she is the hemmed-in Jamesian puritan who wants to live. "Everyone has to *live* sooner or later," she says, still not daunted but with a certain regret. "One can't exist at the bottom of a sandpit all one's life."[7]

Yet, for all that *The Benefactor* is a Jamesian pastiche, much remains which is characteristically its author's. As Ford observed, a pastiche is "an exercise in the manner of a writer," and that is "not exactly the same thing as an imitation."[8]

The most obviously Fordian element is the central figure, for George Moffat is his typical indecisive character. In the present novel he is a gifted, dilettante writer, loosely of the Pre-Raphaelite school, who has produced many little works but nothing truly first-rate. A man who proclaims that that person is happy who sets "phenomena, not events . . . down in his mental journal," [9] both his career and life have foundered because he has seen always most clearly the ends of others rather than of himself. Lacking any very conscious goals of his own, he has been willing to step aside and supply the incentive of applause. And altruistically he has given the bulk of his inheritance to the support of promising talent. Yet nearly always he is ill repaid. Seeing it is their benefactor's compulsion to help those who need a push, they no longer value him when their own ends are achieved. Though pained by this ingratitude, George Moffat still accepts it, without complaint. "That, after all," he says, "is the highest of human qualities. Not to yelp. Not to disturb the neighbours." [10]

The dramatic conflict of the novel develops out of the psychological impact of the earnest Jamesian heroine upon the indolent Fordian hero. Under the stimulus of Clara's conviction that he is a great poet and of her insistence that he strive always to be at his best, he is spurred to serious work on a new volume; and gradually the pair fall in love. But two barriers prevent their union. George is already married, to a woman who had left him many years before, and Clara must nurse her father, a half-demented clergyman. In the end, the Reverend Brede, having yielded to George's well-meant urging that he return to his pulpit, grows violent under the stress and has to be committed to an institution. Thus freed, the lovers tacitly arrange to leave England for Italy. But when the moment of claiming is at hand, George Moffat cannot, will not, go. For an image of her father rises before him, with voices saying: "Oh, Brede. He's in a lunatic asylum, and his daughter ran away with a married man." And George reflects that contempt would fall on his friend's memory: "it would be a final and despicable treachery." [11]

In this refusal, George Moffat is, in a sense, typically Jamesian —

giving up what is to his advantage out of a finer motive. But Ford is not here aping the master so much as expressing an approach toward life shared by both writers, a truth the rest of his novels make clear. Indeed, the point of view is epitomized in the title to *Some Do Not*. Yet the two attitudes can also be distinguished. James's characters choose to deny themselves out of a hard but free choice: renunciation for them is a personal triumph often exhilarating in its moral freedom. With Ford's characters, denial most often is something they cannot help. It is not a victory, for it flows from weakness, and it has little radiance about it. George Moffat's rejection is thus viewed finally through the eyes of the stunned Clara. "If he were right," she reflects, "the right was a bitter wrong to her, and it was fated that all the world might think for others, and never one man for her." Not trusting herself to speak to the man who has thrown her away, Clara is silent. "Self-sacrifice," she slowly says at last. "Doesn't that ever end?" A moment later, she is gone; and the novel is over.

In his handling of Clara's father Ford departs from the Jamesian spirit in still another way. However the American might have been fascinated with the strange subtleties, and even aberrations, of the human mind, the half-truculent, half-bewildered pain of lunacy was not his material. The representation of a powerful anguished passion is, on the other hand, extremely characteristic of Ford, particularly in his best work, and its presence defines a crucial difference in the sensibilities of the two novelists.

Ford's first independent novel in thirteen years, *The Benefactor* shows ample evidence that he had learned much since his juvenile *The Shifting of the Fire* (1892) about the writing of fiction. A true novel of an "affair," it is well integrated and unified, as the early work was not. Implausibility does not discredit its basic situation or characters, as in *The Shifting of the Fire*, where the reader is expected to accept with ease the marriage, out of pique at her fiancé, of a twenty-year-old girl to an octogenarian. Where love in the early novel is thin and assumed, in *The Benefactor* Ford carefully delineates in a succession of scenes the mounting passion of his lovers. Perhaps the most striking difference, however, from the earlier work, and from Ford's share in the two collaborations, is the dramatic heightening, both in the sharply drawn conflict and in the general method. At times, of course, the treatment is somewhat theatrical, even stagey. The Reverend Brede looks, for example, "like an immense spider dropping out of a lurking place." [12] And the Conradian note is sometimes all too evident: when Brede reached his cottage, "he threw the garden gate violently back, and went obscurely crashing into a dark bit of shrubbery." [13] But the impulse is a healthy one, soon to be more finely controlled.

The growth of powers can also be observed in the richer development of scenes. Many display a new understanding by Ford of the value of counterpointing action — of simultaneously presenting speech, mental process, and physical movement and thus increasing dramatic tension and the feeling of a genuine experience. The long final scene, with its impressive, complicated emotional statement, in which Ford keeps shifting his point of view between George Moffat and Clara, is particularly striking in its technique.

Yet if the novel reveals that its author has learned a good deal about writing fiction, Ford is still far from being a master. Much is young, awkward, and inadequately mounted. The unseasoned apprentice can be seen variously: in the ingenuous explanation that the Abruzzi are mountains in Italy, in an overfondness for classical comparisons, and in sentimental passages like the following, in which is described an awakening of love:

It came out then, and, under the steely glitter of the winter stars, shut in by the gathering shadows, and confronted with the purple bluff of the town's little hill, which had on one shoulder a single, oblong, orange pane of a lit cottage window, they were gloriously and glowingly warm suddenly — immensely happy and tenderly desolate; bursting into the speech, and dumb with the irrational mournfulness of a newly-avowed and inevitably crossed love.[14]

Or, again, in such passages of callow sententiousness as: "But it is at once the solace and the curse of mankind that one must for ever picture the just impossible as the supremely desirable." [15] And: "it was because I cared for him too much. One kills . . . those one likes too well." [16]

But, as in *Romance*, it is thinness which is Ford's weakest point, particularly in the handling of his minor figures. Of the success of his two principal characters, however, there is no question. Nor, finally, of the fact that *The Benefactor* — a much more demanding novel technically than *The Inheritors* — is apprentice work of attractive promise.

Before we leave Ford's earliest independent novel of interest, a few observations should be made about its autobiographical aspects, for George Moffat, peculiarly enough, foreshadows the subsequent career of his creator. It is as though having conceived in Moffat a fantasy of himself Ford sought to act it out in life.

Many details connect the protagonist of *The Benefactor* with Ford Madox Hueffer (the double "f" of the surname among them): the character's need for disciples and his "ceaseless incitements to all sorts of technical excellencies" [17] ("I've been thinking over those passages in your chapter four. Mind you, I think they want keying down — bringing in tone. Because it seems to me that if you get the opening chapters so strong — as they undoubtedly are — you won't have anything left for the end . . . in the way of effect"); his warning against adopting a poetic attitude ("But don't you see, my dear fellow? A man either is or is not a poet. If he is, his commonplace *is* the poetic point of view. If he isn't . . ." [18]); and praise of his work by a Continental for being almost that of a Frenchman.[19] George Moffat is even addressed by an admirer, to his great pleasure, as "Cher Maître" — a valuation which was one of Ford's own deep longings, as Stella Bowen has written, and which title he himself was to be called by young writers in the twenties.

Most striking of all, George Moffat prefigures Ford's own indolent attitude toward his powers. As Thwaite, his most loyal protégé, reflects, while running over in his mind "the desultory output of George's life":

"There are volumes enough, and it's all good stuff; it's got charm; it's got his own individuality." It hadn't failed of its success of esteem; but in the light of George's personality the success did not seem good enough. . . . If only he would pull himself together, and deliver one blow to clench all the staves of the barrel.[20]

Ten years after Ford had published these words about his forty-five-year-old protagonist, when he himself had reached the age of forty-two, they could as well have applied to his own career. Behind him he had to his credit forty-one published volumes, nineteen of them novels. The bulk of them were "good stuff," had charm, and their own individuality. And like George Moffat, Ford was preparing to clench the staves in the barrel. He was publishing *The Good Soldier*. There is even in *The Benefactor* another "prophecy" which in its irony is perfectly Fordian. As George Moffat is preparing his "big" book, he becomes famous through the publication of a romance called *Wilderspin* which he himself considers an inferior thing of his youth and unworthy of him. It is not unlike Ford's success as a historical novelist — which was, in fact, still ahead of him — and in particular with *Ladies Whose Bright Eyes*.

That character is fate is, almost surely, the most remarkable truth *The Benefactor* offers us.

A Call

Of his novels before *The Good Soldier*, *A Call* (1910) is Ford's richest and technically most accomplished. First published serially in *The English Review*, it undoubtedly was stimulated by the literary excitement engendered by that magazine, which must surely have provoked Ford to show his contributors and readers what he himself could do in fiction. All signs of the apprentice are gone. During the five years since he had published *The Benefactor* — in works like the *Fifth Queen* trilogy, *The "Half Moon,"* and *Mr. Apollo* — he had been steadily trying and sharpening the instruments of his craft. In the confidently selected detail of *A Call*, its absence of strain, and its supple unfolding — in, briefly, its creative ease — Ford plainly reveals the high artistic level he had attained by the time of his editorship. The work undeniably bears the marks of a master talent. Which is not to say, however, that *A Call* is a masterpiece, for the book is ultimately not a success. The artistic achievement lies rather in its parts. The novel's unit of excellence is the scene, extended and brilliantly mounted, and of these there are an impressive number.

The world of *A Call* is characteristically Fordian, only more deeply rendered than we have so far encountered it: a world of passion and agonized denial, of desire and incompletion, of self-blindness and cruelty. Its conflicts are many, but the fundamental struggle lies between the passional longings of individuals and the repressive exactions of civilization. From without and within, the lives of its characters are confined and pressed upon by social fears, strong behavioral codes, and neurotic compulsions. And in this maze Ford's people endeavor, often deviously, with much crushing strain, and rarely with success, to pluck satisfaction out of existence.

The "affair" examined in *A Call* is an extremely complicated one, involving five entangled personalities. The controlling symbol of the novel, pointedly referred to at the close of the first chapter, is lancers — a quadrille which progresses through a fixed series of steps. Like the dance, the action of the novel evolves through a set of variations, until the pattern of opposed desires with which the book was begun is at the end ironically reversed.

The central figure of the quintet is Robert Grimshaw, a wealthy Londoner of thirty-five (half-English, half-Greek) — and the characteristic vacillator and meddler of Ford's fiction. Torn by desire for two different women and unable to resolve his conflicting passions, Grimshaw discovers at last that hard circumstance has done it for him. As a result, he and others must confront, out of the wreckage, bitterly ruined lives.

Simply put, the two women embody, respectively, the masculine and feminine principle. The first (Katya Lascarides) is marked by a strong will, the active principle to Grimshaw's own passivity. Her ruling passion is obstinacy, and her goal is to possess Robert completely. She and Grimshaw would already be united except for Katya's insistence that they live together without a marriage ceremony, as did her mother and father. "Don't you see," Katya argues (in words whose irony is not felt fully until the conclusion), "she wanted to be my father's chattel, and to trust him absolutely. . . . Isn't that the perfect relationship?" [21] The second woman (Pauline Lucas), on the other hand, is the passive principle to Robert's own mastery, or at least his desire for it — the woman who adores — and

who represents to him "tenderness, fidelity, pretty grace, quaint-
ness, and, above all, worship." [22] Yet, despite their mutual desire,
Grimshaw does not bring the relationship to fruition, but instead is
the chief influence in arranging Pauline's marriage to his best friend
(Dudley Leicester). Though Grimshaw is appalled at his anguish
on the wedding day, he clamps himself in his resolve, asking: "What
have we arrived at in our day and class, if we haven't learned to do
what we want, to do what seems proper and expedient — and to
take what we get for it?" [23] As Grimshaw sees it, the business of his
life is to save himself for Katya and to see that Pauline "has a good
time"—with, of course, him watching her have it. The wealthy
Dudley will be good to her, he reasons, and Pauline, reared to English duty in the traditions of her class, will be the making of her
husband. "That's how Society"—and civilization —"has to go on."
If neither he nor Pauline can have what they want, "the next best
thing is to have a life's work that's worth doing . . . that keeps
you from thinking about what you haven't got." [24] But these words
are self-deceptive. Underlying them is Grimshaw's desire to preserve his access to both passions.

Out of Grimshaw's need to watch over Pauline develops the piv-
otal event of the book. While she is away, her husband meets an old
love, the warm, flirtatious Etta Hudson. And, innocently escorting
her home, Dudley falls victim to her impulsive vanity and is tricked
into her house. Meanwhile, Grimshaw, having observed them on
the street and assuming that Dudley is philandering, decides to telephone Etta, and hearing Pauline's husband answer, asks, with indignation in his heart: "Isn't that Dudley Leicester speaking?" The
consequences of this "call" are far-reaching. For Dudley, who is an
extremely neurotic individual, replies "Yes," and in terror hangs
up, but without recognizing Grimshaw's voice. From this moment,
all of Dudley's troubled symptoms are exacerbated, and he enters
a world of dread, made still worse by Pauline's adherence to her
English code. Convinced that Dudley will never be himself while
he hides the source of his fright, she determines to confront him
with her knowledge, gained from Robert, that there is another
woman. Like Grimshaw, Pauline is a meddler. For when she tells

Dudley that she "knows all about it," his shock plunges him into a catatonic state.

Unlike Grimshaw, however, Pauline is capable of decision, and with impressive, even fierce self-command, she rises to the occasion, fully determined to keep her flags flying. The price she pays, however, is the strain of endless vigilance. And in the end, she appeals to Katya, a skilled student of nervous disorders, to help cure her husband.

The stage is thus set for the end of the "affair"—the last sequence of movement in the patterned dance. Where Grimshaw's intention had been to wait for Katya and to see that Dudley's wife was happy, he finds ironically that Pauline is living in hell, and that for Katya he no longer feels any love at all. Still worse, Pauline has bitterly locked her heart against him. What he must now do, she tells him, is to give Katya a good time and to go on waiting, forever, for her. Her place is with her husband. "I mean to do what's right," she adds, "and I mean to make you." [25]

Desperately tired and lonely, Grimshaw thus yields at last to Katya's terms of union — and upon that capitulation, the final irony snaps into place. As he and Katya stand over the inert Dudley, who is about to be brought out of his trance, Katya considers the emotion which exists between Pauline and Robert, and coolly declares that he cannot, after all, have her on those terms. Instead he must marry her. "So that," the desolate Grimshaw answers, "you get me both ways." And the novel closes with Katya's triumphant reply: "Everyway and altogether."

The presentation of this "affair," as should be expected of Ford, is highly indirect and subtle. Probably none of his novels, even *The Good Soldier*, is more oblique, or requires more active and alert participation by the reader. Its effects are gained almost wholly by suggestion. A character's response, which may be one of great feeling — of fierce jealousy or of desolating despair — will be conveyed merely by some fractional, tenuous externality. Robert Grimshaw's face will grow ashy white, and the reader must remember that it had been so after the break with Katya, and is a sign of anguish; or his hands will fall to his sides, a gesture expressive of helplessness. Or, again, Pauline, after she has barred him, is described as wearing on her lips a faint smile; and from it we must infer that she is taking a certain thin satisfaction in the full confirmation of his love for her. Katya's or Etta's tones will become hard, we are told, and will be followed by sharper, more selfish words: and the reader must be attentive to the speeches that have just been made by Robert or Dudley and recognize their implied concern for Pauline. An interjection like "Oh!" or "Ah!" will express worlds. So will fragments of sentences, or whole sentences whose meanings are broader than they appear. Dudley's valet, for example, observing Grimshaw dully striking his head against a marble mantlepiece, will say to himself only, "Ah! I thought it would come to that." And we are aware that the servant is the person who knows who made the call, and in a single stroke is drawn the entire relationship of the English servant, who does not reveal what he sees, to English master, who is served, observed, and in a sense imprisoned by his servant. Or Pauline will say no more of her feelings about her marriage with Dudley than, as she rakes the fire before which her catatonic husband is sitting, "These coals really are very poor." [26] But the words do not end the section idly.

In seeking to convey the situations and feelings of his characters Ford also employs another device of indirection, the prominent use of which is peculiar to this novel — their displacement to external objects, the method which Ruskin called the pathetic fallacy. Thus Ford describes a daily, frenzied pushing contest between a lamb and Katya's five-year-old niece, Kitty, who stubbornly refuses to speak, a struggle which symbolizes the conflict of obstinate wills between Kitty and Katya. Just as the lamb defeats Kitty in physical struggle, so Katya daunts the girl in her will not to talk, and so later Katya will conquer Grimshaw.

But the most extensively created of these symbolic representations is little Peter, Robert's dog: a polished, light brown dachshund, with large paddling feet and long flapping ears, and "eyes as large, as brown, and as luminous, as those of his master." From the very opening Ford makes a close identification between Grimshaw and the animal, and variously indicates that the infinitely gentle Peter, with his soft and sensitive nose, characterizes Robert's intimate feelings. Probably the most striking example of Ford's use of Peter to stand for Grimshaw occurs when, as Pauline mournfully appeals to Dudley to speak, the little dog approaches, rises on its hindlegs and touches her hand with the tip of its tongue.

Eventually a time arrives, however, as Ford has commented, when the situation and the issues must come out clear and the characters directly confront each other. But this clear emergence does not occur until they have been presented obliquely. Only gradually, for example, does the reader understand, in the description of Pauline's wedding which opens the book, that Grimshaw is passionately in love with her; and Pauline's return of that passion is not revealed until after the marriage, when, her railway coach sliding out of the station and her face like death, she lets drop to the platform the violets Grimshaw has given her. Only then is Robert made to justify his decision. Similarly, Grimshaw's pity for Pauline's situation is not directly spoken until several pages after the dog Peter tenderly touches her hand.

By presenting the narrative through skillful suggestion rather than direct statement, Ford obviously achieves freshness and poetic penetration. The method involves, however, more than the quickening of the reader's intelligence and sensibility. It is also essential to the subject matter, to the capturing of those tenuous crises which constitute the highly civilized existences of his characters. As a result, *A Call* perhaps may always lose more readers than it retains. Ford discovered that very consequence, indeed, when he first published it in *The English Review*. In his "Epistolary Epilogue" to the published novel, he notes his bewilderment at the fact that "all the moderately quick-minded, moderately sane persons who had read the book in its original form failed entirely to appreciate what to me appeared as plain as a pikestaff." In correction, therefore, he put greater emphasis on stage business and added certain passages of explicit conversation. In all, about seven more pages are inserted, the most significant addition being much of the overt statement in the climactic exchange between Pauline and Robert.

Whether Ford or his friendly critics were correct about the original version is difficult to evaluate. Certainly most of what was made explicit in the key scene is implied elsewhere. The direct statement of the theme of modern tragedy is perhaps unnecessary. And Pauline's formal withdrawal from Grimshaw is somewhat theatrical. Indeed, all of the interpolated passages are a shade cruder in style. Nevertheless, the changes, by heightening dramatic emphasis, do have the effect of rounding out the experience and very probably of making it more satisfying. In agreeing to them Ford himself would seem to grant as much. Yet even in its revision the book still remains most decidedly indirect.

The subtlety with which Ford renders the emotions of the characters of *A Call* applies as well to the settings and the seasons. Park railings, greenness of grass, street lamps, hoof sounds on midnight streets, the carpets of drawing rooms, gloved hands — such highlighted details impressionistically fix the scenes in which the characters move. The transition from November to early and then to late spring is never pointed to, simply occurring in the description of the trees or the weight of clothes. The firmness and care with which Ford handles the varied settings is another triumph. The English downs, Regent Street at midnight, Hyde Park and Kensington Gardens, Bushey Park, and the interiors of the houses are all done with swift-stroked but penetrating skill. The characters of *A Call* move in a real world of London.

The novel is also distinguished among Ford's fiction by its closeness to the method of the drama. Like the majority of his works so far treated, its point of view is that of the third-person author, sometimes omniscient, sometimes half in and sometimes half outside the consciousness of one of the characters (most often Grimshaw, occasionally Dudley and Katya). But to a much greater degree than usual, Ford prefers in *A Call* to present his situation externally and to allow his figures to perform like actors, through speech and gesture. In large measure this restriction to the point of view of the onlooker is imposed on Ford by his plot, by the fact that he withholds until near the end the knowledge that Grimshaw made the call. Whatever the cause, however, the result is that Ford has turned out a number of tense, excitingly brilliant scenes.

The effectiveness of these scenes arises from various qualities. Their dialogue is excellent: interesting, surprising in its turns, subtle, and expressively revealing of the various levels within its speakers. The firmness and definiteness of the settings has already been mentioned. Even more important, the scenes almost always have as their issue some intense conflict or feeling: prepared for by the previous sections, the scene itself is an inherently exciting culmination. And, of course, in its turn it pushes the action a further step, out of which develop new complications, and eventually a new brilliant episode. Certain scenes are worth particular attention: the morning after the call when Grimshaw visits the unhappy Dudley and they talk about the secrets that servants know; the masterfully spacious meeting of Grimshaw with the Greek Orthodox archbishop in Kensington Gardens, in which they discuss the nature of the English and the need of man to do kindnesses without regard to rewards; and the several interviews between Grimshaw and Katya or Pauline. Probably no episode in the novel is finer than the one in which Robert Grimshaw goes to Hyde Park to tell Etta Hudson what has befallen Dudley. Not the least of its attractions is the witty, changeful dialogue which arises out of a confrontation between two such clearly marked, wary personalities. But it is admirable as well for the way in which Ford has built it to achieve maximum interest and meaning.

Yet as brilliant a performance as *A Call* is in its many parts, it does not, as earlier noted, altogether come off. The most obvious shortcoming is its ending, out of which no feeling emerges. The complaint is not that the conclusion is blighting, but that we do not feel the moral or emotional impact of that blight. The failure doubtless depends on the configuration of hundreds of elements, but among the more obvious would seem to be an inadequate exploration of some of the characters. In her desire to utterly possess the man she loves, Katya Lascarides is not an obscure or an extremely unusual human being. And Ford has perceptively shown the intense jealousy of the woman of will toward the feminine doll-like rival who clings ("But there's nothing *in* them!"), along with Katya's ruling motivation: "Nobody should be loved but me." Extremely interesting as a modern type, she remains, however, a type, her reactions and aims too single. The reader is puzzled by the mind and feelings of a woman who will accept a man she knows loves and wants another — not because the act is improbable but that the novelist has not made clear why this particular woman would. The failure of the ending is basically the failure of psychological justification. *A Call* lacks that attribute in a novel which Ford so highly prized — inevitability.

Another weakness in the closing third of the book is the dead spot that the personality of Dudley Leicester becomes upon his lapse into a mute state. Dudley's is never a penetrating portrait, yet earlier in the novel a certain definite, downrightly comic personality does emerge. Extremely tall, so strong that his movements have to be forever circumscribed and timid, his shoulder blades always rubbing against mantels or clock faces, he is an upper-class gentleman who has never done anything in his life, and who is prey to a thousand fears, spending much of his time in depressed consideration of what to do next. As a personality, he decidedly exists, one of the centers of the novel's life, particularly when he has his panic about the call and enters the world of dread. But when he slips into his catatonic state, Dudley vanishes from the book, and becomes a thing, "so many clothes carelessly thrown down." [27] Grimshaw reflects at one point that, unlike Pauline, Dudley had given in. "For all they could tell, he was having the time of his life." [28] But this is the only suggestion that a person still exists within that inertness. Thus, when the final scene between Robert and Katya takes place over his still form, the figure of Dudley does not function as the basic living material which, according to Pauline's elected destiny, will center his wife's interest and so drive her and Grimshaw poles apart. Had the scene dramatized the tension between three not two, the conclusion might well have possessed an emotional penetration it now lacks.

The shortcomings of *A Call* also involve its structure. In building his narrative Ford again shows his high technical skill, but one key detail is perplexing – the decision to withhold from the reader until almost the end, and as the climax of the book, the knowledge that it was Grimshaw who had made the call. Such a device enhances suspense, of course, and, at its disclosure, provides the satisfactions of surprise. But in a work of literature, plotting needs to do more than divert. It should also function to express truths about characters and situations which are humanly meaningful and which perhaps can only be thus conveyed. Unfortunately Ford's withholding of information in *A Call* reveals nothing significant that could not have been otherwise presented. Nor at its revelation does it change or sharpen our perception of Grimshaw: it merely presents an additional fact. In his epilogue, Ford emphasizes that Grimshaw is a meddler; yet as the point of the exposure, that fact seems comparatively trivial, in terms of both plot and of human insight.

But even if the device did succeed in revealing Grimshaw more deeply, the effect would have been gained at a large price, for the consequence of holding back the information is to obscure and diminish the effectiveness of the book. Many scenes which on first reading seem unrealized, thin, and uninteresting take on surprising excitement and tension when we possess the crucial fact. Grimshaw's strange agitations, the ash-whiteness of his face, and many of his comments and reactions, become comprehensible. Situations that were irritatingly amorphous suddenly assume shape, and the interplay of speech and event grows fascinating. Grimshaw's visit to Dudley the morning after the call, for example, takes on new dramatic depth and color when we grasp the point of Robert's hinting words about the secret knowledges of servants, his emphasis on the time when newspapers, with their gossip columns, go to press ("about half-past one in the morning – about half-past one," he keeps stressing, "I shouldn't imagine it was any earlier"– precisely the hour the telephone bell had rung). And we understand that he intends that Dudley cringe. So with many other scenes – with Etta, Katya, and particularly with Pauline, whose warm, naive praise of Grimshaw thus often becomes a bitter irony.

The device of presenting scenes from which crucial facts are withheld was in time to become part of the basic equipment of all

Ford's novels. *A Call* may even be termed a first experiment. But in his later use of the technique there is an important difference. In *A Call* Dudley Leicester answers the telephone on page 76 and the reader does not learn the identity of the caller until two hundred and two pages later. In the Tietjens books, on the other hand, the key information is never held back more than the length of a chapter. Although the reader begins a unit in a certain suspenseful puzzlement, by its close the situation is clarified. In *The Good Soldier*, it is true, the suspense is maintained longer. But in neither of these works does Ford withhold only a single fact, but rather a cluster of details which one by one are gradually worked in. As a result, the reader has the life-like illusion of creating his own meanings out of an exciting and rich experience.

Earlier we described *A Call*, published for the audience of *The English Review*, as ambitious. And certainly it is a serious work, vivid, arresting, and penetrating. Yet a good deal of George Moffat remained in its author. At bottom, Ford still had not engaged himself. Not only did he indulge in tricks of the detective story, which undercut the value of the book, but he also failed to restrain his freakish comic impulses. Thus, where he could easily have altered them, he has adopted a number of specific names from Henry James. Etta Hudson's maiden name, which is often used, is Etta Stackpole (Henrietta Stackpole of *The Portrait of a Lady*); one of her servants is named Moddle (from *What Maisie Knew*); Pauline once worked as governess for a family called Brigstocks (*The Spoils of Poynton*); and a character briefly appears named Madame de Mauvesine ("Madame de Mauves").

Many of the themes and motifs of *A Call* have been met before, but here for the first time Ford began to explore them more deeply. Yet he still had not found in it the forms by which his vision, in its profoundest reaches, could be rendered in art. His penetration into his characters and the tension between them is inadequate to its expression. Nor does the plot line permit the natural inclusion of material central to that vision. Thus Ford had to introduce scenes which neither advance the action nor cast light on the chief issue: the fascinating dialogue between the Archbishop and Grimshaw, for example, and certain extended observations about Americans and their unfibering lack of a sense of history and tradition. These scenes express part of Ford's perception, but they have not been integrated into an organized, piercing whole.

For the full objectification of Ford's vision into the heart of life, we must look to *The Good Soldier.*

The Nature of a Crime and *The Panel*

Between *A Call* and *The Good Soldier* Ford wrote two other novels that should be treated in this group: *The Nature of a Crime*, a collaboration with Conrad, and a "sheer comedy" called *The Panel* (1912) in England, and in America *Ring for Nancy* (1913). These may be briefly dealt with.

The Nature of a Crime was first printed in 1909, in two installments of *The English Review*, under the pseudonym "Ignatz von Aschendorf." It did not appear in book form, however, until 1924, when it was published at the instigation of Ford. As he explains in his preface, the work having been called to his attention, he had had "a sort of morbid craving" to see it printed in definite and acknowledged form, in fear that some future philologist might, "in the course of his hyaena occupation, disinter these poor bones, and, attributing sentence one to writer A and sentence two to B, maul at least one of our memories." [29] To Ford's wish Conrad gallantly acceded, and also contributed a preface. Privately, however, he appears to have been indignant — particularly when many reviewers referred to it as a new collaboration. Among the members of his circle it was thought, in fact, that Ford was trying to ride the coattails of Conrad's popularity, then at its very highest. This indignation was a further reason, indeed, for the heavy criticism aimed at Ford's "personal remembrance" of his collaborator which was published later the same year, not many months after Conrad's death; and it sheds some light on the angry, unfair, but damaging attack on Ford and his book made by Jessie Conrad in a letter to the *Times Literary Supplement*.[30] If the truth or falsehood of this complaint cannot be absolutely fixed, Ford is at least open to the charge of indiscretion. The value of the work is such that it might well have been left a prize for some researcher, hyaena or otherwise, of posterity.

Cast in epistolary form and described by Conrad as "in the nature of an analytical confession," the book comes to life only spasmodically. Indeed, it scarcely can be called a novel at all. Its beginning to be sure is striking enough. An unnamed middle-aged letter-writer in London, addressing himself to the married woman he loves, who is visiting in Rome, tells her that he is about to kill himself. As a kind of sophisticated game, he explains, he has been for a long time embezzling funds from an estate of which he is a trustee; but now, its young heir having decided to marry, the accounts are to be audited. After this melodramatic opening, however, the thought of suicide is all but forgotten, and the narrator, in a series of letters, indulges himself in various, frequently acute, reflections on life, its possibilities, meanings, and deceptions. The only real scene occurs midway through the book (Chapter IV) when, in a witty, subtle encounter, the heir uncomfortably visits the narrator to confide that he has had a mistress. Following this chapter, however, the novel plummets swiftly downhill, becoming no more than a fatiguing string of sententious statements on the theme that as a husband the poet is a better risk than the bourgeois (Chapter V), that to the man of action death is a solution, while to the man of thought it is none (Chapter VI), and so forth. The conclusion is hasty and thoroughly mechanical. The lawyers will not, after all, examine the books; the narrator is reprieved. But since his correspondent now has the letters, his future is in her hands. And on this will-she-won't-she, Lady-or-the-Tiger note, the novel ends.

In part this fictional debacle can be explained by its hurried death. Conrad, deciding that such a subject was impossible to treat in collaboration, pleaded with Ford that the work be ended. "The neatness and dispatch with which it is done in Chapter VIII," he wrote, "were wholly the act of my collaborator's good nature in the face of my panic." [31] What probably occurred is that Conrad — who was the chief writer, almost surely, of the bombastic fifth to seventh chapters — recognized once again that the analysis of personal relations was not his forte.

The Panel is Ford's only novel written as an "entertainment"— a gay, frothy work clearly directed at a popular audience. That Ford felt it out of character is plain from his dedication (addressed to Miss Ada Potter): "Why it should have come into your head to inspire me to a task obviously so frivolous and one which will draw down upon my head the reprehensions of the great and serious, and the stern disapproval of eminent and various critics, is a matter that lies between yourself and your conscience." Best described as being in the vein of P. G. Wodehouse farce (and of countless plays and films), the work reveals a surprising deftness, being well built, cheerful, and funny in its dialogue, and generally full of verve and spirit. Indeed, were its surface still more sophisticated and more carefully polished, it might even be a staple of its kind.

The hero of the book is one Edward Brent-Foster, who is the youngest major in the English army, a distinction that he achieved by reading the works of Henry James. For, as he explains, threading his way through their intricacies had so toughened his mind that promotion had been no difficulty at all. Quick-thinking and Irish, Brent-Foster possesses a great gift for lying his way out of situations, a course which — naturally — makes them worse. No fewer than five women surround him: his doting aunt; his jealous and priggish fiancée, Olympia Peabody of Massachusetts (perpetual grand mistress of the Boston Society for the Abolition of Vice); an extremely popular author of erotic novels (the president of the Society for Abolishing Conventional Marriages); a cheerful music hall artiste, Flossie Delamare; and the woman he truly loves, Lady Mary Savylle, whose house his aunt has rented and who pretends to be her lady's maid, Nancy (thus the American title). Much of the comedy centers on the locations of the bedrooms and the curious fact that a picture in Brent-Foster's room is mounted on a panel (hence the book's English title) which pivots to open onto the room behind. In one long scene, lasting many chapters, the five women successively find their way to the major's room, by various chances or pretexts. The action involves such standard situations of farce as concealment behind curtains and under beds; and the complications arise out of the tug of wills between the different characters, including an extremely choleric gentleman who is, of course, the president of the Quietist Church. All ends happily, however, as the unpleasant Olympia is sent off packing, and the Major and Lady Mary are united.

Probably the most delightful feature of the book for the literate reader is its spoofing of Henry James. "So that there we all, in a manner of speaking, are," Brent-Foster is fond of saying, explaining that James's characters constantly make this remark. "And, of course, as you can never make out where they are, it's extraordinarily strengthening to the brain to work it out." [32] The major always makes it a point to ask for James's books at all railway newsstands. That way the master's novels will be stocked — a tactic denounced indignantly by the manager as an evil plot to make his chain handle unsellable merchandise. Satirized too are intellectuals who always buy worthy new books at second-hand from lending libraries. "It's only intellectual people," the manager declares, "only *quite* intellectual people who know how to be really mean." [33]

Ford's Novels Up to 1914

With *The Good Soldier* Ford's pre-war period closes, and it seems appropriate, before turning to the work which is its artistic culmination, to review his production in the novel from 1901 to 1914. In all, including the three collaborations, they number eighteen volumes, written concurrently in the three different genres. But whatever its type, this output may be divided into two subperiods, of which Ford's ejection from *The English Review* early in 1910 would seem the demarcation point. In the first period his work is marked by a slightly soft romanticism, a fondness for vaguely evocative words and for effects based on splashes of color rather than sharpness and lucidity. After 1909, however, with the natural exception of the historical novels, such effects are banished, and Ford's language takes on a far more precise, even clinical quality.

In general, the more attractive work is early — the *Fifth Queen* trilogy, *Mr. Apollo*, and, the peak achievement of the style, *A Call*. Less successful are the later, more clinical performances, of which

The New Humpty-Dumpty and *Mr. Fleight* are the most characteristic. Too dry and unappealing, they are lacking in (for want of
a better word) charm. For, in his soul, Ford was essentially a ro-
manticist.

Nevertheless, his dissatisfaction with the older style was sound.
In *A Call* he had gone as far as he could go with it, and if he were
to say anything more significant, it would have to be in a tougher
idiom. In novels like *Mr. Fleight*, therefore, Ford seems to have
been hardening his instrument and discovering the resources of such
a style. When he began to write *The Good Soldier* — a great work
of the romantic sensibility — it would be in a prose completely
stripped of softness and romantic imprecision.

"The Saddest Story": *The Good Soldier*

To move from Ford's earlier novels to the world of *The Good
Soldier* (1915) is to come upon a rich, new dimension of experience. Where the territory before had been only mildly colored and
resonant, the reader suddenly steps into a country that blazes and
vibrates. Of the difference Ford himself was well aware, dismissing
his earlier books, in fact, as pastiches, specimens of precious writing, or tours de force — turned out "rather desultorily." He had always believed ("very fixedly"), he said, that to be able to write a
novel by which he "should care to stand," he should have to wait
until he was forty. Ceremonially, therefore, on that date ("the 17th
of December 1913"), Ford sat down "to show what I could do" —
to put into his novel "*all*" that he knew about writing. And, he
added, "the 'Good Soldier' resulted." Of its high value Ford was
fully assured. "I have always regarded this as my best book — at any
rate as the best book of mine of a pre-war period," he wrote in
1927,[34] and, four years later, he commented:

I think *The Good Soldier* is my best book technically, unless you
read the Tietjens books as one novel, in which case the whole design
appears. But I think the Tietjens books will probably "date" a good
deal, whereas the other may — and indeed need — not.[35]

And in 1937, dropping qualification, he went as far as to call it his
only novel "at all to count." [36]

And in this high estimate, Ford was thoroughly justified. For *The Good Soldier* is, in fact, one of the literary triumphs of the twentieth century — a creation of the very highest art which must also be ranked among the more powerful novels that have been written. Certainly very few works in English — *The Scarlet Letter*, *Jude the Obscure*, *Sons and Lovers*, *The House in Paris* perhaps — can match the force of its emotion, while none can equal its duration. And this emotional intensity, which begins on a high pitch in the opening chapter, not only sustains itself throughout but steadily tightens until the final moments. The psychological effect of the novel is that of some relentless spiral cutting deeper and deeper into its human material. It is the extraordinary "turning of the screw," not for 140 pages as in Henry James's famous nouvelle, but for a far more exacting 256, and rendered with a visceral intensity completely unknown to James — one we are more likely to associate with the Greeks. *The Good Soldier*, in short, is a rare combination of Flaubertian technique and almost Dostoyevskian laceration and power. It is also a book, it is extremely important to add, whose second reading is astonishingly different from its first: in intellectual subtlety, in tone, and, above all, in feeling.

Originally calling his novel "The Saddest Story" — its title when its opening chapters appeared in the famous first number of *Blast* (June 20, 1914) — Ford was compelled to change this name because of the war. For, as his publisher, John Lane, insisted, such a title as "The Saddest Story" to a book brought out in 1915, the darkest days of the conflict, would only doom it. Appealed to for a substitute, Ford, by this time in the army, suggested with irony to Lane "The Good Soldier" — and was, he says, horrified when six months later the novel appeared under that title, with the sentence, "This is the saddest story I have ever heard," inserted at the beginning, as a kind of saving remnant. This change Ford never ceased to regret, and only fear of confusion prevented him from restoring the original after the war. Indeed, that events compelled him to alter his title was, it should be stressed, among the more unfortunate incidents in his often unfortunate career. For as guide to Ford's intention "The Saddest Story" is far more appropriate than its present one — the most obvious, if not really the most important, defect of which is its misleading indication that the book is about war. It must be granted, of course, that "The Good Soldier" as descriptive of its central character, Edward Ashburnham (and perhaps also of its narrator), is essentially on the mark. But the meaning and significance of the book spring not from the story of only one individual but from the interrelationship of all its characters and events, from its total pattern. Had the novel become known as "The Saddest Story," the title would, in its superlative, even vaunting claim (even in its touch of banality), almost surely have challenged both critics and general readers to meet the book on the very highest terms, a confrontation which even yet has not been made.

Robie Macauley, for example, writing in *The Kenyon Review*, for all his high praise and perceptive comments, classifies the novel as a "miniature" performance and suggests that, were it not for the fact of the Tietjens books, it might be thought of as "the lucky try of a gifted and fortunate minor novelist." Misreading the relationship between Ashburnham and his wife, Mr. Macauley formulates a partial, even mistaken meaning for the novel, and so misses the great scope of the work asserted by its original title. It is not surprising, therefore, that he should dismiss that title by saying that Ford "was always bad at naming his books." [37]

Mr. Macauley, however, is far closer to the spirit of the novel than Mark Schorer, whose critique strategically appears at the head of the 1951 and 1957 reissues of the book. [38] Unlike Mr. Macauley, Mr. Schorer sympathizes with Ford's "understandable" horror at the change. Yet his argument is not that the original was more truly expressive, but that the present title, apparently because of the "libertine" character of Edward Ashburnham, is "peculiarly inappropriate, certainly uncongenial enough." Unfortunately, these same words are far more applicable to Mr. Schorer's analysis. For despite his high estimation of *The Good Soldier* (he in fact deems it a great work), the book in his hands loses much of its real importance and becomes little more than a clever tour de force. By focusing on only this one dimension, Mr. Schorer has unhappily described, and treated, a novel of deep, intensely tragic power as a comedy and, more unhappily still, as a "comedy of humor."

The culminating achievement of Ford's "cat's-cradle" vision, *The Good Soldier* is, at its core, a tragedy. It tells a lacerating tale of groping human beings, caught implacably by training, character, and circumstance, who cruelly and blindly inflict on each other terrible misery and pain: "poor wretches," as the narrator says, "creeping over this earth in the shadow of an eternal wrath." [39] Yet around this awful core, and without diminishing its power, Ford in his complex and subtle art has placed a context of comic irony. This context — which Mr. Schorer has made the center of the book — Ford uses, as we shall see, to provide the novel's ultimate commentary on the nature of human life in the twentieth-century world. Indeed, in its juxtaposition of these two modes, *The Good Soldier* epitomizes in a classic way the altered tragic vision of our modern sensibility.

Let us examine its action more closely. At the heart of *The Good Soldier* is a tormented love triangle bridging two generations. Ford tells us that in writing the work he sought "to do for the English novel what in *Fort comme la mort* Maupassant has done for the French." And the triangle he establishes is essentially Maupassant's in that book. An older man, hopelessly in love with a younger woman, agonizingly stumbles to his doom — caught in a passion as strong as death. In Ford's hands, however, the basic triangle has undergone a fascinating, original transplantation. The older pair become husband and wife, not lover and mistress, and the girl is herself swept away by the action. The cultural situation is thoroughly anglicized, and the drama made enormously more taut, integrated, and powerful. A further change is the adding of two other characters, a wealthy, somewhat bizarre American couple, Florence and John Dowell. For many pages, in fact, the reader is led to believe that the novel is about a four-sided relationship among the Dowells and the Ashburnhams — or, more precisely, about a different triangle, for the American wife, it is soon disclosed, has been Ashburnham's mistress. Only gradually, as the novel moves through a series of bewildering turns in which the "truth" of what unfolds continually shifts — seeming actualities exposed as substanceless or as profound distortions — does the reader finally confront the central trio.

In essence, then, this is the action of *The Good Soldier*; but to understand its issues we must go still deeper into its chief characters and events. It will also greatly help clarity to sort out the intricately rearranged chronology of the book and to review the steps, down almost a score of years, which developed the intense marital hostility between the Ashburnhams.

The nature of their conflict was simple, inevitable, and irreconcilable. In the parentally arranged marriage of the young couple were yoked two critically inharmonious personalities, in temperament, rearing, religion, and conception of the good life. In his actions, Edward —"the good soldier"— was guided by idealistic and sentimental values. Raised in the generous, responsible traditions of his family long established on their English land, he was noted for his paternal acts of kindness to hard-pressed tenants and hapless townspeople and for a selfless bravery. Practical, even materialistic values, on the other hand, motivated the ungenerous Leonora, the product of a beleaguered, impoverished English father supporting a large family of girls in a hostile and exploited Ireland. In contrast to her easy-going Anglican husband, Leonora was a strict, convent-educated Roman Catholic.

At first hidden, these differences eventually grew prominent. To Leonora Edward's generosities were a wild extravagance leading to swift ruin. She suffered also from his insistence that their sons must be raised traditionally as Anglicans; her barrenness she took as a judgment of God. Under these anguished pressures, the latent coldness and efficiency of Leonora's personality grew ascendant — a development which could only alienate a man like Edward. For with his sentimental, pre-twentieth-century view of the cosmos, he expected women to be fragile, flower-like creatures, sympathetic, tender, and providers of moral support for their men. What held the Ashburnhams together was, above all, their marriage vows: as a Roman Catholic, Leonora was unable to divorce, and Edward, as a gentleman, would not. Besides this, Leonora felt a strong physical passion for her handsome husband — an attraction which, to her anguish, he never felt for her. And Edward, on his part, profoundly respected and admired, even feared, his wife for her strength of character and purposefulness.[40]

But, in time, Edward's dissatisfaction and events led him to look outward for the feminine warmth his nature required, so that the history of the Ashburnhams involved not one or two, but actually a succession of triangles, both in England and the East. Through them all Leonora, sustained by the managerial labors she had wrested to herself, anguishedly but discreetly kept silent, in the blind belief that Edward, having tried the various womanly types, would come at last to hers. As she saw it, her duty as a Catholic Englishwoman was to hold her husband and to prevent scandal. Not even the annexation of Edward by Florence Dowell, the American wife, which began at Nauheim on their return from India and which was to last for nine years, could shake this increasingly bitter faith. At last, however, Edward came to his ultimate passion, his young ward Nancy Rufford — a love which ended one taut situation for the Ashburnhams, in that Florence despairingly took her life, but began another that was to be far more terrible.

A queer, angelic, extremely sensitive girl of twenty-two, Nancy Rufford seemed almost a daughter to Leonora and Edward. To her thoroughly innocent, convent-trained eyes, the Ashburnhams were perfectly married; Edward in particular she had always adored, seeing him as a cross between Lohengrin and the Chevalier Bayard. And he, on discovering his fierce, powerful desire for this beloved almost-daughter, as fiercely determined to leave her alone.

The ensuing months were a time of intensest agony for all three — and are the emotional core of the book. For Edward, in the torment of his self-denial and the knowledge that life could offer him no spiritual completion: constant drinking and a steady, slow dying. For Leonora, understanding his passion, and his decision (and hating and admiring him for it): anguish, dull headaches, and a bitter stoical round of duties. And for the girl: the gradual discovery of the true situation and of Edward's love for her — a knowledge which she clasped triumphantly to her heart, perceiving the depth of her responding love for him. Deciding at last to send Nancy to her father in India, Edward clung, however, to the sentimental hope that she would continue to love him – a wish he revealed to his enraged wife, with terrible consequences. For Leonora, determining to crush such a hope, vindictively exposed to the girl the full story of her husband's infidelities and of her suffering and humiliation. And in endless talks in the night, Leonora would also hammer at the girl that she must marry him and save his life – while simultaneously impressing upon her that in the eyes of their Church it could never be a marriage and would mean the girl's eternal damnation. The complex attractions and repulsions among the three characters are electrifying, the most terrible moment occurring when Nancy, in all her naive cruelty, appeared at Edward's bed and offered herself to him: "I can never love you now I know the kind of man you are. I will belong to you to save your life. But I can never love you." [41] (In anguish, Edward ordered her from his room.) With the departure of the girl, affairs at Branshaw settled to a calmer tenor – until a telegram from Nancy (sent from Brindisi) arrived for Ashburnham. So atrociously heartless is the message that Edward, for whom the girl and the love between them is the only meaning in life, kills himself by cutting his throat – horribly, with a penknife. A little later, when the eastward-sailing Nancy reads of his suicide in an Aden newspaper, she becomes permanently mad. Eventually, Dowell, who also had been in love with the girl, brings her back to the Ashburnham house which he has purchased, cast once again in the role of nursemaid. Meanwhile, Leonora, the colder, more efficient personality, has remarried, this time to a more ordinary human type; and, as the book ends, she is expecting a child who will be raised a Romanist. Leonora at last will have her "quiet, comfortable, good time."

Rudyard Kipling once wrote that "There are nine and sixty ways of constructing tribal lays / And every single one of them is right!" [42] Ford, who often referred to this jingle, granted that stories may be told by a multitude of means. But for each story, he insisted, there is one best method. And certainly this claim is true of *The Good Soldier*, for Ford could have transmitted his lacerating tale of passion in no more effective way than through the eyes of Florence's deceived husband, John Dowell.

The artistic advantages of having Dowell narrate the story are enormous. Some are obvious and shared with almost all novels told by a first-person narrator. Characteristically the point of view heightens reality: the narrator personally witnessed and participated in these events—they must be so. The angle of vision is also an invaluable narrative convenience. A review of the action reminds us that the novel concerns itself with a steady, gradual alteration in character and relationship over a span of many years. It is the story of a long psychological struggle in which the individual incidents which crystallize a response and move a character another notch toward alienation and hatred or toward love and passion are in themselves not sharply dramatic, are like the life that most of us live from day to day. As the narrator once observes, in a key passage, the work is called "The Saddest Story" and not "The Ashburnham Tragedy"

just because there was no current to draw things along to a swift and inevitable end. . . . Here were two noble people — for I am convinced that both Edward and Leonora had noble natures — here then, were two noble natures, drifting down life, like fireships afloat on a lagoon and causing miseries, heartaches, agony of the mind, and death.[43]

To present this tale, a narrator is clearly necessary, enabling Ford to set side by side discontinuous incidents which have powerfully affected motivation. Even Dowell's name indicates his function in the story as a necessary center of composition — a "dowel" being, as the second definition in Webster's unabridged dictionary informs us, "a piece of wood driven into a wall, so that other pieces may be nailed to it." (Nor is such a meaning accidental, as can be seen by examining the names of the other characters, which also subtly imply special meanings. It surely is not chance that the two tender, sympathetic women of the novel, Mrs. Basil and Mrs. Maisie Maidan, have been given the name (1) of the basil herb, commonly called "sweet basil," and (2) of that feminine state which has been traditionally thought of as fresh, innocent, and gentle. Nor that the cold sensualist, Florence, bears the family name of "Hurlbird" with its emotional suggestion of ideality violated (the symbolic bird so violently used). Nor that Nancy, the character whom Ford ultimately feels and presents most intensely, bears the name of Rufford, significantly combining both the double "f" of Hueffer and Ford's first name. Nor, finally, that the tormented Edward has been given the name of Ashburnham.)

Dowell as narrator holds together, however, more than a chronologically diffuse action. He also enables Ford to shape the highly complex emotional and intellectual responses he wishes to arouse in his reader. Dowell is not after all a mere narrator, a clinical witness of the story he tells. He himself is engaged in its action.

Before examining Dowell's artistic function, however, we first must try to understand his character. For certainly, superficially considered, it is baffling. Although Ford provides various facts about him — his Philadelphia origin and wealth, for example — these are minimal and tell us little about his motivation. Where Edward, Leonora, and Nancy are "justified" with great detail and care, Dowell's background is scarcely explained at all. We learn nothing, for example, of his immediate family, nor are we given any cause, psychological or otherwise, for his lack of masculine vitality. He has no occupation: "I suppose I ought to have done something but I didn't see any call to do it. Why does one do things?" What he originally saw in Florence is unclear. "I just drifted in and wanted Florence," [44] is the way he puts it: "And, from that moment, I determined with all the obstinacy of a possibly weak nature, if not to make her mine, at least to marry her." [45] That he should never in twelve years of marriage have suspected either her unfaithfulness or her fraudulent invention of a bad heart, which had kept him from any conjugal claims, seems almost fantastic. In Dowell something of the common state of humanity is missing, a lack reflected in the responses of other characters. Edward, he tells us twice, thought of him as not so much a man as a woman or a solicitor.[46] In behavior, he is often peevish, even fatuous. Ford's characterization of Dowell undeniably seems shaped under the comic spirit.

But that is only part of the story. For our sense of the objectively ludicrous in Dowell is very much qualified by the fact that we perceive his emotional life from within. He himself tells the story. And it is also qualified by our knowledge, which gradually becomes firmer and firmer, that this emotional life is that of an individual who is a psychic cripple.

In Dowell, Ford has created one of the most remarkable, certainly one of the most subtle, characterizations in modern literature. Almost completely from within he has caught and rendered the sensibility of a severely neurotic personality. Dowell is Prufrock before Prufrock, and not a mere sketch as in Eliot but a full-scale portrait. He is a man who, incapable of acting, is almost entirely feeling — a creature of pure pathos. Lonely and unrooted, Dowell is an alienated being, as he himself with fascinating indirection indicates in the opening chapters. With "no attachments, no accumulation," "a wanderer on the face of public resorts," always "too polished up," he felt "a sense almost of nakedness — the nakedness that one feels on the sea-shore or in any great open space." [47] That was why the Ashburnhams had meant so much to him. They had, he implies, filled a frightening void. Dowell's absurdity does not induce laughter, but rather a grave sadness. [48]

The narrator's spiritual invalidism is manifest in many ways — his atypical behavior, his almost painful self-deprecation, his peculiar images, and on occasion, certain incongruously repetitive and overly precise observations which Ford superbly uses to reassert this knowledge. (For example, his reference to the marriage rites of the Anglican Church and the use of the word "trotted" in the penultimate sentence of the book.) The plainest reference to his psychological state is brought out when he describes Leonora's reaction at their initial meeting. For at first, she was cautious and probing; but then into her eyes came a warm tenderness and friendly recognition. "It implied trust: it implied the want of any necessity for barriers." "By God, she looked at me as if I were an invalid — as any kind woman may look at a poor chap in a bath chair. And, yes, from that day forward she always treated me and not Florence as if I were the invalid." [49] "I suppose, therefore," he continues wryly, "that her eyes had made a favourable answer. Or, perhaps, it wasn't a favourable answer." The same motif of himself as the patient is reinforced a few pages later.[50]

The clinical origin of Dowell's damaged spirit is not given, but its source does not really matter. Ford has rendered the inner life of that spirit, and that is sufficient. In fact, had more been presented of Dowell's background, the emphasis would have been taken away, as it should not be, from the central characters. "I don't know that analysis of my own psychology matters at all to this story," Ford pointedly has his narrator write at the opening of Part Three. "I should say that it didn't or, at any rate, that I had given enough of it."[51]

The appropriateness of Dowell as the medium through which the careers of the Ashburnhams and their ward are told should by now be clear. Either in actual life — as students of mental disorders well know — or in *The Good Soldier*, the neurotic sensibility, turned in on itself, is apt to be heightened above the normal in its perception of emotional pain. It will be peculiarly receptive to the ache in the universe.

Dowell's sensitivity is further intensified by the recent shock of his sudden, appalled insight into the characters of his friends and their relationships. In quick succession he had been exposed to Edward's confidences, his calmly terrible self-destruction, and the discovery that his wife had been Edward's mistress. As he begins his account, his spirit is still reeling under the reeling impact of his new knowledge.

Dowell's anguish is also rooted in his admiration and highly personal feeling for the Ashburnhams and their ward. In particular his emotion is grounded in his deep love for Edward and Nancy, a love which finds much of its source in their embodiment of what he values in life and in the pathetic identification he makes between himself and them. The depth of his love for the girl, with her rectitude and strange, half-tortured beauty, can be discerned in almost every description and response. They are further united in that each are innocents who for the first time have confronted the full evil of the world. Indeed in the last third of the book the reader all but ceases to see events through Dowell's eyes; although they are told by him, Nancy's seems the sensibility through which they pass.

As for his feeling for Edward, it naturally is more complicated. Dowell, like Nancy, admires Ashburnham for his collective responsibility and for his virtues as a good soldier, a considerate landlord, an upright magistrate. At first, being an American, he had taken these qualities for granted. "I guess I thought it was part of the character of any English gentleman," the duty of his rank and station. "Perhaps that was all that it was — but I pray God to make me discharge mine as well." [52] If Edward had cuckolded him, Dowell could not hate him for it, for Florence did not mean that much to him really, as he comes to see, and Edward, the "luckless devil," had suffered too much torment. Dowell's love, finally, is based on the fact that Edward was what he himself longed to be and could not be. "I can't conceal from myself the fact that I loved Edward Ashburnham — and that I love him because he was just myself. . . . He seems to me like a large elder brother who took me out on several excursions and did many dashing things whilst I just watched him robbing the orchards, from a distance. And, you see, I am just as much of a sentimentalist as he was . . ." [53]

Certainly, however, it is not sufficient for the narrator of such a passionate tale merely to be sensitive to the ache of its events. Otherwise, the effect would only seem distraught and excessive. To be communicated, the emotions must be contained within order. And this risk of sentimentality, particularly dangerous in a work as emotionally ambitious as *The Good Soldier*, Ford has masterfully guarded against.

The most obvious technical resource for the control of emotion is the prevailing ironic tone. The irony which Dowell feels is partly the product of his natural resentment against Florence, Leonora, and Edward, all of whom in varying degrees have misused him. And it is partly a personal defense, the summoning of the intellectual principle of irony to ward off painful feelings. "Forgive my writing of these monstrous things in this frivolous manner," he writes in one connection. "If I did not I should break down and cry." [54] The

irony thus provides for the novel a counterweight, a check on un-
bridled responses. Sensing this control, the reader can accept the
passion as valid.

The greatest ironic resentment which Dowell feels is naturally
directed toward Florence and Leonora. Of Florence spying on Edward and Nancy in the park by the Casino, he writes, "And that
miserable woman must have got it in the face, good and strong. It
must have been horrible for her. Horrible! Well, I suppose she
deserved all that she got." [55] Or, at another point, he comments on
Florence's justification (given to Leonora) that she had deceived
him because of a passion for Jimmy that was overmastering: "Well,
I always say that an overmastering passion is a good excuse for feelings. You cannot help them. And it is a good excuse for straight
actions—she might have bolted with the fellow, before or after she
married me. And, if they had not enough money to get along with,
they might have cut their throats, or sponged on her family. . . .
No, I do not think that there is much excuse for Florence." [56]

As for Leonora, his dislike, based on her unfeminine hardness, her
selfish individualism, and her materialism, is tempered through most
of the book by admiration and by his sympathy for her tortured
position and deep, unsatisfied longings. Words written by Ford
about James apply as well to *The Good Soldier*: "The normal novelist presents you with the oppressor and the oppressed. Mr. James
presents you with the proposition, not so much that there are no
such things as oppressors and oppressed, but that, even in the act of
oppressing, the oppressor isn't having a very much better time than
his victims." [57] Dowell also carefully points out that Leonora's character deteriorated under the pressure of events. Florence, an un-
stoppable talker, broke down Leonora's pride and reserve. "Pride
and reserve," Dowell writes, "are not the only things in life; perhaps they are not even the best things. But if they happen to be
your particular virtues you will go all to pieces if you let them go.
And Leonora let them go." [58] In the end, however, when she is released by Edward's death and remarries, Dowell's dislike emerges
plainly and brings at last to clear focus all the selfishness and craving
for comfortable respectability at the basis of Leonora's personality.

He even literally names her "the villain of the piece." Part of his response is personal. Several times she has sacrificed his happiness for her own, constricted, ends. But his antipathy is also based on her destruction of the two persons he most loved — the "Beati Immaculati" (the "Blessed Immaculates") in the words affixed to the title page — and is expressed in the bitter irony of the following: "So Edward and Nancy found themselves steam-rolled out and Leonora survives, . . . married to a man who is rather like a rabbit. For Rodney Bayham is rather like a rabbit and I hear that Leonora is expected to have a baby in three months' time." [59] The most terrible ironic thrust, however, is the *coup de canon* which ends the book. With the knowledge that Edward is going to kill himself, Dowell brings Nancy's telegram to Leonora. "She," the closing sentence reads, "was quite pleased with it." [60]

Dowell's ironic view of Edward, as might be expected, is more prominent in the earlier stages of the novel, when he is still suffering from the knowledge of betrayal. Thus, his opening physical description of Edward: "When you looked [at his eyes] carefully you saw that they were perfectly honest, perfectly straightforward, perfectly, perfectly stupid." [61] Or again of Edward after the Spanish dancer barred her door to him: "I dare say that nine-tenths of what he took to be his passion for La Dolciquita was really discomfort at the thought that he had been unfaithful to Leonora. He felt uncommonly bad, that is to say — oh, unbearably bad, and he took it all to be love. Poor devil, he was incredibly naive." [62] Later, as Edward steadily increases in stature, Dowell's ironic tone toward him disappears only to emerge at key moments to serve as a subtle check to excess, and as relief. Thus after Nancy has been sent away and Leonora quietly exhibits her sense of triumph, Edward is heard to say beneath his breath, "*Thou hast conquered, O pale Galilean*," and Dowell comments: "It was like his sentimentality to quote Swinburne." [63] Even Nancy, whom he presents with such tenderness, is not completely free from Dowell's irony, a check which only redoubles the sense of bitterness. Thus in describing the form of her insanity, he writes: "She hadn't made any fuss; her eyes were quite dry and glassy. Even when she was mad Nancy could behave herself." [64]

Ford further guards against the dangers of a merely aching consciousness as his transmitting medium by adopting the methods of poetry. Imagery, allusion, juxtaposition, cadence — these characteristically poetic means — are all drawn upon by Dowell to formulate emotion. A man as feeling as he, if he is to be expressive, must be in fact a poet or nothing.

It is by images particularly that Dowell seeks to communicate his feeling of a personality or a situation. Thus, he writes of Florence:

She became for me a rare and fragile object, something burdensome, but very frail. Why, it was as if I had been given a thin-shelled pullet's egg to carry on my palm from Equatorial Africa to Hoboken. Yes, she became for me, as it were, the subject of a bet — the trophy of an athlete's achievement, a parsley crown that is the symbol of his chastity, his soberness, his abstentions, and of his inflexible will. [65]

And of Maisie Maidan, he observes:

Why, even I, at this distance of time, am aware that I am a little in love with her memory. I can't help smiling when I think suddenly of her — as you might at the thought of something wrapped carefully away in lavender, in some drawer, in some old house that you have long left.[66]

Of his feeling when Leonora for the first time, as he puts it, paid any attention to his existence, he writes: "She gave me, suddenly, yet deliberately, one long stare. . . . And it was a most remarkable, a most moving glance, as if for a moment a lighthouse had looked at me." [67] The rightness of this extraordinary image for its purpose is stunning. That is precisely how the impact of a hard, coldly integrated personality like Leonora's would feel to a tremulous soul like Dowell's. At a more intense moment, as when the leagued Leonora and Nancy are daily censuring Edward, the images may literally become lacerating.

Those two women pursued that poor devil and flayed the skin off him as if they had done it with whips. I tell you his mind bled almost visibly. I seem to see him stand, naked to the waist, his forearms shielding his eyes, and flesh hanging from him in rags. I tell you that is no exaggeration of what I feel.[68]

At times Dowell's quest to image a feeling is baffled, and his struggle for a form is brought to our conscious attention. Of a crucial scene between the couples, when the relationship between Florence and Edward is faintly emerging, he writes: "I was aware of something treacherous, something frightful, something evil in the day. I can't define it and can't find a simile for it. It wasn't as if a snake had looked out of a hole. No, it was as if my heart had missed a beat. It was as if we were going to run and cry out; all four of us in separate directions, averting our heads." [69] And on another occasion, when he is introducing Leonora, he attempts a peculiar image of the way Leonora looked in an evening dress. Not well, he thought, because it was always black, cleanly cut, and had no ruffling; her shoulders were too classical for it. "She seemed to stand out of her corsage as a white marble bust might out of a black Wedgwood vase." His own awareness of the strangeness of the image is indicated by the sentence that follows and closes the paragraph: "I don't know." As if to say, it is at least a try. His meaning is not so vague, however, and is reinforced by a more obvious image in the next paragraph when he observes that although he always loved Leonora, he had never had any sexual feeling toward her:

As far as I am concerned I think it was those white shoulders that did it. I seemed to feel when I looked at them that, if ever I should press my lips upon them, they would be slightly cold — not icily, not without a touch of human heat, but, as they say of baths, with the chill off. I seemed to feel chilled at the end of my lips when I looked at her. . . .

In short, there was little of femininity about Edward's wife. In so many words, however, this is never said, not even in the expressive sentence which follows: "No, Leonora always appeared to be at her best in a blue tailor-made." [70]

These examples are, by and large, bold and self-aware. Dowell is the conscious imagist trying to find forms for his experience. But the function of other images is subtler, more a part of the general emotional atmosphere. As an example we may take the second paragraph of Chapter Two, in which the dominant mood has still to be established. Perplexed as to how to tell his story, Dowell writes:

I shall just imagine myself for a fortnight or so at one side of the fireplace of a country cottage, with a sympathetic soul opposite me. And I shall go on talking, in a low voice while the sea sounds in the distance and overhead the great black flood of wind polishes the bright stars. From time to time we shall get up and go to the door and look out at the great moon and say: "Why, it is nearly as bright as in Provence!" And then we shall come back to the fireside, with just the touch of a sigh because we are not in the Provence where even the saddest stories are gay. Consider the lamentable history of Peire Vidal. Two years ago Florence and I motored from Biarritz to Las Tours, which is in the Black Mountains. In the middle of a tortuous valley there rises up an immense pinnacle and on the pinnacle are four castles — Las Tours, the Towers. And the immense mistral blew down that valley which was the way from France into Provence so that the silver-grey olive leaves appeared like hair flying in the wind, and the tufts of rosemary crept into the iron rocks that they might not be torn up by the roots.[71]

In this paragraph Ford is both summing up in juxtaposed images the emotional dimensions of the novel and shaping the reader's responses and expectations. There is the warm, reassuring fireplace set, however, in the vast elemental context of the sea, the wind, and the stars; the moon which is not the soft, comforting moon of romance (this will not be that story); the sudden, by no means accidental, introduction of the "lamentable" story of Peire Vidal; and the shift to the motoring trip to Las Tours, with all its wracking emotive diction: *Black Mountains*; *tortuous valley*; *immense mistral* blowing down that valley (the earlier wind grown savage); *olive leaves like hair flying in the wind* (in the classic image of grief); and, finally, moving imagistically to the ultimate condition of the characters themselves, *the tufts of rosemary* (the name of no other flower, with its suggestion of love, purity, and tenderness, could have been more appropriately selected) *crept into the iron rocks that they might not be torn up by the roots*. A paragraph which has begun in comparative calm ends with great violence, and the reader's readiness for the cruel story before him is by so much more prepared.

Still more subtle kinds of imagery emotionally pave the way for a fact or a response. In describing the slowness at first of his courtship of Florence, Dowell observes: "Perhaps that was because it took place almost entirely in the daytime, on hot afternoons, when the clouds of dust hung like fog, right up as high as the tops of the thin-leaved elms. The night, I believe, is the proper season for the gentle feats of love, not a Connecticut July afternoon, when any sort of proximity is an almost appalling thought." A key sentence in the next paragraph, dealing with Florence's preferences in a husband, explains the emotive purpose of this passage: "And — she faintly hinted — she did not want much physical passion in the affair." [72] Even more subtle yet are those images which vivify a place and, by extension, a character. An exquisite example is the candle shades in Edward's study. Their greenness is reflected in the glass of his bookcases, and his face is always seen when he is there by the light in their openings. As a result, the room conveys the feeling of being suffused in a green coolness, as though it provided for him a kind of sanctuary, a place of refuge and meaning in a world otherwise searing. It is almost as though Ford had peculiarly in mind, so that it came out an imagistic pun, Marvell's "green thoughts in a green shade."

But if the poet Dowell draws heavily on the emotional resources of imagery, he does not neglect the power of allusion to shape and prepare feeling. Thus he frequently mentions the Protestant leader, Ludwig the Courageous, who "wanted to have three wives at once — in which he differed from Henry VIII, who wanted them one after the other, and this caused a good deal of trouble." [73] The reference is significant both as preparation for the story of Edward and for the establishment of the religious conflict which shortly follows. Classical myth also is evoked by Dowell when he writes near the end: "I seem to see poor Edward, naked and reclining amidst darkness, upon cold rocks, like one of the ancient Greek damned, in Tartarus or wherever it was." [74] Similarly, the Hebraic-Christian myth of the Garden of Eden is suggested, though never overtly, in the brilliant scene when Edward is falling in love with Nancy while Florence looks on. The powerful effect is that of a blessed Adam and Eve spied upon with passionate envy by the serpent.

One of the key emotive methods used by Ford in *The Good Sol-*

dier is the device of setting side by side details which do not naturally connect, and thus compelling in the reader an imaginative, poetic leap and resolution between them. Such effective juxtaposition can be seen in Chapter Two, for example, in Dowell's apparently aimless but decidedly meaningful shift from discussing the character of Florence to telling the Provençal story of the troubador Peire Vidal and the crucial part played in it by La Louve, the heartless She-Wolf. Another example is Dowell's digression about his amusement, on a trip all four made, at seeing from the train window a brown cow hitch its horns under the stomach of a black and white one and pitch it into a stream. "I chuckled over it from time to time for the whole rest of the day. Because it does look very funny, you know, to see a black and white cow land on its back in the middle of a stream. It is so just exactly what one doesn't expect of a cow." [75] In two more pages Leonora will be in the position of the overturned cow, as Florence begins her formal annexation of Edward. In a similar way the gray-faced head waiter of the hotel at Nauheim is juxtaposed with Edward. When Leonora wishes to appropriate a table reserved for others, the waiter objects. Although he knows that the Ashburnhams would give him much less trouble and tip him far more handsomely than the legitimate table holders, he is intent on doing his steadfast duty, which is the right and just thing. The notion of honor is thus subtly introduced, and the waiter's code is an analogue of Edward's.

In managing prose rhythm to help achieve his emotive ends, Ford demonstrates the utmost mastery. Economical and simple in diction, unpretentious in sentence structure, his language moves through an intricacy of cadences which richly but unobtrusively supports the complexity of thought and feeling. Conversational in tone, it is yet a prose which is as tightly drawn as can be imagined — a fact which becomes clearer on subsequent readings of the novel. Probably Ford's most striking rhythmic device is the effect of finality with which many paragraphs end. After moving appropriately through a series of sentences, the line of thought will suddenly be thrust into place in the concluding statement — like a bolt shooting home. Most often the thrust is ironic, like "Well, I suppose she deserved all that she got." [76] At other times it will be a statement which has an impact because of revelation, surprise, or shock: "And, by God, she gave him hell." [77] "Outside the winter rain fell and fell. And suddenly [Nancy] thought that Edward might marry someone else; and she nearly screamed." [78] In the closing, most intense, section of the novel, no paragraph lacks its final jolt—in sensibility as though one's heart were being struck at again and again. Together with the tight control of the prose itself, the effect is an extraordinary feeling of constant pressure.

But in rendering emotion, Ford does not employ oblique means only. At the most intense moments he can be powerfully direct. Perhaps no word occurs more frequently in *The Good Soldier*, for example, than agony and its forms. It is, in fact, the emblem of the work. Or consider such direct statements of the situation as:

are all men's lives like the lives of us good people — like the lives of the Ashburnhams, of the Dowells, of the Ruffords — broken, tumultuous, agonized, and unromantic lives, periods punctuated by screams, by imbecilities, by deaths, by agonies?

Or, again, Dowell's explanation of why a man must go to the woman he loves for renewal of his courage and solution of his difficulties: "We are all so afraid, we are all so alone, we all so need from the outside the assurance of our own worthiness to exist." [79]

The technical importance of Dowell in shaping the responses of the reader is not confined, however, to various poetic, ironic, and stylistic elements. He also enables Ford brilliantly to manage feelings by controlling the tempo and tension of the novel and the degree of its psychological penetration. The structure of *The Good Soldier*, as a result, is extraordinary in its gripping suspense, narrative drive, and emotional concentration.

The use of Dowell to bridge time, which we noted earlier, may now be examined more closely. Ford's problem was not unlike one James faced in writing a famous tale in which he wanted to present the spiritual changes in a young woman over a considerable period. To do this he selected a narrator who reports his encounters with her on four separate, revealing occasions, hence the story's title,

"Four Meetings." In his book on James, published not long before *The Good Soldier*, Ford took special note of this tale by devoting three pages of discussion to it (including this sentence which seems particularly appropriate to Dowell: "Mr. James knows very well that he was giving just an extra turn to the tragedy of the story by making his narrator so abnormally unhelpful").[80] And in one important respect, the story would seem to have served as his technical model, for Ford focuses the action on three specific encounters among his characters. Thus, although the chronicle of *The Good Soldier* spans many years, it concentrates on the initial meeting of the two couples at Nauheim; the death of Florence and Edward's discovery of his love for Nancy in the same place nine years later; and the two-month period which follows at Branshaw after the Ashburnhams return to England. As a result the novel gains greatly in dramatic unity and immediacy. Unlike James, however, Ford is not limited to these major dramatic occasions. (It is partly the difference between the tale and the novel.) For, as we have seen, much of the book traces the careers, motivation, and actions of the characters in the periods before the couples meet and in the interval between the episodes. The reader becomes acquainted with them in full dimension, so that the crucial incidents take on considerable authority and depth. The important technical point, however, is that Dowell (or Ford) presents only the highlights of the "justifying" actions. One of the most unusual features of the novel in fact is that very few of its episodes last more than a page. A very important scene continues two pages, and only a few are longer. The novel has no lengthy exchanges of dialogue. In a scene of dramatic confrontation, the reader will be led up to the height of the incident; a character will speak an intense, key speech and may or may not be answered; and the episode is finished, its point burning like a brand into the reader's consciousness. Being extremely concentrated, the method wins for the book an emotional penetration rare in fiction.

This emotional penetration is, naturally, not attained only through concentrated impressions. It requires as well a plot development that will couple concentration with the highest degree of narrative tension, and this Ford achieves. The effect, as was said, is a series of surprises, brought about by new insights into facts and relationships — the constant turning of the screw.

Basically Ford uses the device of beginning in the midst of action. His tactic is to grip the reader's attention by presenting as forcefully as he can an emotional conflict at the peak of its intensity, and then, having aroused the desire to know more about it, to develop the background which led to the situation. His special skill is in so presenting the expository material that the tension is not quickly resolved, but keeps pulling the reader on and on. For these purposes Dowell is admirably contrived. His state of shock at what he has only recently discovered, together with his somewhat foolish, ineffectual character, goes far toward justifying the rambling method with which he tells the story. He himself is still in process; his personal attitudes toward the various other characters are not finally formed. As he begins to write, he does not even know the final outcome of the action: the closing two chapters, written on his return with Nancy from Ceylon, are completed months later. One probably need not add, however, that the ramblingness of the narrative is only seeming. "Not one single thread must ever escape your purpose," [81] Ford always insisted, and none does in *The Good Soldier*.

To understand how Ford's method works in practice, let us stop to examine his remarkable opening chapter. In it, most of the basic facts of the novel are laid out. But nearly all of the disclosures are only by the way, for Dowell, at least for the moment, is not really interested in the facts. In this, his first attempt to set down the story, he is concerned with the significance of his experience, not its details. The controlling theme of the chapter is sounded in the first paragraph when he writes: "My wife and I knew Captain and Mrs. Ashburnham as well as it was possible to know anybody, and yet, in another sense, we knew nothing at all about them." The conflict which almost involuntarily shapes Dowell's needs, then, is that between appearance and reality. What is appearance? he in effect asks, and what reality? And is not appearance really reality, after all, if one has lived by it? "If for nine years I have possessed a goodly apple that is rotten at the core and discover its rottenness only in nine years and six months less four days, isn't it true to say that for

nine years I possessed a goodly apple?" The chapter provides a series of illustrations of his puzzlement. As he had seen it, Florence in
their twelve years of marriage had almost never been out of his
sight; how could she have found the time to be unfaithful with
Edward, to engage in her long conversations of worldly wisdom
with Leonora, or carry on her protracted negotiations between the
pair? Or the Ashburnhams, who seemed to be the model couple,
and never spoke to each other; who seemed appropriately and perfectly wealthy for their status as county family, and who suffered
long grinding poverty to keep up appearances. To him Leonora
appeared to have all a woman could want, yet she had once tried
desperately to take a lover. Or what of Edward? He was a man who
very much disliked to hear gross smoking-room stories: "You would
have said that he was just exactly the sort of chap that you could
have trusted your wife with. And I trusted mine — and it was madness." [82] Again and again Dowell returns to his theme and announces
that he does not know, that it is all a darkness.

As a consequence, the essential facts emerge only as part of the
illustrations Dowell offers of his perplexity, and in this form, although they arouse great dramatic interest, are in themselves insufficiently structured. The reader wants to know more.

Interest is captured as well by the cosmic size with which Dowell
responds to his experience, on a scale which also announces the large
promise of the whole work. "Why do I write?" he asks, and explains
that his reasons are many:

For it is not unusual in human beings who have witnessed the sack of
a city or the falling to pieces of a people to desire to set down what
they have witnessed for the benefit of unknown heirs or of generations infinitely remote; or, if you please, just to get the sight out of
their heads. [83]

And he goes on to add: "Someone has said that the death of a mouse
from cancer is the whole sack of Rome by the Goths, and I swear
to you that the breaking up of our little four-square coterie was
such another unthinkable event." And, once having released the
floodgates of feeling, he continues, with passionate eloquence, to
compare that long, tranquil nine years to stepping a minuet:

Upon my word, yes, our intimacy was like a minuet, simply because on every possible occasion and in every possible circumstance we knew where to go, where to sit, which table we unanimously should choose; and we could rise and go, all four together, without a signal from any one of us, always to the music of the Kur orchestra, always in the temperate sunshine, or, if it rained, in discreet shelters. No, indeed, it can't be gone. You can't kill a minuet de la cour. You may shut up the music-book, close the harpsichord; in the cupboard and presses the rats may destroy the white satin favours. The mob may sack Versailles; the Trianon may fall, but surely the minuet — the minuet itself is dancing itself away into the furthest stars, even as our minuet of the Hessian bathing places must be stepping itself still. Isn't there any heaven where old beautiful dances, old beautiful intimacies prolong themselves? Isn't there any Nirvana pervaded by the faint thrilling of instruments that have fallen into the dust of wormwood but that yet had frail, tremulous, and everlasting souls?

The emotional intensity of Dowell's response is not the only element, however, which compels the fascination of the reader. Interest is also aroused in the narrator's sudden reversals of mood. For the first five paragraphs the tone is matter of fact. But with the explanation of Dowell's purpose in writing, it begins to take on feeling, first of a public kind in the image of the destruction of peoples, and then shifts, as we saw, to a very direct personal response. The next paragraph bridges both, and the following paragraph about the minuet, already quoted, is an intense elegiac lament. But instantly the mood is broken. "No, by God, it is false!" the next paragraph begins, and continues with bitter intensity:

It wasn't a minuet that we stepped; it was a prison — a prison full of screaming hysterics, tied down so that they might not outsound the rolling of our carriage wheels as we went along the shaded avenues of the Taunus Wald.

Once again, however, the mood changes, becomes more tranquil:

And yet I swear by the sacred name of my creator that it was true. It was true sunshine; the true music; the true plash of the fountains from the mouth of stone dolphins. For, if for me we were four people with the same tastes, with the same desires, acting — or, no, not acting — sitting here and there unanimously, isn't that the truth? If for nine years I have possessed a goodly apple . . .

And the following paragraph is a further shift to a deeply personal lament, which in mid-course makes a new transition to the theme of appearance and reality. Opening with an echo of the previous paragraph's closing words, "I don't know . . ." it reads, in part:

I know nothing — nothing in the world — of the hearts of men. I only know that I am alone — horribly alone. No hearthstone will ever again witness, for me, friendly intercourse. No smoking-room will ever be other than peopled with incalculable simulacra amidst smoke wreaths. Yet, in the name of God, what should I know if I don't know the life of the hearth and of the smoking-room, since my whole life has been passed in those places? The warm hearthside! — Well, there was Florence . . .

Because of the intensity of these feelings and their sudden, surprising reversals — the way Ford has constantly modulated the emotional values, as Caroline Gordon has pointed out — the sensibility of the reader into whom they are inducted is kept at the stretch, constantly alerted and swept emotionally onward — by the desire to know more and by the very experience itself.

Beginning with such "a strong situation," to use the Fordian phrase, a novel faces the crucial and extremely difficult technical problem of sustaining and still further heightening interest. It cannot be allowed to slide downhill, except briefly as a rest between intensities. To understand how Ford solved this problem, it will be illuminating to examine his handling of the five chapters (covering sixty-five pages) which make up the rest of Part One. The central aim of the opening chapter, we saw, was to arouse in the reader the desire to learn more, particularly about the unusual relationships among the characters introduced. What, he is compelled to wonder, is the meaning of the connection between Florence and Edward, Edward and Leonora, Dowell and his wife? The reader's attention thus caught, Ford can then tantalize by concentrating on the individuals rather than the relationships. His method can be seen in a survey of the action of the succeeding chapters: description of Florence (Two); introduction of Ashburnhams and depiction of their first meeting with the Dowells (Three); the launching, obliquely seen, of the liaison between Edward and Florence

(Four); mainly exposition (Five); the incidents leading to the grotesque death of Maisie Maidan (Six), which concludes the chapter
and part. But although the reader acquires considerable knowledge
about the characters and situations in these pages, he still is left in
mysteries. He does not yet know, for example, the background of
the Dowell relationship nor the identity of the "girl" who is several
times mentioned, nor the true natures of Edward and Leonora. He
will move into Part Two and then Part Three still dominated by
vibrations of uncertainty that were struck in the first chapter.

  This delay in unfolding the central dramatic issues, together with
the length of exposition, might well (for all the force of the reader's
curiosity) be exasperating and dull, and scarcely intensifying. But,
in this case, not so. What prevents monotony and actually contributes to tightening interest is Ford's superb management of irony,
emotional intensity, and rhythm, each of which contributes to
raising in the reader's mind a rich set of onward-pulling tensions.

  During most of these chapters — in which Dowell is trying to
make the reader see what the characters are like — the prevailing
tone is chatty and ingenuous, providing a basic rhythm which is
relaxed and (seemingly) casual. But out of this almost neutral manner emerge suddenly, as frequent variations and with enhanced effect, moments of cutting ironic statement and emotional intensity.
The reader is continually being jolted into renewed interest. Nor
does Ford ever allow him to forget for long the dominant mood of
anguish and portentousness of the opening section. While the exposition is being "worked in," the mood constantly is re-established
through a sudden cry of lament by Dowell or by his citation of
someone's passionate speech.

  The most potent reinforcement occurs, however, at the chapter
endings, which, like so many of Ford's paragraphs (and each of the
four parts), close always with an intense climax. Chapter Two, for
example, is predominantly a low-keyed account of Florence.
Shortly before its end, however, Dowell shifts to a description of
his arrival at Branshaw, on appeal from the Ashburnhams. Seated
beside Edward on the dog-cart, he found the place pleasant and
delightful, "the very spirit of peace." Leonora greeted him from

the door; the "girl" was probably out with the hounds; "and" (the chapter slams shut) "that poor devil beside me was in agony. Absolute, hopeless, dumb agony such as passes the mind of man to imagine." So also, in Chapter Three, in which the major purpose is the description of the characters and their meeting at Nauheim. The couples having joined forces at a common table, the section concludes with a pointed, thrusting formality:

And then Florence said: "And so the whole round table is begun." Again Edward Ashburnham gurgled slightly in his throat; but Leonora shivered a little, as if a goose had walked over her grave. And I was passing her the nickel-silver basket of rolls. Avanti! . . .

The actors in their places, Destiny can begin.

All these various methods of developing tensions are brilliantly combined in Chapter Four, together with an immediate, intensely dramatic situation which gives new vitality to the narrative. (The scene is also basic to a deeper understanding of the novel.) Although the chapter essentially describes the beginning of the affair between Florence and Edward under the horrified eyes of Leonora, once more the management is indirect. Dowell's ruling purpose in the chapter, in fact, is rather the theme of appearance and reality, to which, as it opens, he has returned. After describing the placid, congenial routine of the couples, the narrator, in his chatty, rambling manner, relates as an illustration of his theme an expedition all four had made. Under Florence's leadership they had gone to inspect a castle where Martin Luther was said to have slept and where was kept a pencil draft of the Protest which he, Bucer, Zwingli, and Ludwig the Courageous had signed. Dowell is at pains to say that he thinks Florence got some of her facts wrong. He tells of the cheerful mood she had been in that day, how he had laughed at the two cows, and how relieved, seeing her so gay, he was to be "off duty." He describes her triumphant display of the document, and her explanation that that is why they were all called Protestants. And then there begins a startling and dazzling shift of mood. Suddenly the easy, chatty surface that has been developed for over ten pages erupts into the intensest violence. It is to what happens next that Dowell referred when he spoke of the treachery in the day and of the snake looking out of a hole. For Florence had continued, looking up into Edward's eyes:

"It's because of that piece of paper that you're honest, sober, industrious, provident, and clean-lived. If it weren't for that piece of paper you'd be like the Irish or the Italians or the Poles, but particularly the Irish . . .

"and" (the statement gets a paragraph to itself) "she laid one finger upon Captain Ashburnham's wrist." At once the scene is suffused with the sense of fear. In Edward's face Dowell sees absolute panic. "I was horribly frightened and then I discovered that the pain in my left wrist was caused by Leonora's clutching it. 'I can't stand this,' she said with a most extraordinary passion; 'I must get out of this.' " Together Dowell and she flee down the stairs. "Don't you see?" Leonora cries. "Don't you see what's going on? . . . Don't you see that that's the cause of the whole miserable affair; of the whole sorrow of the world? And of the eternal damnation of you and me and them. . . . Oh, where are all the bright, happy, innocent beings in the world? Where's happiness? One reads of it in books!" And the passage continues to the end of the chapter:

She ran her hand with a singular clawing motion upwards over her forehead. Her eyes were enormously distended; her face was exactly that of a person looking into the pit of hell and seeing horrors there. And then suddenly she stopped. She was, most amazingly, just Mrs. Ashburnham again. Her face was perfectly clear, sharp, and defined; her hair was glorious in its golden coils. Her nostrils twitched with a sort of contempt. She appeared to look with interest at a gypsy caravan that was coming over a little bridge far below us.

"Don't you know," she said, in her clear hard voice, "don't you know that I'm an Irish Catholic?"

The scene is a masterpiece of ambiguity and irony. Details about religion, or rather about religious figures, have been in the foreground for at least four pages, and superficially Leonora's passionate comments would seem directed toward Florence's attacks on Catholics. As such, except for their excessive emotion, they are even, from a Catholic point of view, apposite. But it is what Leonora discerned in Florence's physical gesture that has really moved her, and sent her hopes for recovering her husband crumbling. (She is also concerned for the pain that Maisie Maidan would feel.) Her recovery, therefore, does not merely involve her recapturing personal command. As the "clear hard voice" implies, her remark about being an Irish Catholic is the reclamping down of public control, a determined return to the smoothness of appearances.

Having given in Chapter Four fresh dramatic vitality to his narrative, and a new set of perplexities to his reader, Ford can, in the next section, safely deposit much background material, brightened, however, by his usual sudden surprises of irony and emotion. At its completion the groundwork for the story has been laid; and Part One ends with its briefest and, appropriately to its final position, its most intense section. The power of this closing chapter springs from various qualities. Fundamental is the force of the emotions treated: the violent exchanges between Leonora and Florence ("You come to me straight out of his bed to tell me that that is my proper place. I know it, thank you. . . . Yes, you would give him up. And you would go on writing to each other in secret, and committing adultery in hired rooms. I know the pair of you, you know. No, I prefer the situation as it is"); Maisie Maidan's discovery that not her own husband but Leonora had paid the money to bring her to Nauheim ("I did not know you wanted me for an adulteress," reads her letter. "Oh, Mrs. Ashburnham, you knew the world and I knew nothing. I thought it would be all right if you thought it could, and I thought you would not have brought me if you did not, too. You should not have done it, and we out of the same convent. . . ." At which, on reading it, Leonora screamed); Dowell's declaration of his hatred of Florence ("For I hate Florence. I hate Florence with such a hatred that I would not spare her an eternity of loneliness. She need not have done what she did"). The highest peaks of intensity in the chapter occur, however, in two sharply contrasting passages, several pages apart. "They are dead," Dowell writes, in the first of these; "they have gone before their Judge, who, I hope, will open to them the springs of His compassion." It is not for Dowell to blame or to think about it.

It is simply my business to say, as Leonora's people: *"Requiem aeternam dona eis, domine, et lux perpetua luceat per eis. In memoriam aeternam erit. . . ."* But, what were they? The just? The unjust? God knows! I think that the pair of them were only poor wretches creeping over this earth in the shadow of an eternal wrath. It is very terrible . . .

It is almost too terrible, the picture of that judgment, as it appears to me sometimes, at nights. It is probably the suggestion of some picture that I have seen somewhere. But upon an immense plain, suspended in mid-air, I seem to see three figures, two of them clasped close in an intense embrace, and one intolerably solitary. It is in black and white, my picture of that judgment, an etching perhaps; only I cannot tell an etching from a photographic reproduction. And the immense plain is the hand of God, stretching out for miles and miles, with great spaces above it and below it. And they are in the sight of God, and it is Florence that is alone. . . .

(In the context the two embracing figures seem to be Edward and Maisie Maidan; actually in Dowell's mind they are Edward and Nancy, who has not yet been introduced. But the confusion is not a mere narrative trick: Ford clearly means to blend the two girls in the reader's awareness, for they are alike in their feminine gentleness, in contrast to the hardness of Leonora and Florence.)

The other passage ends the chapter and the part. If the first offers the grandest, most powerful image in the book, the second presents surely the queerest. The death of Maisie Maidan has been conceived as a terrible consequence of the relations between the other characters. Yet when finally described, it is a strange blend of the comic, the romantic, and the grotesque, and thus peculiarly shocking. After reading the girl's letter, Leonora in dread hurries through all the public rooms of the hotel to seek her out. She had not wanted to search Maisie's rooms first.

Now, as soon as she came in, she perceived, sticking out beyond the bed, a small pair of feet in high-heeled shoes. Maisie had died in the effort to strap up a great portmanteau. She had died so grotesquely that her little body had fallen forward into the trunk, and it had closed upon her like the jaws of a gigantic alligator. The key was in her hand. Her dark hair, like the hair of a Japanese, had come down and covered her body and her face.

Leonora lifted her up — she was the merest featherweight — and laid her on the bed with her hair about her. She was smiling, as if she had just scored a goal in a hockey match. You understand she had not committed suicide. Her heart had just stopped. I saw her, with the long lashes on the cheeks, with the smile about her lips, with the flowers all about her. The stem of a white lily rested in her hand so that the spike of flowers was upon her shoulder. She looked like a bride in the sunlight of the mortuary candles that were all about her, and the white coifs of the two nuns that knelt at her feet with the faces hidden might have been two swans that were to bear her away to kissing-kindness land, or wherever it is.

The juxtaposition in a climactic position of these two images is not without larger point, as we shall see later.

As with Ford's development of Part One, so it is with the rest of the novel. A leap is made forward to some passionate moment; then the novel doubles back to bring in the expository or justifying material that led to that moment. The first two chapters of Part Three, for example, tell of Edward's discovery at Nauheim of his love for Nancy and his decision to leave her alone. But not until sixty-five pages later does the narrative resume the account of this relationship as it continued at Branshaw. In between, Ford mainly traces in much greater detail than before the intense marital history of the Ashburnhams, from the standpoints of both Edward and Leonora. When at last he does take up the story of his principal triangle, he introduces it with a brief scene depicting Nancy's appearance at Edward's bed. He then portrays in a chronological fashion most of the highly charged events that led to this visit, which itself is presented later in context and at greater length. Similarly the penultimate chapter, written after Dowell has returned from Ceylon, begins by articulating the theme of the novel and proceeds to illustrate it.

Still other technical factors enhance Ford's narrative drive. Since *The Good Soldier* is characterized by brief scenes which concentrate only on dramatic highlights, it naturally follows that the book — unburdened by the need to carry an often clogging freight of stage management and exposition for each new episode — can be much swifter than the usual novel. The drive of the book also is strengthened by Ford's management of his rhetorical structures, by what might be called his lock-stepping prose. The stunning effect with which he closes many paragraphs of itself tends to pull the reader on, but Ford goes further. By often tightly linking his paragraphs to each other, he allows the reader no pause, either emotional or logical. An unusual number of paragraphs, for example, begin with the coordinate conjunctions, "And," "But," and "For," or with connecting phrases like the following (all taken at random from Chapter Five in Part Three): "So she went at it." "Indeed, in a way, she did him very well — but it was not his way." "It was probably also very good for Edward's health . . ." "That was the most unsettling to Edward of all his affairs."

The greatest of Ford's narrative triumphs, however, is not so much that he prevents interest from slackening as that, consummately modulating the values of his novel, he has steadily intensified the force of its emotion. The power of Part One, although considerable, is mild compared with what follows. Through a combination of literary devices, mostly involving his narrator, Ford in the opening chapters has skillfully kept his basic emotional materials at several steps removed. Because Dowell tends to fill the foreground during the early stages of the novel, the intense emotions of the other characters, of which he is reporter, come to the reader only in isolated bursts; and not deriving from integrated centers of personality which the reader can as yet be assured of and understand, these passionate outbursts remain "unplaced" and muted in penetrative force. Similarly, emotional power is moderated by Dowell's ironic tone. And finally, distance is achieved through the high degree of indirection with which the experience of the novel is transmitted — the peculiar juxtapositions which often require of the reader subtle, thoughtful yoking; and the abundant use of intellectual imagery. Later in the novel these screening elements begin to dissipate. The reader moves closer and closer to the characters, until their emotional responses are rendered with almost excruciating directness.

Among the most extraordinary of many extraordinary qualities about *The Good Soldier* is that although Ford has presented an account of drifting lives which, considered chronologically, fail to move toward any swift or inevitable end, he has nevertheless produced an artistic work which is singularly distinguished by its sense of swift inevitability. Ford's canons of economy and movement to produce the sense of relentless destiny in a novel are perfectly embodied in *The Good Soldier*. Every word is carefully chosen to advance the action; digressions relax tension, yet are only seeming digressions; the narrative moves faster and faster and with increasing intensity (*progression d'effet*). Finally the entire novel draws to one inevitable culmination, which, as Ford said, should reveal "once and for all, in the last sentence, or the penultimate; in the last phrase, or the one before it — the psychological significance of the whole." [84] In *The Good Soldier* this culminating moment occurs one page from the end. All the facts of the story have been recorded, and the book seems to be trailing away without any final climax. Suddenly remembering, however, that he has not told how Edward met his death, Dowell depicts the scene at Branshaw when Nancy's telegram arrived. Until this point in the novel the telegram has been several times referred to indirectly, and vaguely described as "atrocious." Now Ford sets down the actual message, and its bright, hard words provide the final turn of the screw, the ultimate clinching cruelty. At one instant, and with a shock of perception, the reader understands both why Edward had to end his life and why Nancy, on learning of his suicide (and knowing its cause), had to go mad. In the face of such cruelty in the human heart, withdrawal from life is the only conceivable course for such sensitive beings. The reader has been magnificently prepared to feel the horror of it. All forces have contributed to the inevitable end.

Finally, one further point of Ford's art ought not to be overlooked — the size and depth given to the novel by its great number and variety of marvelously executed scenes, each of which is a model of artistry, with its own individual angle of attack, appropriate tone and mood, structural rhythm and prose cadence. There are episodes, for example, of social comedy: the two Hurlbird aunts in their Stamford home (with its picture of General Braddock), delicately trying to warn Dowell against their niece; the pathetic post-midnight elopement of Dowell and Florence in Waterbury, Connecticut, and its aftermath: the couple, "listening to a mocking-bird imitate an old tom-cat" [85] while they dully wait in the woods for dawn; the photographing of Leonora and her six sisters at their impoverished manor house and the other hopeful expenditures made for the visit of the Ashburnhams and their marriageable son; Edward at Monte Carlo with the Spanish dancer; Leonora striking Maisie Maidan in a hotel corridor and her attempted recapture of poise on discovering that Florence had been a witness; or Dowell's fateful meeting with the odious Mr. Bagshawe, who knew of "Florrie" Hurlbird's affair with Jimmy. There are also the splendid scenes of graver import: Dowell's almost stream-of-conscious memory (a technique unusual in the book) of his catatonic state after Florence's death; Dowell and Leonora in the dead-world of Branshaw after Edward's suicide, with the rabbits already beginning to nibble the lawn; the narrator's magnificent, extremely moving disquisition on the growth and meaning of a man's love for a woman; the sequence, purely quivering in its feeling, when the simple Nancy discovers (through reading the newspapers) the existence of marital infidelity, perceives the bitter hate between the Ashburnhams, and, with a sense of age and wisdom and of superiority over Leonora, at once recognizes her own proud love for Edward; or the terrible scene at the end in which, with Dowell looking on, Edward and Nancy, those restrained "good people" of England, bid each other goodbye at the railroad station without any sign of emotion. ("The signal for the train's departure was a very bright red," Dowell writes; "that is about as passionate a statement as I can get into that scene.") [86] Only a reader of the novel can understand the full variety and brilliance of such episodes, how admirably they have been selected to impel the action, or how masterfully they establish the breadth and solidity of the work.

The intense, complex experience of *The Good Soldier* and the means by which Ford successfully mounted it have by now been isolated. Still before us, however, is its larger significance. What, ultimately, is Ford saying in the novel? In his examination of character and of the agonies of human relationships the intention is apparent enough. But, like Flaubert, Ford does not express his full meaning obviously. Rather he subtly implies it, asking the reader to actively participate in understanding it. There are mysteries in *The Good Soldier*, and the mind cannot rest until it resolves them.

Earlier the novel was described as a classic rendering of the modern tragic outlook. What was meant, more specifically, was that in it Ford has presented a genuinely tragic experience but in circumstances, peculiar to the twentieth century, which condition that experience in a special, meaningful way.

Those elements which make for the tragedy of the action are classically Aristotelian: its sense of inevitability, its reversals of situation and meaning, its high poetry. Its protagonist, Edward Ashburnham, is a man much above the ordinary. He lives according to the high values of generosity, kindness, duty, and responsibility to those who depend upon him, and he can act for the right with will and determination. "The unfortunate Edward," Dowell writes. "Or, perhaps, he was not so unfortunate; because he had done what he knew to be the right thing, he may be deemed happy." [87] If Edward at his introduction seems, like Dowell, essentially a creation of comedy — an indulgent libertine, athletically handsome but basically stupid and vacuous — his dignity and stature steadily grow during the book (the reversal begins on page 93) until at its close he is an extremely impressive, noble figure. By no means a perfect man — the tragic protagonist never is — he is a good man who has never been guided by base motives. As Dowell makes clear, he was not a promiscuous libertine, but a sentimentalist. [88] Sentimentality in fact is Edward's basic human weakness, his fatal flaw — even, as, ironically, it is the source of much of his virtue. Most importantly, *The Good Soldier* arouses in the reader the cathartic emotions of pity and awe at the spectacle of its admirable, greatly suffering protagonist overwhelmed by hard cruelty in so terrible and unfeeling a way.

These are the classic attributes of tragedy, but this experience is significantly qualified by elements that are not tragic. The sense of destiny, for example, is merely formal. The lives of the characters actually trail away to no seeming conclusion. Nor does the tragic experience of Edward and Nancy move in the larger context of a universe which is purposeful, either in the classical Greek deterministic meaning or in that of the Hebraic-Christian Divine Plan. Instead Ford has placed the pair in a world in which, there being no purpose, there is hence no meaning to life on earth, only an ultimate knowledge of futility. At one place Dowell writes of himself and Leonora: "I cannot tell you the extraordinary sense of leisure that we two seemed to have at that moment. It wasn't as if we were waiting for a train, it wasn't as if we were waiting for a meal — it was just that there was nothing to wait for. Nothing." [89] This motif of nothingness, which is actually announced in the opening chapter ("And there is nothing to guide us. . . . It is all a darkness"),[90] is re-sounded almost at the very end of the novel when Dowell presents his final description of the insane Nancy: "It is very extraordinary to see the perfect flush of health on her cheeks, to see the lustre of her coiled black hair, the poise of the head upon the neck, the grace of the white hands — and to think that it all means nothing — that it is a picture without a meaning." [91]

The religious framework of the world, with its vision of harmony between God, man, and nature, has been shattered. This catastrophe and its consequences Ford crystallizes through brilliant juxtaposition in at least two key places in the novel. The first is the somewhat bathetic contrast (in the concluding chapter of Part One) between the powerful, compelling image of the palm of God and the comic, half-mocking (and half-weeping) image of the death and doll-like religious funeral of Maisie Maidan. More striking still, and more obvious in its meaning, is the conjunction of the only comments which are spoken by Nancy after she goes insane. "Credo in unum Deum Omnipotentem" is the first, and about it Dowell sadly, wearily comments: "Those are the only reasonable words she uttered; those are the only words, it appears, that she ever will utter. I suppose they are reasonable words; it must be extraordinarily reasonable for her, if she can say that she believes in an Omnipotent Deity." [92] Almost at the end of the book Nancy speaks the other: a single word, repeated three times, "Shuttlecocks." That is how she felt between Leonora and Edward, and that was the way Edward had felt between the women. And that is the word, Ford is saying, for man's buffeted, purposeless existence in the world that has come into being.

We can now understand also the full ambiguity and subtlety of the scene in which, when Florence had disclosed a copy of Luther's Protest, Leonora cried out: "Don't you see that that's the cause of the whole miserable affair; of the whole sorrow of the world? And of the eternal damnation of you and me and them . . ." Her words, as we saw, are addressed essentially to the quietly meaningful touching by Florence of Edward's wrist. Although a staunch Roman Catholic, Leonora in reality is not a religious woman at all, operating rather according to the rigid code of the Church, to its letter rather than its spirit. Yet the reader does not yet know this fact and the words make their significant effect in his mind. By them Ford is saying that the rise of Protestantism, which symbolizes the entire modern, sceptical, fragmenting impulse, is the source of the destruction of the old consoling religious framework and the whole present sorrow of the world.

This sense of a nothingness at the heart of the universe can also be seen, of course, in the questionings of Hamlet and the rages of Lear. But the distance between Shakespeare's world, in which only chinks in the spiritual framework are spied, and our own period is great. As the modern era moves on into the time of the high prestige of science and Darwinism, the religious structure holds less and less power over the minds and actions of men. And with the change comes the disappearance of the heroic attitude. ("I am not Prince Hamlet," declares Prufrock; and Dowell says of himself in heaven: "Well, perhaps they will find me an elevator to run.") [93] Gone also is the deep assurance that evil must, for all its ravages, be overcome. In *Lear* the disaster of the King and Cordelia is meliorated by the bitter deaths of Goneril and Regan. In *The Good Soldier* Edward and Nancy, who are the spiritual descendants of Lear and his youngest daughter, are destroyed, while Leonora, for whom the evil sisters are an essential prototype, triumphs without final punishment. In the rendering of man's spiritual plight in the twentieth century, *The Good Soldier* is thus a major artistic document, an objective correlative of its age.

This twentieth-century world Ford represents specifically through various symbols. One is his selection of a pair of Americans as the peripheral characters to his tragedy. Ford conceived of his fictional Americans — as we observed in *The English Girl* and *A Call*, and as may be seen in his presentation of Millicent de Bray Pape in *The Last Post* — as unrooted creatures and, hence, as faint, ineffective personalities. Several times Dowell speaks of himself in these terms, and his wife he once calls a "paper personality" who at her death dropped completely out of recollection. Florence is also characterized by her American busybody but mindless desire to bring "a little light into the world." This meddling Dowell point-edly defines through a digressive anecdote about her uncle, who on his world tour took with him thousands of California oranges to give as "little presents" to strangers. The absurdity of the venture is epitomized brilliantly in the following passage:

When they were at North Cape, even, he saw on the horizon, poor dear thin man that he was, a lighthouse. "Hello," says he to himself, "these fellows must be very lonely. Let's take them some oranges." So he had a boatload of his fruit out and had himself rowed to the lighthouse on the horizon.

"And so, guarded against his heart," Dowell adds (in a double sense), "and having his niece with him, he went round the world."[94] This is the American in action, innocent of what lies below the sur-face of life, and often, as in the case of Dowell's wife, cheerfully doing evil.

Another meaningful symbol may be seen in Ford's depiction of Florence dead on her bed: "looking with a puzzled expression at the electric-light bulb that hung from the ceiling, or perhaps through it, to the stars above."[94] Strikingly paralleling this description is a movement of Edward's just before he takes his life: "He just looked up to the roof of the stable, as if he were looking to heaven . . ." We may note the contrast. For Edward, the agrarian stable (with its connotation even of the birth of Christ) and the searching appeal for heaven. For Florence, an electric light bulb, an almost by now classic symbol of the industrial substitution for Godhead, and the stars which coldly swing in the empty spaces above.

In dramatizing the nature of this dominant modern spirit, Ford did not rely, however, only on texture and subtly revealing incidents. He also built the point into the structure, so that the form itself defines and crystallizes its scope and large meaning; from beginning to end, the main action is transmitted through the sensibility of the narrator — an individual who brilliantly objectifies this lamed modern spirit. The ultimate importance (and final justification) of Dowell in the novel is as a concrete, functioning embodiment of the state of mind formed by the new conditions of the twentieth-century world: alienated and unrooted, helpless and "less than human," pathetic and absurd. As symbolic context, Dowell gives the tragedy a remarkably contemporary dimension. Ford has been praised for dramatizing in the Tietjens cycle the transition in England from one order of society to another, particularly in the composition of its governing classes; but in *The Good Soldier*, his *constatation* of change is still more penetrating. It is not limited to England, or its governing classes, or the public events of a decade. Rather it directly concerns itself, as we have noted, with a basic alteration that has steadily been going on in the attitudes and psychology of Western Man in general.

Having perceived the deeper significance of Ford's narrator, we must also consider the underlying meaning of his final fate. As owner of Branshaw Manor and nursemaid to the mad Nancy, neither of which roles gives him any satisfaction, Dowell's end suggests a grim, sad prophecy. Ford appears to be saying by it that the modern estranged spirit, symbolized by Dowell in particular and Americans in general, will supplant the older types and values (Edward, Nancy, and Branshaw; the seat of the stabler feudal attitudes based not on abstract capital but tangible land; even a Leonora). Yet this spirit, being sick, will not be the possessor of the dying, blighted remains, but, like Dowell, their joyless caretaker.

Ford's story, in the end, however, focuses not on the ascendancy of the future, not on the "new" man, but rather on the predicament and death of the old. Dowell (and Florence) are not, after all, at the center of the experience of *The Good Soldier*. That position is reserved for the three English characters who move in the spiritual

environment the Americans represent. As personalities (and creations) they are in sharp contrast with the Dowells, are strengthened
and deepened by their social, familial, and religious roots. They
strive to put a face on life, to give it meaning and purpose, to shore
value, even if only sentimental, against the ruins. None of them are
personal ciphers, as modern writers frequently have made their en-
trapped characters. If in a sense they are victims, it is not in a simple
reflex way; they are not mere products of society. In abundant
measure they possess the will and passion to victimize themselves.
Their personal strength gives them their grandeur and makes them
worthy of such tragedy as Ford sees that the twentieth century
enables.

But in the end, of course, futility is the context in which they
move. Theirs is not the resolution finally of great tragedy, which in
its heroism confirms the optimistic view of man's ability to transcend himself spiritually. Instead, for Edward and Nancy, it is the
resolution of withdrawal, by suicide and insanity, from a world
which is too horrible. Souls of a certain greatness have suffered
greatly, but hopelessly and to no larger purpose — their values,
lacking sanction, sentimental. This is the tragic absurdity (or absurd tragedy) of human life in a world bereft of meaning. The
novel in every way earns its superlative claim. It does, indeed, tell
"the saddest story."

TIETJENS, THE GREAT WAR, AND ENGLAND

THE imaginative world which Ford created after the war of 1914–1918 — the world of Christopher Tietjens and of England — was the logical culmination of his fiction. Looking back over the earlier novels from the vantage point of the twenties, we can readily see the ways in which the Tietjens books — and *Some Do Not*, in particular — pull together the various strands of his pre-war production. In them are combined the large public canvas of the social satires and the characterization in depth of the novels of "small circles." And from Ford's absorption in his historical novels derives much of their emphasis on the English past as evaluative standard. Yet, as inevitable and climactic as this post-war creation now seems, it easily might never have been written.[1]

The Good Soldier was, in fact, to have been Ford's last novel. As he wrote in 1927 in his dedicatory letter to that book, he considered himself the Great Auk who had laid his one egg: the one book which "was enough for any man to write." He could therefore die, and leave the way to "Ezra, Eliot, Wyndham Lewis, H. D. and the rest of the clamorous young writers, who were then knocking at the door."[2] Nor was this statement a pose, as ample evidence testifies. When Stella Bowen begged him after the war to start a new book, he told her "that he never wanted to write another word." [3] Writing, he said, made him nervous, cross, and ailing; he preferred to grow vegetables, raise pigs, and to sink into a quiet obscurity. But in time, with the renewal of his strength and the constant encouragement of his friends, and of Stella Bowen, who insisted that his books were of the highest importance, he once again began to write.

The value of this warm support cannot be overestimated. In its absence, it can be said without hesitation, Ford almost surely could not have summoned the energies needed to create the Tietjens world. Before he began to write, as he openly tells us, he had "dreaded the weaknesses in myself that I knew I should find if I now made my prolonged effort. I was still tired and I have always been lazy." [4] Had Ford not been so encouraged, modern letters would be much the poorer. It would be missing some of its most memorable characters; at least one superlative, very likely great novel; and, finally, an artistic record, of high cultural importance, of the crucial transition in England — and the Western world — from the way of life of the nineteenth century to that of the twentieth.

The Great War

For all the horrors, brutalities, and destructions of the World War of 1939–1945, historians will very probably insist that its impact on the British — and European — way of life and spirit was much less terrible or revolutionary than the Great War of 1914–1918. Casualties in part tell the story. In the Great War nearly one million men of the British Empire military forces were slain, and over two million more were wounded. In World War II, almost two thirds less were killed and the wounded were about half. For those engaged in World War I the dominant quality was the emotion it aroused, as the years dragged on, and the waste and the casualties mounted, of its senseless futility. In the second war the enemy, led by Hitler and the Nazis, represented, on the other hand, a barbarism that civilized men could be inspired to battle and whose destruction was unquestionably worth achieving. The feeling of mad futility in the earlier struggle was reinforced even more significantly by the nature of the fighting. Nothing could be more demoralizing than trench warfare: the mud and slime, the immobility, the desperate waves sent over the top into decimating fire to wrest from the hands of the enemy a few yards of territory. World War II, with its swiftly altering battlefronts, did not seem as futile. Its soldiers could witness at least change from their actions.

Most of all, the appalling impact of the Great War lay in the circumstance that the European, and particularly the British, spirit was psychologically unprepared for its violence. The later generation, which had become accustomed to the horrors of modern warfare and which knew the shocks of world economic depressions, had little about which to become illusioned. Where it was the complete child of the twentieth century, the generation before had grown up in the nineteenth-century peace and had shared the nineteenth-century expectancy of the steady advance of human civilization. Since Napoleon Europe had known only small wars, which were often fought with a certain decorum. The military life, with its occasions for feats of personal bravery and its colorful rituals and uniforms, was honored, particularly as a check against a softening, unheroic commercial civilization. The mind of 1914 was not ready for barbed wire, concentrated artillery bombardments, trench fighting, poison gas, and the enormous wastage of materials and of men. Soldiers did not wear gay uniforms — although at first they tried to — but mud-colored khaki. And individual bravery had little status in operations which involved the mobilization of more than sixty-five million men. To a Europe conceiving itself as civilized, the revelation of its own barbarity was soul-shattering; the old values, the old inspiring words, seemed meaningless, had played mankind false. World War I began in one century and ended in the next.

The Tietjens novels undertake to register this transition in British life and values. Its "subject," as Ford describes it, is "the world as it culminated in the war." [5] And the books are, in large measure, a lament for the world that expired and for the senseless deaths in staggering numbers of the finest flower of England's manhood.

But before launching into the discussion of this significant work, let us first examine the two novels, related in theme, which Ford wrote before he began to create *Some Do Not*.

The Marsden Case and No Enemy

Although *The Marsden Case: A Romance* (1923) and *No Enemy: A Tale of Reconstruction* (1929) were published six years apart, both were written in the period before Ford left England to live in France, as is implied in the dedication to *No Enemy*, and as he categorically stated later. Not only do both works refer centrally to the war, but they are also more directly autobiographical than any other of his novels. Indeed, Ford was afterwards to deny (correctly) that *No Enemy* was a novel at all. Nominally fictional, it is plainly another memoir, its author thinly veiled under the name of Gringoire, the reminiscing central figure.[6] And as the work proceeds, the mask of fiction is put more and more aside.

No Enemy focuses mainly on Ford's wartime reflections and experiences in France and Flanders, at the front and behind the lines. *The Marsden Case*, on the other hand, is a legitimate novel set in England shortly before and during the conflict. The book tells two stories. The first is the complicated tale of a sensitive, and much beset, young man named George Heimann. The offspring of a brilliant British earl named Marsden, who in disgrace had exiled himself to Germany, George does not, however, discover this fact until just before the war — whereupon his sister, Marie-Elizabeth, becomes frantically determined to be acknowledged. Out of fear for his father's safety, George hurries to Germany, and there finds that the earl, who had been a fervent believer in close ties between the two nations, has in despair hanged himself. Interned for seven months, the young man is finally repatriated to England where he is then denounced by the sensational press as a German agent and encounters a multitude of official harassments. Driven to the border of sanity, George also attempts to kill himself. But in the end, the heritage is established. And George, dropping his prior objections, agrees to become the fourth earl of Marsden. He also marries a gifted actress-singer named Clarice Honeywill. "Thus, simply, they entered Paradise."

The other tale, peripheral to the events of the Marsden Case, but more interesting and deeply felt, involves Ernest Jessop, the novelist-narrator. Ford thus tells the story of George Heimann by concentrating on one of Jessop's harried literary days before the war and then by impressionistically describing his strain and isolation as an army officer. The chief drama of Jessop's situation springs out of his sympathy for George Heimann and, above all, from his poignant, hopeless love for Clarice Honeywill, whose heart is the younger man's. In the end, after the Armistice, Jessop feels himself thoroughly cut off from his times by the barren tract of years and of change that stretches between him and his earlier life.

Of *The Marsden Case*, Ford wrote in May, 1923, to Edgar Jepson (to whom the book is dedicated): "I believe that, as a 'treatment,' it is the best thing I've done — but the subject is not a very good one." [7] Although the novel is far from being as "done" as *The Good Soldier*, Ford's estimate is otherwise sound. The narrative idea would seem to have overborne him, but the "treatment"— the exacting craft which creates characters, settings, and atmosphere — is on many counts admirable. Thus, the book achieves a remarkably real sense of the strained atmosphere of pre-war London after Sarajevo and a fascinating thickness of detail, emotion, and attitude. It is in Part One that Ford shows his particular skill as he shepherds his diverse, sizable, and clamorous cast of characters swiftly through an accelerating series of different episodes and settings on a single, crowded day — from publisher's office to the London street, to a ladies' afternoon literary gathering (where Jessop goes to lecture), to Miss Honeywill's apartment, to, finally, a basement cabaret club, where a shadow play by Jessop is put on. [8] And the narrative of the book is yet further varied and enhanced by the narrator's presentation of dramatic episodes from the past lives of the Marsden characters — a time-shift method similar to that in *The Good Soldier*. Probably the finest asset of the novel, however, is the narrator himself. Knowing and experienced, complexly burdened and humanely ironic, Ernest Jessop, who possesses qualities of personality unlike any other character Ford created, provides a valuable life-giving center of personality and composition. The force of the book is further deepened by the position in time from which he tells the story — from after the war, with the poignant knowledge of the later deaths in battle of some of the characters, and of the irrevocable loss of the world described. The narrative, as so often in Ford, thus moves with a compelling, elegiac dramatic irony and sense of destiny.

The major fault of *The Marsden Case* is structural, for rather than increasing in tension and interest from the first part to the second, the book declines. Indeed, the novel suffers from a split personality, its two halves being inconsistent in tone and method. (Curiously enough, the same lack of unity characterizes *No Enemy*: in its first half the observations and recollections of Gringoire-Ford are presented through the medium of a visitor to his small country farm; in the second part, the device is dropped and Gringoire speaks directly to the reader.) The first half of *The Marsden Case* is fundamentally dramatic and is concentrated into a period of about twelve hours; the second, covering the years of the war, is predominantly narrative and diffuse in its action. In the first half Jessop exists in a complex, independent fashion. The reader may infer that he is based largely on Ford himself but does not need to, since the character has a rounded reality of his own. In the second half, aesthetic distance tends to diminish, and Jessop grows more like the voice of the specific Ford of the memoirs. In the process the tone also changes, and he loses something of his inner force, becoming less complex and interesting, more passive and pathetic.

But the second part of *The Marsden Case* is not a total collapse. Although it is predominantly expository, and hence risks tedium, the writing itself is neither poor nor hasty. And, at times, certain first-rate, finely built scenes do emerge. Probably the most striking is the episode when Jessop speaks his love to Clarice and for a time has, as he puts it, "amazing hopes." The sequence culminates (by means of a time-shift) at a Belgian railway station in 1917 when Jessop's "impracticable love" is blended with the departure of his train up the line. The complex emotional orchestration in the scene — through surprise, situation, and irony — is remarkable.

The novel has yet other virtues. Particularly interesting is its sense of rueful comedy: in a quiet way *The Marsden Case* is a funny, satiric book. Consider the two harpy journalists; the lamentably inaccurate American newspaperman, Pflugschmied; the underhanded publisher Podd; the loyal parliamentary secretary, Carstones; the "advanced" Miss Jeaffreson (the author of a *Child's Guide to Nietzsche*) and her lugubrious attorney brother; or the temperamental scenery designer at the night club. Peculiarly comic as well are the scenes of stiff punctilio with which George Heimann is treated by the Germans, even when he attempts to escape. Or George's exit visa personally signed by the Kaiser, who unhelpfully lauds him as "a friend of Germany." Or again Ford's comic description of the dismay of the British civil service at being confronted with George's case.

Interestingly enough, the entire book ends by being a sharp satiric thrust, as is revealed by Ford's labeling it a romance. For an orphan at last ascends to an earldom, marries his beloved, and lives happily ever after — all in a context of ruin and disaster. The whole last chapter, in fact, in a subtle, unobvious way, is a parody of the traditional ending of the nineteenth-century novel which Ford often ridiculed. The main characters are gathered together at Geneva after the war; good fun is had at the expense of the inaccurate American journalist; and generous words are said by the earl about Jessop, who feels himself a lost outsider, and who in a sense is satisfyingly taken in. But the satiric note which undercuts this whole "good-humored" scene is the prolonged image of a waiter crawling on hands and knees toward the boots of the earl to clean away the soup he had accidentally spilled on them. Life, Ford would seem to be saying, in a note of proletarian class consciousness that is new to him, has resumed as before.

The Tietjens Cycle: *Parade's End*

Thoughts of the Great War always touched Ford's pen with eloquence and feeling — an emotion generated above all by his sense of its terrible destruction of the finest spirits of his country. England had suffered more, he felt, "at least in her mentality," than any other combat nation, since she had fought over half the war with enlisted men. "It had been impossible for a young man sound physically and of healthy imagination not to volunteer in the years between 1914 and 1917," with the result that the most vigorous and alert of England's young had been killed or mangled in body and spirit. "Those who remained and filled all the posts in 1919 were the physically unfit and the mentally frigid. So those poor boys came back; maimed and bewildered to a world administered by those born to detest them." Thus, the Tietjens novels become not only a lament for those lives and the world that was lost with them, but also a condemnation of the supplanters — the official "intelligentsia" who "had *embusquéd* themselves in government offices, in munitions works, in prisons or in the posts vacated by fighting men." [9] What had happened to England seemed epitomized by a disbanding ceremonial planned for a Kitchener battalion — symbol of the old army — when the fighting would be done.

The end of the show was to be: the adjutant would stand the battalion at ease; the band would play *Land of Hope and Glory*, and then the adjutant would say: *There will be no more parades.* . . . Don't you see how symbolical it was . . . For there won't. There won't, there damn well won't . . . No more Hope, no more Glory, no more parades for you or me any more. Nor for the country . . . nor for the world, I dare say. [10]

England, which had marched so splendidly and proudly down the long centuries of its history, had suffered a death blow. Glory and hope had faded. A great nation, and perhaps even a great civilization, had come to its "Parade's End"— the title Ford applied to his over-all conception.

About the main action of the Tietjens cycle and its genesis, Ford has written at considerable length. [11] And since, unlike Henry James, he rarely discussed the particular mechanics of his own novels, his remarks have an unusual interest. If the steps by which his conception evolved were possibly arrived at after the fact (to fit the needs of his narrative in *It Was the Nightingale*), nevertheless the stages, together with his explanatory background, do give valuable insights into the purpose and dynamics of his work.

His intention, he said, was to dramatize "the public events of a decade"— roughly from 1908 to the end of the war. (In this, he very probably had in mind Flaubert's similar purpose in *L'Education sentimentale*.) Stated differently, Ford's aim, as we have already seen, was to render a picture of the world culminating in the war. But the "world," Ford knew, could not be made his central character. "Perhaps it ought to be done. Perhaps that may prove to be the culmination of the novel." [12] But he, at least, had to rely on the "old device" of a world seen through a focal character: in short, Christopher Tietjens. To sustain interest in Christopher's observations of the crumbling world, he would have to be weighted with tribulations —"with a permanent shackle and ball on his leg . . . something of a moral order and something inscrutable." [13] And he would have to bear this burden with patient self-control, to win the reader's sympathies. In fact the very nature of the subject required such a strong-minded, composed individual: "No one else could have supported at once the tremendous pressure of the war and private troubles of a very dire description." [14]

This central character would not be heroic, however; he would be deprived of any glory. His most marked activities would be critical. He would observe bad management from the War Office in Whitehall down to brigade headquarters; and criticizing this ineptitude when it seemed his duty, he would get "into many and elaborate messes." Thus Ford's "intrigue" would become screwed up tighter and tighter.[15]

Next was the problem of rank and social status. Christopher clearly had to be an officer of sufficient authority for his reports to reach the higher commands. And he had to be a gentleman. Theoretically, Ford observed, every wearer of His Majesty's uniform is a gentleman and the social equal of his fellows, although rank must be remembered. But on the private, social side, the rigid class barriers continue to exist: "You may, at mess, sit next to the son of your milkman. He may be a fine fellow of faultless deportment and as such you will treat him and even respect him. But the moment you go to your own quarters — and they may be merely a hole in the mud — the normal civilian hierarchy reasserts itself." (By the time he was preparing his novel, Ford noted, he himself had arrived "at the stage of finding the gentleman an insupportable phenomenon.") [16]

His central character, however, was also to be a member of the governing class, which, Ford explained to his mainly American audience, is separated from and "absolutely above the merely gentlemanly class." As a rule this body is recruited from the sons of landed proprietors, old titled families, higher army officers and "what, in England, one called Good People," and its members monopolize the first-class government departments — the war and foreign offices, the treasury, the diplomatic corps. Distinguished by being authoritative, cynical, and instructed in the ways of mankind, "they are permanent unless they come personal croppers over a woman, or through overintelligence or on account of financial disasters." The gentlemen of the country, Ford added, decide whether the nation will be temporarily conservative or liberal, but the permanent officials see to it that the country follows its ancient traditions. "So at least it was before and during the War — and it was with those periods alone that I meant to deal." [17]

Thus Christopher Tietjens was made a member of the ruling classes, who was to become *persona non grata* by a combination of all three disgraces: over-intelligence, financial disaster, women. These were to comprise his "private troubles of a very dire description." In shaping these troubles, Ford also drew, he said, on various private biographies. Part of Tietjens' situation was taken from the career of a man, who, except for his disaster, would have been in the foreign office. Having picked up a woman of comparatively good family in a train between Calais and Paris, he was afterwards told by her that he had got her with child and was persuaded to marry her; later he learned that the child might well be another's, and that his wife was unfaithful. He would not free himself by going to court, however, holding that a decent man should not initiate divorce proceedings. Nor would his wife divorce, being a Roman Catholic. Borrowing from the unhappy career of a wealthy

American, Ford moved on to the next step. Deserted by his promiscuous wife, the American fell overwhelmingly in love with another woman. Ironically, however, his wife took that moment to return to him permanently. And with this stage, we have the outline of the basic triangle running throughout *Parade's End*, and its major dramatic tension: Christopher's relationship to his willful, unfaithful, and returned wife, Sylvia, and to the "other woman," Valentine Wannop, bluestocking, athlete, and suffragette.

In developing the "personality" of Tietjens — as distinguished from his dramatic situation — Ford tells us that he drew on the characteristics of his close friend, Arthur Marwood, the mathematician who had been his partner in *The English Review* and who had been an important widening influence on Ford's horizons. Although broadly acquainted with creative artists and with people who were well-traveled, cultivated, and gifted, the Hueffers had had, according to Douglas Goldring, "little social experience of a general sort and few contacts with conventionally educated members of the British ruling class." [18] In Marwood, Ford discovered a new species of Englishman: the "English gentleman" par excellence — for certain purposes, the "real" Englishman. This admiration is also testified to by Ford himself, in frequent references to his friend.[19] In *Thus to Revisit* (1921), written several years before Christopher was conceived, Ford offered the following description and "tribute" to Marwood.

He was too unambitious to be a writer but, large, fair, clumsy, and gentle, he had the deepest and widest intelligence of all the men I have ever met. He had the largest general, the largest encyclopaedic, knowledge that, I imagine, it would be possible for any one man's skull to hold. He could discourse, and accurately, about the rigging of fruit schooners, about the rotation of crops on sandy soils, about the home life of Ammianus Marcellinus, the vocabulary of Walter Pater, the hidden aims of Mr. Chamberlain, systems of irrigation, the theories of Mendel, the rapture of Higher Mathematics, Napoleonic strategy, consubstantiation, or the Theory of Waves. . . . He had no personal ambitions, being a Yorkshire Tory Squire, a distinguished mathematician and the Fellow of some Cambridge College — Trinity, I think.[20]

In *It Was the Nightingale* Ford provides a description of Marwood identical in personality and appearance with Christopher Tietjens. He possessed dark hair startlingly silver in places, keen blue eyes, a florid complexion, and "immense, expressive hands"; his figure was heavy and shapeless. Ford reports that his friend used to say of himself next to Conrad's vibrating small figure: "We're the two ends of human creation: he's like a quivering ant and I'm an elephant built out of meal sacks!" [21] Deliberate, strong, slow in movement, and omniscient, Marwood was, beneath his reserved surface, however, "extraordinarily passionate"—"with an abiding passion for the sort of truth that makes for intellectual accuracy in the public service." [22]

Marwood died before the war ended, but later when Ford in his novelist's imagination began to cast about for the type of his central character, he thought of his old friend and asked himself how the spectacle would have looked to him. What could be better, Ford considered, "as a medium through which to view struggles that are after all in the end mostly emotional . . . than the sceptical, not ungenerous, not cold, not unconvincible eyes of an extinct frame of mind?" For Toryism, by the time of Ford's relative youth, he explained, had "gone beyond the region of any practicing political party. It said for a year or two: A plague on all your houses, and so expired." [23] Elsewhere, he described Marwood (and, of course, Tietjens) as "the last English Tory"—"omniscient, slightly contemptuous and sentimental in his human contacts." [24]

In his various comments on the volumes Ford went to great pains to insist that he himself should not be identified with Christopher. These books, he asserted, "like all my others, constitute an attempt simply to reflect — not in the least to reflect on — our own times." [25] His aim, he said, was to project how this world would have appeared to his friend: "and that is the exact truth of the matter." [26] "Like all of us," he added, his central character is neither unprejudiced nor infallible: his reactions and reflections "are not, *not*, NOT presented as those of the author." [27] Each of the epistolary dedications in the series, with some exasperation, reiterates this point: "State, underline and emphasize the fact how you will it is impossible to get into the heads of even intelligent public critics the fact that the opinions of a novelist's characters as stated in any novel are not of necessity the opinions of the novelist. It cannot be done." [28]

To make a direct equation between Tietjens and his author would certainly be mistaken, as anyone acquainted with the novelist's biography must know. Ford was very likely to collapse under adversity, was a splendid talker, had small feeling for literal fact or science, was passionately devoted to the arts, and was cosmopolitan in outlook. Tietjens, on the other hand, is characterized as a stolid, rock-like individual, sparing of speech, a classicist with small liking for any literature written after the eighteenth century, extremely fact-minded, a statistician, and — except for his love of France — an insular, anti-empire Briton. If Ford shared some of Marwood's class prejudices, he certainly did not regard them with his partner's spleen; he was, as he often said, too much a novelist for that luxury. In particularities and the emphatic nature of his character, therefore, Ford's caveat is sound.

Yet it also tends to mislead, for not a few of Christopher's traits and circumstances derive, in fact, from Ford rather than Marwood: his non-English name; his war service and loss of memory; [29] the dishonoring of his checks; [30] his decision to live a self-sufficient, agrarian life on a hillside, and many of the circumstances that occur there; his unerring taste in furniture; [31] his golfing expeditions with a cabinet minister; [32] and, quite characteristically, his Francophilia. The two partners of *The English Review* also shared certain physical and temperamental characteristics. Like Marwood (and Tietjens), Ford was large and slow in reactions, had a remarkable memory, and frequently was described by acquaintances, including Conrad and Wells, as "omniscient" in manner.

Ford's disclaimer, therefore, cannot be taken at complete face value. "No author, however rigid his technique of self-concealment," we have already quoted him, "can conceal utterly his moral or material preferences — at least in his characters." [33] The very fact that Ford chose to see events through the eyes of Marwood suggests his affinity. Christopher surely could not be so magnificently realized a character had there not been in Ford considerable self-identification and love. More decisively, we need only examine Tietjens' values and the ones he rejects, which do not vary significantly from those which emerged from Ford's pre-war novels, as codified in Chapter Three. He is the Christian Gentleman (Anglican, not non-conformist), feudal in his values, and devoted to the ideal of service. Generosity, kindness, loyalty, stoical reserve are his major virtues. He looks with disfavor on the changes wrought in English life by industrial capitalism and the empire. For him they are marks of a national decay from once admirable, orderly standards. Nor do Christopher's values depart from the generous, good-pastor spirit of Ford's own life, most particularly in his kind behavior and encouragement to young practitioners of the arts. The type of Tietjens, finally, is not new to Ford's novels. In earlier chapters, we have seen parts of him invested in Mr. Bettesworth of *The Portrait* and Mr. Blood of *Mr. Fleight*, and, less arrogantly, in Count Macdonald of *The New Humpty-Dumpty*. If Tietjens is scarcely a literal transcript of his creator, he is equipped with not a few autobiographical details and, what is still more to the point, embodies Ford's own essential standard of values — a conclusion about which various critics, such as Douglas Goldring, Robie Macauley, Walter Allen, Elliot P. Gose, Jr.,[34] are in agreement. By attributes, values, or both, Christopher Tietjens exists, therefore, in a definite line of continuity.

Still more significant for our present purposes, however, than his similarities are the ways in which Christopher is different, both conceptually and artistically, from the earlier Fordian characters. In the novels written before the war, Ford's typical protagonists were, as we saw, unimpressive personalities, curiously ineffective, vacillating, diminished in dignity, force, and emotional depth. We need only recall Etchingham-Granger, the Fordian John Kemp, George Moffat, Don Collar Kelleg, Robert Grimshaw, Count Sergius Macdonald, Aaron Fleight. Tietjens is decidedly otherwise. Only Henry VIII of the *Fifth Queen* books approaches him in forcefulness of personality, not at all in resolution. Characterized by rock-like strength and definition of character, fortitude, clarity, and purposefulness, Christopher is conceived in broad, heroic proportions. Although like the earlier creations he is essentially passive, a stoical adherent to his code, unlike the great majority of his predecessors Tietjens reveals by his actions that he can be effective when circumstances warrant it — as, for example, his presence of mind at the uproarious Duchemin breakfast table or at the wounding of the cart-horse in the fog, or afterwards at the base depot and in the trenches.

More important still are the differences in the artistry with which he is created. Where the pre-war characters (excluding those in *The Good Soldier*) tend to be sketches, he, on the other hand, is magnificently rounded and textured. Christopher Tietjens must be placed, in fact, among the undeniably great characters of English literature. His very outlines are compelling to the imagination: large, extremely powerful in body and mind, yet stolid, diffident, and unambitious. Tietjens arouses much the same fascination men have always felt for personages whose great strength is unused but dramatically potential: he shares in the deep appeal of the myth of the sleepy Bear-Son (like him, a younger one), who someday will wake to tremendous deeds. But Christopher is not merely archetypal. His inner life is richly rendered. He is a fully human, complex personality. For all the rock-like definiteness of his public character, in his spirit is embodied a cluster of dramatic and life-giving contrarieties. Phlegmatic and clumsy in body, he is deeply passionate, with almost a poet's sensibility. Arrogant and frank, from both class position and intelligence, he is yet tolerant, considerate, generous. A staunch traditionalist, he disregards formalities, is careless of his dress. Although he does not love his wife, he yet accepts her return for the sake of honor and their child. Living in the strongly sexual presence of Sylvia, he denies himself any relations with her. Intensely loving their child, he yet carries within him the dreadful knowledge that the boy may not be his. And when he wrongly suffers public obloquy, he refuses to clear his name, out of fidelity to his code and from simple disdain at demeaning himself by explanation.

Equally important, Tietjens alters and grows. He is a character in process. In large measure this sense of development derives from the reader's gradual discovery of the various facets and contradictions of personality that lie concealed under his arresting exterior, a matter of Ford's art of unfolding his character. But change also occurs in Tietjens himself, involving fundamental shifts in direction and state of being. The most dramatically effective are his growing love for and commitment to Valentine, and the pitiful and ironic loss of his great memory from shell-shock: fate's punishment of his sin of *hubris*.

Besides these, still another difference distinguishes Tietjens from his predecessors — a historical event. Before the war Ford's criticism of modern institutions and values could easily enough be set down as the attitudes of a crank. But with the terrible disaster which modern civilization, developing along the tendencies Ford rejected, came to in the struggle, his attitudes assume much of the power of prophecy: the Great War was frightful public objectification of a moral and spiritual decay. As a result, the values Ford and Christopher stand for no longer have the air of mere nostalgic ineffectuality, but instead take on a striking attractiveness, and a persuasive power. If Christopher is a man who is the product of such values, one is made to feel, they cannot be absurd. In a world where all truth is flux, and men in their day-to-day lives tend to do nothing heroic because unable to commit themselves, Tietjens' point of view and example are genuinely compelling.

Christopher is not, however, the only memorable character in the work. Ford has created more than a dozen and a half imaginatively striking and rounded personalities. Although many make brief appearances, no fewer than six are major in proportion, prominence, and creative success. Like Tietjens, much of their force comes from their being distinct classic types, in myth or society. And like him also, they are filled out by the novelist's art to become living, particularized individuals.

The most important after Christopher are the two women in his life. As a type, Sylvia Tietjens is corrupt beauty — the cruel, ravishingly attractive temptress. Her introduction, in fact, is under the sign of Astarte: the intensely bored Sylvia dabbling in forbidden rites and moving, in a gold sheath dress, amidst a Continental circle of decadent upper-class women. Yet for all her sophistication, celebrated in the pages of the rotogravure, Sylvia is strongly ascetic, deeply marked by the discipline of her puritan Roman Catholic upbringing. The attraction of men is only an external need, egotistic and social; at core, she is cold and continent. Enjoying the fascination she exerts on males, and the fear aroused among their wives — herself a fish-eagle among gulls — Sylvia treats her suitors with disdain. On returning to Christopher, she thus determines to be faithful; her consolation will be the pleasure of making him wince. In time, however, she herself falls intensely in love with her husband, her hell being that this desire emerges only after his heart is Valentine's. Thereafter, her course is vindictively to torment and even ruin him.

Like Christopher, Sylvia is not a new Fordian character. As the rejected beauty vengefully punishing the protagonist, she made her first appearance in his gallery in The "Half Moon," as the witch-woman, Anne Jeal. And, subsequently, she appeared in various forms as Katya Lascarides in A Call, Countess Macdonald in The New Humpty-Dumpty, and Augusta Macphail in Mr. Fleight. (Although Leonora in The Good Soldier in her cruelty shares in the type, she is, by reason of her detailed suffering and greater complexity, a significantly different character.) Compared with these forerunners, Sylvia is, by far, the most impressive and exciting. Ford achieves this distinction in large measure through the brilliant surface his art has given her. Her stunning clothes, her languid manner, her savage tongue and scornful insolence vividly establish her. Ford has also been careful, as he was not in earlier versions, to develop an adequate motivation, conveying with impressionistic power and penetration the disruption of her spirit through a violent sexual experience.[35] Sylvia is better motivated in yet another way. The constancy of passion with which the earlier women persecute their men tends in time to take on an unreal, even insane aspect, since in normal experience expressed hostility must eventually discharge itself. Sylvia's protracted hatred is objectified apart from any mad (and uninteresting) willfulness by the fact of her being a Roman Catholic wife who cannot divorce. Bound by indissoluble marriage vows to a being whose presence, and even existence, torments her and continually re-provokes her hatred, Sylvia, in her almost unflagging desire to injure Christopher, is thoroughly credible. It was a solution to Ford's problem of formulating such emotion in his fiction which he first arrived at, as we have seen, in his conception of Leonora. But life, of course, had itself offered the clue.

Sylvia is still further humanized by moments in which she feels heartfelt pity, even a deferring tenderness for Christopher, particularly after he has suffered his war experience. "Somewhere or other there must surely be / The face not seen: the voice not heard" are root-striking words, known by Sylvia and quoted by her husband, which penetrate to her deepest, buried longing for union and fulfillment: "The echo of them remained with her like something terrible and alluring: like a knife she would some day take out and with which she would stab herself." [36]

In sharp contrast with Sylvia is her rival. For Valentine Wannop is the classic type of the boy-like girl — fresh and open-hearted, sprightly and intelligent. She is the tomboy of freedom and self-reliance, but also of quick and feminine sympathy for the male predicament; intrepid when danger threatens, yet fearful earlier and after: chaste, but frankly knowing: a Rosalind, essentially, with touches of Viola. Her biography is still further compounded of opposites. Although both her parents are of the intelligentsia — her father a famous Cambridge professor, her mother a noted novelist — Valentine has not been formally educated, but rather has been encouraged in athletics. At the same time, she is something of a bluestocking, and almost professionally competent in the classical languages — a talent which leads to delightful scholarly debates with Christopher. Entitled to move in good social circles, she yet has been forced by poverty after her father's death to work as a housemaid, for which reason she is both a socialist and a militant suffragette. As a character, Valentine is unique among Ford's creations. Katharine Howard of *The Fifth Queen*, Clara Brede of *The*

Benefactor, Eleanor Greville of *An English Girl* share some of her spirit but little else. Certainly none of them can compare in liveliness or fullness.[37]

Still another attractive personality is Christopher's older brother, Mark Tietjens, an imaginative creation perhaps even more enduringly impressive than Sylvia or Valentine. Mark's great charm as a character is not easily summed up. In part it lies in his very definiteness. For Mark is a decidedly insular, laconic Yorkshireman, a brilliant official in a high government office in London, who moves incuriously and unemotionally through a fixed set of unvarying routines — supremely content with agreeable physical pleasures like buttered toast, mutton chops, and the Thursday races. Even his grim and uncomfortable apartment, furnished with horse-hair-upholstered mahogany and illuminated by means of ground-glass skylights, expresses his amazing self-containment. With his bowler hat and umbrella, old race glasses dangling across his tightly buttoned suit, his brown complexion and bulging eyes, Mark is imaginatively as striking as any creation of Dickens. Reasonable claim may be made that he typifies the individualist, eccentric, nontheoretical, practical-minded Englishman. Yet Mark, who is a first-rate comic creation, is not a mere caricature. He has more than one dimension. Although a singularly provincial Englishman (narrowed down still further to the North Riding), he is a Francophile. For many years he has had a French mistress who attends to his domestic wants and who amuses him by reading various items, enlivened with her comments, from the newspapers. And for Christopher and Valentine he feels genuine admiration and a warm affection. Intensely committed to his insular compass, Mark is, in fact, a man of strong passion.

The two brothers form a fascinating combination. Both are taciturn, somewhat arrogant Yorkshiremen with a shared belief in the importance of correct forms and with considerable brotherly feeling. Both have associates close to them who are treacherous, Scots, and of a lower social standing. They even can understand each other without saying a word. In a sense the two are twins, Mark accenting the creature side of existence and Christopher the spiritual — Mark, *homme moyen sensuel*; Christopher, a Christian saint. In *The Last Post*, however, Mark assumes something of Christopher's role and becomes the voice of the dying order — saying farewell, and offering a testament of faith.[38]

Two other impressive Fordian creations are Vincent Macmaster and his eventual wife, Edith Ethel Duchemin, who, being climbers, are more social than mythic types. A friend of Tietjens at Clifton and Cambridge and afterwards in London, where they are colleagues in the same government office, Macmaster is the son of a poor Scots shipping clerk; through hard labor, deprivation, discreet caution, and support from Christopher, he has been steadily rising. The special path Macmaster has chosen to win a career in a first-class government office is through the arts, as a critic; and his monograph on the poetry of Dante Gabriel Rossetti is his chief vehicle. Smallish, a Whig, with a trimmed, pointed beard, a sharp nose, and stubborn black hair ("drilled down with hard, metal brushes"), and vain in his appearance, Macmaster is an excellent foil for Christopher.[39]

Edith Ethel is herself something of a Rossetti female —"an old fashion woman," as she remarks. Dressed in a very large-sleeved dark-blue dress, upon which is a necklace of polished amber, she moves enigmatically and with assurance among roses, polished brown woods, and gleaming silver. Macmaster's initial attraction to Edith Ethel is further intensified by his discovery of her marital martyrdom (her husband, the much older Reverend Duchemin, is a violent lunatic); and both fall in love, circumspectly and in the style of their Pre-Raphaelite sensibilities. At the husband's death, the two marry and together set out to rule an aesthetic salon. Beneath the fastidious surface of Edith Ethel lies, however, a personality which is hysterical, vulgar, and spiteful.

Still another arresting portrait in Ford's gallery is General Lord Edward Campion, the type of the conventional, obtuse British officer. Uncle to Christopher, for whom he has much affection, he yet persists in misjudging the young man. Since to him Sylvia can do no wrong, it is Christopher who must be at fault. Armed with his military man's characteristic distrust of intelligence and of imagination, Campion feels the more confirmed in his judgment by the very fact of Tietjens' brilliance. Christopher is unsound, he sorrowfully reflects: the type who upsets the established order, and on whom society cannot depend, a kind of Dreyfus. As a man, Campion is decent and well meaning, and a first-rate general. For him and his soldier's code, Ford displays considerable sympathy.

In addition to these half-dozen excellently-handled characters, Ford has created many others who appear more briefly: Mrs. Sattherthwaite, Sylvia's mother, sophisticated, forceful, and death-haunted; the Irish working-class priest, Father Consett, a saint consumed by fascination with the game of bridge; Christopher's father, taciturn and intense; the Reverend Duchemin, the lunatic, obscene-tongued clergyman, cultivated and scholarly, a former disciple of Ruskin and associate of the Pre-Raphaelites; Horsely, the bull-sized, booming-voiced first curate, and manager of Duchemin in his wild fits; Mrs. Wannop, the overworked writer who cultivates reviewers with business-like efficiency and who depends on Christopher for her facts; Ruggles, the Scot who shares Mark's quarters and who unweariedly collects a dossier of discreditable information about Christopher; and Marie-Léonie, Mark's mistress (who appears principally in *The Last Post*), the image of the orderly, clean, delightful French housekeeper.

Through these characters and many others, Ford presents his picture of the world which culminated in the war. The action is much as he has indicated. A good man, Christopher is assailed on all sides by those who, judging by appearances or their own baser selves, fail to understand his motives or who misrepresent them. A thicket of rumor flourishes about him, composed largely of the putative and actual sins of others. Trying to help Macmaster detach himself from an inappropriate amour, Christopher typically becomes himself connected with the lady. In the public mind also, it is Christopher, not the discreet Macmaster, who is having the affair with Edith Ethel. And when Mrs. Duchemin fears that she is pregnant by Macmaster, rumor makes Christopher the parent of a real child and then transfers the part of mother to Valentine. Tietjens is falsely accused also of living on his wife's money; and a suitor of

Sylvia's tries to ruin him by marking his bank account overdrawn. Sylvia herself hounds her husband in every way, even to damning him to Campion as a socialist — terrible accusation to the general — as proved, she says, by his self-image as Christ the Saviour. While in the army Christopher again gets into still further difficulties by countermanding foolish orders — such as a barbarous experimental treatment of horses in winter, or the abuses of Canadian volunteers by the military police. In the process are revealed the corruption and blindness of motive of the English governing classes.

Historians may perhaps not completely concur with Ford's unattractive picture of the "inheritors" who stayed at home. And at times the almost unadulterated stupidity, self-seeking, and treachery which he presents seem incredible. But against this criticism, two answers may be offered. One Ford made himself. He does not insist, he said, that his account is objectively accurate. What he was trying to render, he explained, was an atmosphere which prevailed among the fighting men, who were "truly, very lonely out there"—"some millions of men, suspended on a raft, in limitless space"— an atmosphere that was very like that created by Henry James in *What Maisie Knew*.[40] To the soldier in the trenches the greatest concern was home. Under the impact of war he became, indeed, *homo duplex*: "a poor fellow whose body is tied in one place but whose mind and personality brood over another distant locality." [41] Reading the daily papers that reached the lines from home, the troops began to feel "a curious dislike" of the civilians which was never to die. "I don't know what was going on at home: political intrigues, no doubt; strikes possibly. But there seemed to prevail a tenuous, misty struggle of schemes — just the atmosphere of 'Maisie.' " [42] It was this atmosphere, then, which Ford wanted to recreate. His may not be a complete view, but then no views ever are. Who will say, for example, that the picture of English manners and morals created by Thackeray in *Vanity Fair*, which is even more corrupt, was not basically true?

The other answer is to regard the issue of historical accuracy as irrelevant to a literary creation. The primary aim of the Tietjens books is, after all, to present a literary symbol of the formal end of a way of life, made concrete by the actions and personalities of its characters. The ultimate test, as Walter Allen has suggested, voting in the affirmative, is whether Ford's creative power enables him to impose his picture imaginatively upon the reader.

Despite the base attacks of his society, Tietjens stoically retains his own self. His ideal is that of touching pitch and not being defiled, and he performs his duties according to his code. When he learns that his father, believing the stories of his wrongdoings, had not died accidentally but had killed himself because of a broken heart, he can only say: "Oh! Ah! Yes! . . . I suspected that. I knew it, really. I suppose the poor dear knows better now. Or perhaps he doesn't. . . . It doesn't matter." [43] In the army, he works heroically under great fatigue and with no praise to shepherd the men in his command. Son of a saintly mother, Christopher is almost a modern saint himself. In the blight of his war duties, Christopher is sustained in his spirit by a vision of the life of the poet George Herbert — an Anglican saint — at his Bremerton parsonage.

But if Tietjens does not seriously change in his inner equilibrium, he does come, however, to certain recognitions of what his relation must be to the new world that has replaced the feudal structure he loves. The old order, he realizes, cannot support any longer his way of life. Although Groby, his ancestral Yorkshire home, will be his at Mark's death — his other older brothers having been killed in the war — Christopher relinquishes all claim to it. Wrested from its Catholic owners when the Protestant monarch, "Dutch William," supplanted the Stuarts, Groby will go instead to Christopher's son by Sylvia, who is a Catholic, so that the curse will at last be off the land. In a sense, Tietjens makes a separate peace. In the trenches he asks for a world where a man can stand up on a hill. Meaning and order must be found not in the structure of society in the twentieth century, where they do not exist, but in one's daily life, in relation to the natural landscape, and in one's human duties. The model exalted is the clean, orderly, tasteful relation of the French peasant to his world, his love of tending things that grow, and his pleasure in the small but full qualities of life. *Mon verre n'est pas grand, mais je bois dans mon verre.* In the end Christopher breaks with society and lives with Valentine.

This fundamental conflict between Tietjens and the world he found himself in Ford develops in four different novels: *Some Do Not, No More Parades, A Man Could Stand Up, The Last Post.* Published separately, each was written to stand by itself — a practice which is usual, because of commercial demands, in series dealing with the same sets of characters; otherwise, argue publishers, sales would be confined to readers of earlier volumes. As example, *No More Parades,* the second novel, sold far more copies in America than the first, becoming, in fact, a best-seller. (The independence of the different Tietjens volumes Ford himself made clear in his dedication to *No More Parades,* which is, he writes, not so much a "continuation" of *Some Do Not* as a "reinforcement.")

Each of the four books presents Christopher in different circumstances. *Some Do Not,* to be examined in more detail later, shows him in England. Its first half, which is pre-war (about 1908) establishes the various characters, the atmosphere, and the basic situation; its second, occurring in the middle years of the war, presents the intensifying conflict between Christopher and those who distrust, fear, and hate him. Already he has been in combat and been shell-shocked; and at the end he is about to return, all but disgraced, to the war.

No More Parades and *A Man Could Stand Up* shift the action to France: the first, behind the lines; the second, in the trenches. The atmosphere of distrust of the civilians at home dominates these books in particular. The middle pair also support (far more than the first and fourth volumes) still another recorded Fordian aim — the writing of a work "that should have for its purpose the obviating of all future wars." Remarking that he had always had the greatest contempt for novels written with a purpose, Ford acknowledged, however, that in the Tietjens books he had sinned against his gods to the extent of trying to show his readers that war is undesirable. For himself, war had not been very dreadful.[44] But "the desperation and horror that wars caused to other people impressed me with such mass and such vividness that I was ready to put my principles behind me." However, he did not intend to violate his literary conscience by piling up horrors, or by exaggerating them, for that policy ultimately defeats itself: "After you have seen two or three men killed or mangled your mind of necessity grows a carapace round itself and afterwards witnessing the slaying of thousands hardly moves you unless those men belong to your own unit." Instead Ford reasoned that if he could present not merely fear or horror or death or even self-sacrifice, but "just worry," then that might be a "note" of which the world would not easily weary. Fear, he said, ends in callousness; but "worry feeds on itself," until it "so destroys the morale that less than a grasshopper becomes a burden." "And it seemed to me that if the world could be got to see war from that angle there would be no more wars." [45] Ford's treatment of the conflict in these two novels is in keeping with his remarks. The tempting dramatic potentialities of personal combat are all but ignored. There is little actual fighting, and the horror of wounds and of mangled deaths are few and uncalculated to shock and stagger the senses.

In *No More Parades*, the action is mainly divided between a base depot (from which Christopher must dispatch troops up the lines for an expected offensive) and a hotel in Rouen. The major incidents are the bloody death of one of Christopher's men by an artillery shell and the unauthorized visit of Sylvia to the base. In the background, but impinging on the local events, are rumored machinations in Whitehall to get England to remove its army from France for service in the Near East, in order to safeguard Britain's essential interests, namely the Empire. (There is even the hint of a separate peace with the Germans.) In retaliation, the French foment railway strikes to impede the transport of British troops. At deeper political issue in these maneuverings is the supreme command, opposed by London and desired by Paris — and passionately favored by Christopher. The issue of the single command is also the dominant external concern in *A Man Could Stand Up*, in which is foreshadowed the establishment of the command — an event that did not happen, we may be reminded, until April 14, 1918. (In *The*

Last Post, yet another action in Whitehall outrages several of the characters, Mark Tietjens in particular: the unwillingness of the British government to press toward and occupy Berlin at the Armistice.)

The climax of *No More Parades* involves an air raid at Rouen, followed by an ugly episode in the Tietjens' hotel room. As the married couple are preparing for bed — Christopher exhausted and his lungs bad, Sylvia expecting to satisfy her violent desire for her husband — they are burst in upon by an ex-lover of Sylvia and by a general with whom she had provocatively flirted. For throwing out his superior officer, Christopher is put under arrest. At the end of the book, he is released by General Campion and told that he will be sent up to command a battalion at the front.

In *A Man Could Stand Up*, Tietjens is presented in the lines during one of the powerful late German offensives. The climax of the book occurs when a shell explodes beneath the feet of Christopher and of several of his men. One of the troops, a gentle boy who reminds him of Valentine, is killed. Another loses an eye. The section describing Tietjens at the front is framed by two shorter parts, set in London on Armistice Day and focusing on Valentine. The opening unit presents her discovery by telephone, as the eleven o'clock reports go off, that Tietjens, the painful, sensitive burden she had put out of her mind, has returned. Ford's setting of this part — an English girls' school where Valentine is instructor — is by no means chance, for it is a characteristic symbol of British society. Traditional at such institutions, where the future social leaders of England are educated, is the vigorous discipline, and the close regulation of the lives of the girls, even to the wearing of a plain uniform. In fear that the young women may suddenly break from the reins, hurry to London, and riotously celebrate with the troops, the headmistress has ordered Valentine to occupy them with physical exercises while the whistles sound. As Valentine speaks on the telephone, part of her mind fears the flight of the girls in her absence, while the other part kindredly wishes to join them. Thus, in trenchant particularity, is embodied the larger, similar conflict between the regimenting authorities and the intense desires of individual

Englishmen, and people everywhere, to cast off restrictions. The closing section, occurring later in the day, reunites Christopher and Valentine in his empty rooms — stripped of its furniture by Sylvia (as England has been of its treasure, human and otherwise). And its final episode depicts the wandering into these rooms of various scarred and wounded associates of Christopher who have come to celebrate, though not without unfriendliness toward Valentine by their women, the end of the war.

In *The Last Post*, the war is over and the setting is a Sussex hill farm where Christopher has withdrawn to live with Valentine, who carries his child. The action occurs in a single afternoon. During the course of the novel, the various characters of the Tietjens series are brought together, and others are introduced for the first time: Mark's mistress, Marie-Léonie (or Charlotte); Christopher's son, also named Mark; Gunning, the English peasant hired hand; and Millicent de Bray Pape, the obnoxious American woman who has rented Groby. Oddly enough, Christopher himself does not appear until the very end of the book. Instead the central character is his brother Mark, who, since the end of the war, out of choice has neither spoken nor moved. Lying under a thatch shelter behind Christopher's house, a great view before him, and meditating on the world of people he has rejected, this strangely willful man communicates with others solely by eye blinkings. The novel unfolds mainly through a series of inner monologues, beginning with Mark and returning to him in the middle and again at the end. In between, we enter the thoughts of Marie-Léonie (twice), Gunning, Mrs. de Bray Pape, Sylvia, and Valentine. The action is provided chiefly by the invasion of the envious Sylvia into this agrarian sanctuary; Sylvia is driven to her act in part also by anxiety at her ultimate outrage against Christopher: her having prevailed upon Mrs. de Bray Pape to destroy the Groby Great Tree. As old as Groby itself, and an imposing symbol of it, the uprooting of the tree had collapsed a side of the building, including most of the ballroom, the old schoolrooms above it, and Christopher's boyhood bedroom. In the great, now mangled, dovecote, the American has erected a new power station. The death of the tree marks the end of the traditions of the

Tietjens, and Christopher, having been at Groby, appears at the very conclusion of the novel, holding a piece of its wood in his hand. Symbolically the curse upon Groby has been removed. The Tietjens' usurpation of property is at an end. And the new life, in the form of Christopher and Valentine's child, can begin.

The four novels of the Tietjens series, although published separately, have in recent years been gathered together under the comprehensive title of *Parade's End*. But should Ford's work be considered, in fact, as a tetralogy? Or is it more accurately a trilogy, with *The Last Post* as sequel? Robie Macauley, in his introduction to *Parade's End*, has supported the first position, urging that the four should be considered as one book: "I think it can be comprehended in no other way. . . . Without *The Last Post*, the novel would have been sadly truncated." Acknowledging that the work could never "turn out" as an ordinary novel must, he asserts that the recapitulation and final statement of *The Last Post* are "indispensable." [46] Support for Macauley's position, which he himself does not cite, may be found in the epistolary dedications to the books, in which Ford declares his structural intention. After observing, in the introduction to *No More Parades*, that his protagonist had been shown in the first volume at home during wartime and that in the second he is seen going up the line, he adds: "If I am vouchsafed health and intelligence for long enough I propose to show you the same man in the line and in the process of being re-constructed." And in the dedicatory letter to the next book, Ford wrote that *A Man Could Stand Up* is "the third and penultimate" of the series.

Nevertheless, despite Macauley's assessment and these observations from Ford, the sounder approach is to view the enterprise not as tetralogy but trilogy — with the fourth volume as a kind of afterthought, separate from the main design. For by the completion of *A Man Could Stand Up*, Ford, however he may have felt earlier, had clearly altered his intention. In his dedication to *The Last Post*, for example, we find him writing that if it were not for Isabel Patterson's "stern, contemptuous and almost virulent insistence" on knowing "what became of Tietjens," he never would "have conducted this chronicle to the stage it has now reached." Indeed, it is curious that his statement calling the third book the penultimate in the series is dated May 18, 1926, while the novel itself is not marked as finished until more than two months later, July 21. Still more decisive evidence that Ford considered the work a trilogy appears in a letter of 1930. In reply to a proposal that the Tietjens books be issued as an omnibus volume, Ford suggested the title, *Parade's End* (rejecting *The Tietjens Saga* as difficult, and liable to confusion with *The Forsyte Saga*), and added: "I strongly wish to omit *Last Post* from the edition. I do not like the book and have never liked it and always intended to end up with *A Man Could Stand Up*."[47] Nor was this significant judgment expressed only privately. Three years later in *It Was the Nightingale* Ford again indicated his view of the matter by referring several times to the Tietjens books as a "trilogy," and even quoting as its closing words: "On an elephant. A dear meal sack elephant. She was setting out. . . ."—the ending of *A Man Could Stand Up*.

To depart from Ford's final, definite judgment is unwise, particularly since the texts themselves support his verdict. As we have seen, the Tietjens cycle cannot be approached — even as a trilogy — as though it were conceived and executed as a perfect artistic whole, since commercial demands required that each volume stand separately. Nevertheless, between the first book and the end of the third there is a definite, clear unity of subject — the subject Ford himself said he had in mind — that of the "world which culminated in the war," presented through the focus of Christopher Tietjens, the central observer. *Some Do Not* begins symbolically in peacetime in a shiningly appointed railway car, and *A Man Could Stand Up* ends in a bare, stripped room on Armistice night among the damaged victims of the war. England itself has been stripped, and there will be no more parades. The over-all conception of the three books is gaunt, stark, and complete. After them, the action of *The Last Post* can only be considered an addendum, a fact signalized by Ford's removal of his central character from any prominent role. Unlike the first three volumes, the last, as Ford saw, does not come meaningfully under the banner of *Parade's End*. To include it there is only to obscure the force and impact of the basic conception.

Nor is the fourth volume consistent in its fundamental method. The approach of the earlier novels is essentially realistic. Although their characters and events possess a meaning beyond themselves, the significance is implicit, hinted through the texture of actuality. *The Last Post*, on the other hand, is only nominally realistic, its particularity of character and event the merest coloring. Rather, its method is symbolic: the characters and the action overtly serving Ford's *idea*. Less individuals than forces, the characters are like allegorical figures in a pageant. Valentine is motherhood impending, Christopher huntsman and family protector, Sylvia (described in one passage as "it") a diabolic marble statue, Marie-Léonie domesticity, and Mark the presiding magician and deity (willing against Sylvia's influence). The Groby Great Tree, finally, is the highly conscious symbol of the curse upon the Tietjenses. The note of unreality, of a primarily symbolic world, is in fact struck at the opening by the extreme peculiarity of Mark's personal withdrawal. *The Last Post* is a novel plainly of another style altogether from the first three.

Beyond this point the case against including *The Last Post* in the main plan need not go. Ford's own assessment and the disunity of subject and method are decisive. Yet a further argument perhaps may be offered — based on a critical judgment. The book should be excluded finally because it violates the essential spirit and master mood not only of the first three volumes but of Ford himself.

In their conception of the moral nature of the universe, the earlier works move with balance on the tension between belief (or wish) and fact. To Tietjens the world has a cosmic order, with heaven, man, and nature in appropriate relation and coherence — as is suggested in the memorable passage in *No More Parades* in which he compares heaven to a vast, well-run English estate.[48] Yet the world that Ford presents is cruelly out of harmony. The devil, in the form of Sylvia, has the ear and sympathy of the great and the power to hound and persecute a good man. Christopher's father has killed himself. Christopher's child may well not be his own. Even

Christopher is willing to concede that "his projection of a hereafter" is "probably done with." Heaven had become rather "a revival meeting on a Welsh hillside. Or Chatauqua . . ." And God? "A
Real Estate Agent, with Marxist views." He himself hopes that before the end of the fighting he will be "out of it," and "just in time
for the last train to the old heaven." [49] Although Christopher's version of order obviously attracts his creator personally, Ford in the
trilogy does not affirm that that vision is truth. Rather, the reader
feels it to be the conception of an individual character with a particular personality and heritage, who himself recognizes it as a "projection." It appeals pleasantly to his imagination and, still more
deeply, is necessary to his psychic balance. Elegiac lament, not spiritual assurance, lies at the core of the trilogy, lament for the decay
of a once coherent civilization and for the beleaguered state of traditional human values. Ford's emotional and philosophical response
is not very different from the Beowulf poet's as the body of the
dead hero is consumed on the pyre and his people uneasily anticipate their future, or from Malory's at the passing of Arthur and his
realm. He looks back at an age with muted longing and forward
without enthusiasm. The broken, harsh world in which the main
character moves is, in fact, very much the kind of world, if we may
judge from nearly his entire fictional canon, which sadly embodies
Ford's own deepest, firmest sense of reality.

In *The Last Post*, however, the tension between fact and wish is
swept away, and the two are made one. The whole mood of the
first three books is inverted, as all cruel dislocations resolve into
order. Christopher's son is self-evidently his own. Christopher's
father did not commit suicide. (Nor was he, as Mark suspected, the
real sire of Valentine: thus erasing the possibility of incest between
the lovers.) And Sylvia, the devil, on discovering that Valentine
carries Christopher's child within her, abruptly relinquishes her
persecution and agrees to free her husband. Through the enormous
sky and black night, the earth wheels tranquilly, the animal creatures of the world in awe sensing its rush. The great night is eternity and the Infinite, and in it we see "The spirit of God walking on

the firmament." Thus, all is fundamentally well. Ford's verdict at the end is the familiar: "God's in his heaven: All's right with the world." The contrast with the first three books is extreme.

To some readers, this resolution may be satisfactory — the appropriate ending to the series. To most, however, it will seem decidedly unconvincing, and a kind of betrayal. The facts of social and spiritual disorder heaped up earlier have been overwhelming, and in essential ways are supported by the thoughtful reader's own perception of the realities of his times. Suddenly, however, the evidence is denied, and the contrary affirmed as truth. Nor is the resolution dramatic, proceeding through a series of developed, experienced steps. It is simply cursory and arbitrary, an author's reversal externally impressed upon the action. As a result, the act of faith, rather than being valid, seems inevitably, by contrast with what has gone before, a too facile, contentless gesture.

The ending of *The Last Post* is, in short, a sentimental indulgence. It shares kinship with the unfelt, pseudo-Shakespearian conclusion to the *Fifth Queen* trilogy, in which Ford succumbed to the temptation of a crescendo close to a lengthy work, and even more with the original sentimental ending to *Ladies Whose Bright Eyes*, which he afterwards repudiated. This easy sentimentality — so counter to Ford's typically beleaguered, alienated sense of the world — may well be precisely the reason why he did not like the book and did not want to include it with the first three. It was a fairy tale, a wish, the symbolization of something he wanted to be. But in his heart he did not believe it.

Ultimately, however, the issue of trilogy or tetralogy is academic. Whether entitled *Parade's End* and *The Last Post* or called *Parade's End* alone, the Tietjens cycle as a whole will not stand importantly to Ford's credit as a novelist. The true achievement of his Tietjens creations is the first volume, *Some Do Not*. The succeeding books will not last. Where *Some Do Not* is a magnificent and rich work of the novelist's imagination in almost all aspects — characterization, narrative suspense, authoritative atmosphere, and emotional power — the rest are thin productions which peter out the vein.

The larger conception of the trilogy, in brief, is splendid, but it is not filled out.

And essentially this judgment is also Ford's, given covertly and without detail but unambiguously in *It Was the Nightingale*, where he comments that after *Some Do Not* his works had considerably deteriorated. The reason, he said, was an attack of writer's cramp. After the completion of the book he "began at St. Jean Cap Ferrat" (*Some Do Not* from earlier reference), the cramp became so severe he could not hold a pen. And so he took to using a typewriter —"to the considerable deterioration of my work"[50] —and "then, worst of all, to dictating."[51] The typewriter and the stenographer, Ford remarked, made him too fluid. "It is as if they waited for me to write and write I do. Whereas if I have to go to a table and face pretty considerable pain I wait until I have something to say and say it in the fewest possible words."[52]

The failure of the novels after *Some Do Not* lies precisely where Ford has indicated: in their excessive fluidity. Because they are not composed with scrupulous care or by a fully engaged mind, the imaginative vitality established for the Tietjens world in the first book is mostly lost. In writing these volumes, Ford had ceased to be an artist. Documentation of this point can be brief, for the same faults characterize all three.

The unfortunate consequences of Ford's hurried carpentry are evident in a variety of ways, but probably the central casualty is his management of the interior monologue, which (unlike *Some Do Not*) dominates all three books. The device, particularly fashionable at the time of their composition, possesses decided advantages for developing the inner life of a character. Its weakness, however, which follows from its associative principle, is an inherent looseness of structure. Like free verse, its very freedom makes it all the more difficult to do well. The author must not only render successfully the illusion of a character's flowing stream of thought, but he must also contrive, without harming that illusion, to maintain interest and excitement and to advance his narrative. And neither of these ends does Ford achieve in the later books. Too facilely exploiting the liberties of his method, he inevitably has

come away empty-handed. Far too often the details which he puts
into a thought process are not there to build his character inwardly
but to explain the events of the earlier books. And since the exposition required is elaborate, the process can only become deaden-
ing. Converted into a garrulous expository machine, the character
thus has insufficient life of his own. Similarly, thoughts occurring
originally in the mind of one character are often repeated later
in exactly the same words in another's, without justification either
in cause and effect or proximity — only in the needs of plot machinery. There is a tendency also to resort to a same few motives,
the effect of which is to restrict the inner life of the characters.
To Valentine, for example, Tietjens is always a bear, and the same
tags of Latin and English poetry constantly reappear. Nor is any
distinction made in the interior monologue between characters.
Each sounds like every other, with the same tone, cadence, and
recurrent mannerisms of speech —"Something like that," "oh, say
— ," "*call it*"— which are in fact the mannerisms of Ford's personal
voice as a memoirist.

As a result, the characterizations in the three volumes are on the
whole thin and unsuccessful. If, earlier, Ford was highly praised
for creating in his Tietjens world so many first-rate, imaginatively
compelling characters, the praise was thoroughly earned. He has
done precisely that, and triumphantly, as any reader of *Some Do
Not* must allow. But after the first volume these great characters
unfortunately narrow into dullish stereotypes. Christopher becomes merely a burdened stoical figure with almost absurd tendencies toward *noblesse oblige*. Losing her complexity and style,
Sylvia is reduced to an incredibly vulgar (and extremely unpleasant) monster. The same flattening out may be seen in other of the
characters who reappear, such as Valentine, General Campion,
Edith Ethel, and Mrs. Wannop. Permanently set, they do not
change or grow. Whether in appearance, behavior, or mental configuration, Ford ceases to observe them freshly. In the first volume, the fact of Christopher's erudition and intelligence is con-
vincingly demonstrated in his conversation; in the later books this
brilliance is merely asserted, by the easy device of having someone

utter an admiring: "You do know everything!" Nor is the deterioration of Ford's splendid characters compensated for by the fullness with which new ones are created. Those introduced in the later
volumes — Captain Mackensie, General O'Hara, Colonel Levin, the
line captain, the men in the trenches, the peasant Gunning, Millicent de Bray Pape — remain counters. Only Marie-Léonie has genuine charm and surprise.

No less unhappy is the effect of the interior monologue on the
narrative strength of these three books. Very little in them is deeply
engaging because the method is basically a non-dramatic prison —
much of the "action" occurring posthumously, so to speak, in the
mind of a character. And since the focus is not on the conflict itself
but on the character's thoughts about it, the few dramatic scenes
which do take place tend to be muffled and oblique. The method
as implemented also makes for an over-all linear impression, in pale
contrast to the rich and various world of *Some Do Not*.

Finally we should consider still another important casualty of
this easy fluidity: the prose. Lack of genuine care is revealed by
numerous tests. The same words recur again and again in brief
space. Paragraph three of *No More Parades*, for example, repeats
hanging about four times; the next does the same with *very annoy-
ing*. And although such a device might be defended as a calculated
intensity, a demanding art recognizes (as in *The Good Soldier* and
Some Do Not) that it is more truly expressive not to dissipate
verbal power by repetition. Certainly it is difficult to justify the
technique's being used in two successive paragraphs. Ford plainly
was exploiting an easy trick, not artfully creating.

This same reliance on easily-bought effects may be seen in the
routine, unexpressive quality of many of the sentences and phrases
("A tall, purple-faced man in a perfectly impossible tin hat who
was scared to death") and in the over-use of intensives. Vague
adjectives, like "immense," "extraordinary," and "intolerable," are
employed a stultifying number of times. The exclamation point
also is excessively used, often in conjunction with an equally mechanical handling of choppy, explosive rhythms and emphatic italics. On two pages, 519 and 520, for instance, the exclamation point

is employed twenty-two times; one page (545) has seventeen, others (484, 647) fourteen. And if these instances mark an extreme, they are only the high points of a general tendency toward a factitious emotional heightening. Some sentences, finally, are downright bad:

She had strong temperance opinions and, immediately after the death of her husband, she had emptied the contents of his cellar, which were almost as historic as his castle, into the sea, a shudder going through county-family and no, or almost no, characteristics.[53]

Or:

The telephone, for some ingeniously torturing reason, was in a corner of the great schoolroom without any protection and, called imperatively, at a moment of considerable suspense, out of the asphalt playground where, under her command ranks of girls had stood electrically only just within the margin of control, Valentine with the receiver at her ear was plunged immediately into incomprehensible news uttered by a voice that she seemed half to remember.[54]

That the last three volumes of the Tietjens cycle are inferior to Ford at his best needs to be acknowledged. Yet it would be a serious error, of course, to dismiss them out of hand. They are not without their admirable qualities. And a somewhat detailed survey of these qualities will be worth our attention.

Probably the best of the three is *No More Parades*. It is told with considerable skill and with an authentic power of feeling, especially in its depiction of the life of the army. Its finest section is at the beginning, at the wintry base depot, during which the complex pressures that weigh upon Christopher are vividly created. The very first page strikes the note of the situation: inside Tietjens' sackcloth hut, with its blazing paraffin heater. The sound of shellfire is in the distance:

An immense tea-tray, august, its voice filling the black circle of the horizon, thundered to the ground. Numerous pieces of sheet-iron said, "Pack. Pack. Pack." In a minute the clay floor of the hut shook, the drums of ears were pressed inwards, solid noise showered about the universe, enormous echoes pushed these men – to the right, to the left, or down towards the tables, and crackling like that of flames among vast underwood became the settled condition of the night.[55]

And gradually the men in Tietjens' charge are sorted out, each with his own nagging private claim and worry: the two Welsh miners squatting on their heels at the fire, one of them angry at Christopher for not allowing him leave to see his wife who, he senses, has taken up with another man; the Canadian sergeant-major uncertain whether he had packed his new pigskin wallet — the one he had wanted to look very smart with on parade; the deranged, brave officer who may disrupt Tietjens' urgent work at any moment; the other ranks filing by and making out their sometimes complicated wills to be read and signed by Christopher, who is already burdened with an enormous amount of paper work. And beyond the immediate scene is the heavy image in Tietjens' mind of why all these creatures were assembled, and where they are going:

He seemed to see his draft: two thousand nine hundred and ninety-four men he had had command of for over a couple of months. . . . He seemed to see them winding away over a great stretch of country, the head slowly settling down, as in the Zoo you will see an enormous serpent slowly sliding down into its water tank. . . . Settling down out there, a long way away, up against that impassable barrier that stretched from the depths of the ground to the peak of heaven. . . .[56]

Vivid too is the later episode in the hotel ballroom at Rouen, with the wicker furniture, the dimmed lights, the gramophone playing, and the bombing — all as chorus to Sylvia's passionate willing that Christopher submit to her desire for him. Well presented also is the closing section at the base depot, in which Tietjens and Campion have a final interview which emerges into trust. At its conclusion, the cook-houses are inspected, and a sense of military order is for the moment achieved, as seen in the passage which completes the book:

The general tapped with the heel of his crop on the locker-panel labelled PEPPER: the top, right-hand locker-panel. He said to the tubular, global-eyed white figure beside it: "Open that, will you, my man? . . ."

To Tietjens this was like the sudden bursting out of the regimental quick-step, as after a funeral with military honours the band and drums march away, back to barracks.[57]

The most powerful incident in *No More Parades*, however, is the death of O Nine Morgan — the Welshman Christopher had protectively denied leave. "A man, brown, stiff, with a haughty parade step, burst into the light. He said with a high wooden voice: 'Ere's another bloomin' casualty.'" The streak of fatal injury to half his face and to his chest is depicted, and Tietjens is astonished that a human body could be so lavish of blood. As he bends over the figure — the heat from the brazier overpowering — Christopher hopes he will not get his hands covered with blood, "because blood is very sticky. It makes your fingers stick together impotently. But there might not be any blood in the darkness under the fellow's back where he was putting his hand. There was, however: it was very wet."[58] The image is to recur again and again to Tietjens' mind, and beyond any other incident in these novels it catches Ford's deepest mood and vision. It is also a significant, appropriate echo of the episode with the injured horse in *Some Do Not*, which will be described later.

In *A Man Could Stand Up*, Ford's writing is again most compelling in the scenes involving the men and the effects of war. The episodes in the trenches, if not superlatively done (what Conrad would have made of such a setting!), are still interesting for their quiet, unheroic rendering of the details of such combat. There are one or two spectacular passages, of course — as the following virtuoso description, set under the theatrical lighting of the Verey flares:

Tietjens became like a solitary statue of the Bard of Avon, the shelf for his elbow being rather low. Noise increased. The orchestra was bringing in *all* the brass, *all* the strings, *all* the wood-wind, all the percussion instruments. The performers threw about biscuit tins filled with horse-shoes; they emptied sacks of coal on cracked gongs, they threw down forty-storey iron houses. It was comic to the extent that an operatic orchestra's crescendo is comic. Crescendo! . . . Crescendo! CRRRRRESC. . . . The Hero *must* be coming! He didn't!

Still like Shakespeare contemplating the creation of, say, Cordelia, Tietjens leaned against his shelf. From time to time he pulled the trigger of the horse-pistol; from time to time he rested the butt on his ledge and rammed a charge home. When one jammed he took another. He found himself keeping up a fairly steady illumination.

The Hero arrived. Naturally, he was a Hun. He came over, all legs and arms going, like a catamount; struck the face of the parados, fell into the trench on the dead body, with his hands to his eyes, sprang up again and danced. With heavy deliberation Tietjens drew his great trench-knife rather than his revolver. Why? The butcher instinct? . . . The man's shoulders had come heavily on him as he had rebounded from the parados-face. He felt outraged. Watching that performing Hun he held the knife pointed and tried to think of the German for *Hands Up*. He imagined it to be *Hoch die Haende*! He looked for a nice spot in the Hun's side.

His excursion into a foreign tongue proved superogatory. The German threw his arm abroad, his — considerably mashed! — face to the sky.

Always dramatic, Cousin Fritz! Too dramatic, really.

He fell, crumbling, into his untidy boot. Nasty boots, all crumpled too, up the calves! But he didn't say *Hoch der Kaiser*, or *Deutschland über alles*, or anything valedictory.[59]

Or in the more restrained image of no-man's land which Christopher sees from an observation post:

There were still the three wheels, a-tilt, attached to slanting axles, in a haze of disintegrated wire, that, be-dewed, made profuse patterns like frost on a window. There was their own apron — a perfect village! — of wire over which he looked. Fairly intact. The Germans had put up some of their own in front of the lost trenches, a quarter of a mile off, over the reposing untidinesses. In between there was a perfect maze: their own of the night before last. How the deuce had it not been *all* mashed to pieces by the last Hun barrage? Yet there were three frosty erections — like fairy sheds, halfway between the two lines. And, suspended in them, as there would have to be, three bundles of rags and what appeared to be a very large, squashed crow. How the devil had that fellow managed to get smashed into that shape? It was improbable. There was also — suspended, too, a tall melodramatic object, the head cast back to

the sky. One arm raised in the attitude of, say, a Walter Scott High-
land officer waving his men on. Waving a sword that wasn't there.
. . . That was what wire did for you.[60]

But passages like these are few. Ford's picture of the lines is, for
the most part, a muted compound of reflections, relationships, and
details. A listing may suggest its quality. It is made up of such matters as the anxiety of the troops about the wind: when it comes
from the east, the Germans can use their poison gas, and will resume
their offensive; and the Tommies' underlying fear of being driven
into the North Sea. Of the sound of subterranean digging, and the
voice that Christopher once hears from below his camp-bed:
"*Bringt dem Hauptmann eine Kerze.*" [61] Of the spiritually broken
commanding officer (whom Tietjens has replaced), the victim of a
war which has lasted too long and destroyed too many of his
friends. Of Christopher's concern, as he foresees the breaking up of
trench warfare, that the men of his battalion know how to keep in
communication with their neighboring units. Of such mundane but
interesting matters as the variance in the nature of the trenches
themselves, as the soil changes from red gravel to marl to pure al-
luvial soil and even bog; and what to do with the springs they trav-
erse (Christopher has devised a unique siphon-drain). And such
lyric details as the clear, sweet sound of a bugler in the near distance, playing: "I know a lady fair and kind / Was never face so
pleased my mind." [62] Or the astonishing fact of skylarks nesting on
the battlefield. Or such touches of class comedy as Christopher's
promise, in a moment of strong affection, to give each of his men a
ticket for Drury Lane next Boxing Day, and the cheery reply:
"Mike it the old Shoreditch Empire, sir, n we'll thenk you!" [63]

The strengths of *The Last Post*, set in the post-war world, are of
a different sort: mainly pastoral and domestic. The writing is im-
bued with Ford's love of country things: the pleased detailing of
the great view of four counties from Mark's outdoor bed; the hay-
grass, and the raspberry canes by the hedgerows; the careful bot-
tling of the cider; the ducks on the pond; the hedge-sparrow at the
dripping set out for the tomtits; the collecting of the eggs in the
hen-house. Attractive also is the detailed portrait of Marie-Léonie,

her daily routine and verbal meanderings, which always end on the theme with which she has begun. And, unusual for Ford, but engaging, are the monologues in dialect form, of the peasant Gunning and the cabinet-maker Cramp. Thus, the "country reaction" to Marie-Léonie:

She was 'Er Ladyship, a good mark, a foreign Frenchy. That was bad. She was extraordinarily efficient about the house and garden and poultry-yard, a matter for mixed feelings. She was fair, not black-avised, a good mark; she was buxom, not skinny, like the real Quality. A bad mark because she was, then, not real Quality; but a qualifiedly good mark because if you 'as to 'ave Quality all about you in the 'ouse tis better not to 'ave real Quality. . . . But on the whole the general feeling was favourable because like themselves she was floridly blond. It made 'er 'uman like. Never you trust a dark woman and if you marries a dark man 'e will treat you bad. In the English countryside it is like that.[64]

Beyond these quieter elements, there are several intense, if somewhat theatrical, confrontations between various characters, particularly Sylvia's with the pregnant Valentine. But most fascinating in *The Last Post* is the very conception of Mark's willed retreat from the world, and those two stunning moments at the end when he speaks aloud.

The decline of the later Tietjens novels is clear enough. Yet a provocative question remains: why? Such explanation is the task primarily of the biographer, of course, rather than the critic, whose business is to say whether the art-work is achieved or not. We may venture to guess, however, that between the completion of *Some Do Not* and the publication of *No More Parades*, some event occurred to crucially undermine Ford's self-confidence. To set oneself to write a great novel is to be, above all, audacious and supremely assured. Ford, as we know, always felt uncertain of his own great powers, and Stella Bowen and others have written of how setbacks could easily drain his self-belief. And for such a confidence-sapping event we do not need to look far, for in this period Ford was dealt not one but two hard personal blows. The first was Jessie Conrad's assault on him (in the December 4, 1924, issue of the *Times Literary Supplement*) for his book on her husband, in which Mrs. Conrad unjustly condemned him before the world (the account being quickly picked up in New York) as being, in effect, a liar and false pretender. This assault alone would have battered Ford's ego but it was not all. Earlier in the same year (January 19, 1924), Violet Hunt had reopened the whole unhappy past by writing a letter to the weekly *Westminster* referring to Ford as her husband and signing herself "Violet Hunt Hueffer"; and once again Mrs. Elsie Hueffer brought suit against Violet, the case coming up on February 10, 1925, two months after Mrs. Conrad's letter. If this were not enough, in the following year Violet Hunt published *The Flurried Years* (1926), an intimate account of her relation with Ford, the divorce scandal, and the several court hearings. The book was no doubt an act of aggression on Violet's part, who was almost surely stung at being identified with the vindictive Sylvia, as she writes in the memoir that people had done. So that at these various hostile acts, Ford, a reserved person who dreaded the exposure of his private life, may well have felt the heart go out of him. He himself, as we have seen, has ascribed the deterioration of his work to writer's cramp, but such an explanation inevitably must seem superficial. The influence of work conditions is subtle, but to the artist functioning as artist they are scarcely likely to be crushing unless there is a deeper cause. Surely it is not unreasonable to speculate that Ford's suddenly intensified physical difficulty after *Some Do Not* was a psychosomatic manifestation resulting from the jolts administered to his personal pride, that it was a symptom of the artistic abdication evident in the pages of the last three books rather than its cause.

One cannot but feel the loss to modern literature in the decline of the Tietjens books. Had they been continued on the scale and with the care and imagination with which they were begun, they would be among the largest, most impressive productions of twentieth-century fiction. As it is, they have the unfortunate tendency to leak away in the mind of the reader the impact of the characters who live with such vitality and excitement in the first volume. The world of letters and the arts, however, is full of such accidents, splendid conceptions well begun but left in fragment. Art, like every other human enterprise, is beset by chance, and the critic's task is to value not what might have been, but what has flowered. Regret, in short, should not blind us to the very real achievement of *Some Do Not.* And by itself the first novel goes very far toward fulfilling the ends of the larger conception. Of the vital incidents of the later books, it lacks only the picture of the Armistice night closing, which ultimately images Ford's theme of "Parade's End." The base-depot episode and Christopher's concern for his men are, in fact, very largely suggested in *Some Do Not* by his reflections during his visit to the War Office. And the theme that a man of disturbed private life cannot be a satisfactory officer and trustworthy member of society, which Campion impresses on Christopher in the later books, is actually dealt with in the first — in the conversation in which Campion calls him "a regular Dreyfus": "fellows like that *unsettle* society. You don't know where you are. You can't judge. They make you uncomfortable." A man like Dreyfus is worse than guilty — "the sort of fellow you couldn't believe in and yet couldn't prove anything against. The curse of the world. . . ." (To which, Christopher replies, as if in self-revelation: "Ah.") [65] And the motif of the hard, frugal life of Christopher's desire, although developed more fully afterwards, also is introduced [66] in the first volume. In a very real sense, in *Some Do Not* Ford has said all that he had to say — about his people and his theme.

Some Do Not

A work of fiction distinguished by the breadth, richness, and variety of the world it has created and by the great emotional poignancy and power it has caught and expressed, *Some Do Not* can only be described as a masterpiece of the novel, excellent in each of the multitudinously demanding aspects of the form. And in the following pages, an attempt will be made to articulate something of the nature of its art and craft.

The theme of England lies at the roots of nearly all Ford's fictional works, but none of his other novels approaches *Some Do Not* in the range or depth with which the life of his native country is portrayed. Since Ford's intention was to show the impact on the nation of the Great War, its Englishness is hardly accidental: the British milieu required elaboration. It needed to be given the thick, complex feel of actuality — had, in James's phrase, to be "done." Thus the novel is rich with the peculiar motifs, amply developed, of English life: the role and character of the governing classes; the class structure and the demarcation between those "born"and those of undistinguished lineage; political struggles between Conservatives and Liberals; the pervasive dominance of Victorian sexual morality, and the diversity of English types: military man (Campion), banker (Lord Port Scatho), country squire and landowner (Christopher's father), politician (Waterhouse), industrialist (Paul Sandbach), arbiters of society (Lady Claudine and Glorvina), fashion leaders (Sylvia), and the presiders over aesthetic salons (Edith Ethel). Touched upon as well are such motifs as the typical Englishman's distrust of abstract thought; his fondness for his countryside, its birds and flowers; his love of cricket, golf, and animals; his poorly prepared food (*Das Pillen-land*, as Christopher reflects); and, particularly, his historical and literary heritage. Far more than any other novel of Ford's, too, its vocabulary draws on indigenously English words, including dialect and slang: *higgler, coulter, lurcher, haulm, whin, hop oasts, horse-coper, tweeney, quiff, snaffle, squits,* to cite a few.

This world of England is, however, undergoing radical change. Signs of the ferment are present in various cries for social reform: Waterhouse wants economic revisions, Port Scatho seeks to liberalize divorce laws, Valentine campaigns for the female vote, and her brother is ardently a Marxist. Yet these agitations are only symptoms of still deeper shifts in the arrangements of society. The fundamental change is, as it was in *The Good Soldier*, from a basically feudal order, which is rooted in agriculture and the life of the country, to the modern industrial system, founded on capital and centering itself in the giant city. And this movement by which one way of life in England is supplanted by another is, in the ultimate sense, the subject of *Some Do Not*.

It is through the careers of his principal characters that Ford chiefly gives expression to his theme. The richness and vitality with which he has endowed them, imaginatively and credibly uniting complex desire, particular personality and mythic type, has already been described in detail. We may now examine how, set in the context of the larger world, they also, in what happens to them, serve Ford as symbols of that world and give the novel its emotional power.

At the dramatic heart of *Some Do Not* is a deeply poignant love story, that of Christopher and Valentine; and the chief action of the novel is their affair, from first meeting through the growth of their passion to its final outcome. Paralleling their relationship, however, is another, in significant contrast, between Macmaster and Edith Ethel. In depicting the private worlds of both pairs of lovers, Ford has been remarkably successful, sensitively rendering their emotions at all stages with depth and imagination. He has also understood that in reality a love story never exists apart. Being social as well as private and physical, the relation between the sexes is inevitably implicated in the larger world of which the lovers are members — its values, wise and foolish, its habits and rituals, its fears and taboos. What men esteem in society abstractly, they desire concretely in their mates, for our lovers objectify what we love or lust after. So it is with these two couples, minor and major.

The Macmasters live according to appearances, skillfully adapting to the requirements of a corrupt, superficial society — climbers aiming to make successful, publicly honored careers, and ready in the process to discard acquaintances who are no longer useful, Valentine and Christopher among them. While their fellow countrymen at the front die by the thousands, their own concern is to increase their influence and prestige at home and to be the preservers, as Edith Ethel tremulously puts it, of what beauty remains. The hypocrisy of their lives is especially made clear by the course of their relationship. Although both prate of a higher, more delicate sensibility and morality, and Vincent approvingly quotes poetic lines by Rossetti urging the separation of lovers who may not love, ironically it is they, not the other couple, who are adulterous. When by chance their liaison is revealed, they are terrified, and the romantic Edith Ethel lashes savagely out at her lover in the manner and language of Billingsgate.

Christopher and Valentine, on the other hand, are unselfseeking personalities, direct, courageous, and loyal. Often critical of the state of society they find themselves in, they possess sufficient fortitude to persist in their course despite society's sanctions. Both are deeply affected by the carnage and stupidities of the war. Christopher, though a good soldier, is infuriated by the condition of the enlisted men and the treacherous self-aggrandizement of the authorities. Valentine, a pacifist, is simply moved by the mutilations piled on mutilations, deaths piled on deaths. In the working out of their own relationship, they are in ironic contrast with the Macmasters: "I stand for monogamy and chastity. And no talking about it," Christopher had said, scoffing at the "polysyllabic" mouthings of Rossetti and aesthetes like him. "Of course if a man who's a man wants to have a woman he has her. And again, no talking about it." Long acting on his principle of monogamy and chastity, Christopher decides, however, the day before his return to France, to ask Valentine to be his mistress, and wins her consent. But the fates decree otherwise. Between the afternoon of their compact and the night of their consummation, circumstances arising directly out of the social disorder of wartime conditions prevent it. And in the end, each is unwilling to mar the ideal of their mutual love and regard. Some, like the Macmasters, "do"; and some, like Christopher and Valentine, "do not."

The ultimate symbolic act occurs when Macmaster, wanting to impress his superiors, presents as his own one of Christopher's brilliant and prodigal mathematical formulations and is richly rewarded for his treachery by important promotions and illustrious honors. The incident and society's bounty comprise the final irony of the novel, dramatizing its larger meaning of social deterioration.

The effectiveness of the central action and the expressiveness of Ford's theme are still further enhanced by the elegant simplicity of the design in which he has embodied them — the classic form which E. M. Forster has likened to an hourglass. The characteristic shape of the hourglass comes, of course, from the manner in which the lines of its two equal and separate halves flow together at the center, cross, and seem to exchange their relative positions. Thus it is with the form of *Some Do Not*.

At the beginning, the shining star in the social firmament is Christopher Tietjens, well-born, secure, admired, and deferred to; and toward him Macmaster looks upward, ruefully acknowledging the truth of the words, "The Gods to each ascribe a differing lot: Some enter by the portals: Some do not!" By the middle of the book the lines of relationship have begun to converge; and at the end they are reversed. Dishonored, vilified, and self-denied, Christopher wearily goes to his bed, prepared to leave in the morning for Waterloo Station and the war. Macmaster, on the other hand, is celebrating as reward for his statistical coup the bestowal of the knighthood he has long coveted.

Like the hourglass also, the novel is separated into two equal (142 and 144 pages respectively) and thoroughly demarcated halves, which in their contrast of time and setting splendidly serve to dramatize Ford's theme. Part One takes place in an England still undisrupted by the national disaster fate has in store for it. Although an impending war is hinted, the country is securely at peace. Its traditions, its values of honor and uprightness, and its social structure are still intact. It is England under the old dispensation. Appropriately, the scene of the action is almost completely rural, in the southeastern English countryside. Part Two, on the other hand, is set entirely in London in the midst of the war. The closely woven social fabric has been rent and frayed in numberless places. The youth of the nation are being bled abroad, and at home schemers press their selfish game. Backbiting, malicious gossip, and character assassination thrive. Rectitude and honesty in the military corps (Campion) and in finance (Port Scatho) have turned into the vindictive unscrupulousness of Major Drake and of Brownlie, Port Scatho's nephew, who covets Tietjens' wife and exploits the bank to ruin him. It is the new dispensation. To it from the old, time has flowed in the hourglass. The contrast between the two parts is thus the analogue of that between the two couples: where the Macmas-

ters move in drawing rooms, the major pair find their most congenial home in pastoral England.

Although the society and atmosphere of each part are dominated
by the ethos appropriate to it, the two worlds of the novel are not,
of course, completely homogeneous. Signs of the rising forces in-
trude into Part One, for example, when two "city men" from London disrupt with raucous vulgarity the even tenor of the golf-
course club house. The progress of the "unborn" Macmaster and
the overly civilized, unrooted spirit of Sylvia also are indications of
the emerging conditions. And the bold suffragettes' raid on the
golf-playing cabinet minister is still another example.

The most striking invasion into the old order by the new occurs,
however, at the close of Part One. In the first half of *Some Do Not*,
the horse is, significantly, the means by which the characters are
transported. In London, it is a hansom cab —"the only conveyance
fit for a gentleman," says Christopher, who loves horses and is marvelously skilled with them; in the country, it is a fly and, notably, a
horse-drawn dog-cart. A motor car never appears. Suddenly, however, at the end of the part, an uncontrolled automobile roars out of
the dawn mist and mortally wounds the horse that is pulling Christopher and Valentine. Excitingly dramatic, the action also is intensely symbolic. The death blow is triple: physically to the animal
by its supplanter, the motor car; and figuratively by the industrial
order, of which the automobile is fact and sign, to the world in
which the horse thrived, and also to the kind of men it produced.
(The very name of chivalry, we should be reminded, derives from
the horse.) At the very end, Christopher, sobbing with grief, waits
beside the injured beast and, in the last line, the cart of the knacker—
the merchant who trades in the carcasses of horses — lumbers into
sight. The symbols are simple, natural, and fundamental, as valid in
the real world as in the imaginative. The episode is the crux of the
novel — the connecting place between the two bell-like compart-
ments of the hourglass. In one exciting moment and image is summed
up the theme and foreshadowed the new world which will domi-
nate the second part about to open.

The form of the novel and the conflict between the two orders are, of course, not as sharply drawn as analysis here makes them. *Some Do Not* is a novel about human beings first of all, not an allegory of black and white. Nor does Ford line up his characters with deadly neatness on contrasting sides. Valentine, for example, is a suffragette and socialist; and the driver of the car which destroys the horse is, in fact, a figure of the old order, General Campion. (The fact that Campion, a man in a position of national leadership, is thoroughly incapable of controlling the machine, though he refuses to admit it, has no doubt its own point, however.) Nor are the major figures mere machined products of the cultures that produced them. Complex human beings, they share in other systems of triumph and defeat than those of a society they may or may not be in tune with. The lines of the hourglass, which form the basic pattern of development and meaning, are therefore counterpointed, and the novel enriched, by other conflicts. Thus, although Macmaster comes to a dominating social position, he is not free from shame before Christopher at the means of his triumph, or from the reader's contempt. Nor does Christopher as a man decline merely because the world that created him is deteriorating. That world may be gone, and his own position in it have become isolated and extreme, with stoicism as the only valid philosophy. But Christopher himself is not destroyed. Having an insides and will, he affirms his values despite the altered circumstances of society. Principles are necessary, he declares as he waits for the knacker's cart, for "Principles are like a skeleton map of a country — you know whether you're going east or north." [67] Christopher's moral superiority, of clarity and principle, is symbolized in the final chapter of Part One. The mist which shrouds the dark countryside in vagueness is a rich symbol of the confusion in which all of England wanders, including the radical Valentine who moves on foot immersed in it. Only Christopher, perched up on the dog-cart, the mist extending level from his neck, his head (like Neptune's in the *Aeneid*) in the clear — only he has a view of objects in the distance and of the stars and the moon above.

Nor, in the end, is Christopher content merely to sit waiting for the knacker's cart. Living in a world which he dislikes and which is hostile to him, he yet must choose a course of action in it. Although this choice is not overtly dramatized in *Some Do Not* (as it is in the later volumes), it is symbolized, however, in the progress of his walk, in Part Two, with Mark and later with Valentine through the streets of London. Christopher's argosy starts at his rooms in Gray's Inn, which are dominated by the persecuting figure of Sylvia; proceeds through the urban, industrialized city; and ends with Valentine in the pastoral environs of St. James Park. The course of his walk takes him past the symbols of power and of careers in twentieth-century London: Fleet Street (the press), the Middle Temple (the law), Whitehall (government and the military). Only as he moves along the Embankment does his way leave the city masonry, and then the Thames is described as looking like "dirty silver" and the prospect called a "grim effect of landscape," as though Ford were accenting the dominance over the river of the industrial city. Firmly implied in the journey is Tietjens' rejection of the urban world and his decision to carve out a life with Valentine in a place of greenery and naturalness of growth.

The theme of *Some Do Not* and the characters and form which help give it expression have been considered; we now need to examine more closely the manner in which Ford has told his story. How, more specifically, has he given to it its qualities of richness and variety, of narrative excitement, and emotional force? What, in short, are his highly effective tools of composition?

The chief technical means which Ford has employed in *Some Do Not* are particularly appropriate for a work which combines in one both the novel of society and the novel of character. For the first, the public, a broad canvas is needed; for the second, the private analysis in depth. Within his design Ford has handsomely achieved his diverse ends. Through the over-all organization, the selection of point of view, and the use of the time-shift, he has knit together Space — of historical time, social types and milieu, and diverse settings — with Depth — of personality and rendered emotion. It is a work at the same time both extensive and concentrated.

The keystone of Ford's achievement is his arrangement of the action. Although exploring a large and various social world, he very skillfully has brought his material into tight dramatic unity by framing the action of each of the two halves into brief periods of time. Part One covers less than two days, while Part Two, which takes place roughly ten years later, occurs within three hours (excluding the final epilogue-like chapter set ten hours afterward).

The first element which makes this flexibility possible is the point of view — the third person (an angle of vision all but inevitable for any large-canvased novel) and which Ford has not employed with such technical variety and richness of effect since the *Fifth Queen* books. As earlier, he does not restrict himself to any single mode of the third person. Sometimes he writes as the disengaged "omniscient" observer, placing his characters in their social time and place, and striking his "public" note; but this novelist's voice is mainly informational, without any Thackerayan "dear-reader" tone or moral comment. Chiefly it enables him to speed his narrative, setting a scene quickly and avoiding a disproportionate expository machinery. The novel thus begins: "The two young men — they were of the English public official class — sat in the perfectly appointed railway carriage." And "omnisciently" the theme is elaborated:

Their class administered the world, not merely the newly created Imperial Department of Statistics under Sir Reginald Ingleby. If they saw policemen misbehave, railway porters lack civility, an insufficiency of street lamps, defects in public services or foreign countries, they saw to it, either with nonchalant Balliol voices, or with letters to the *Times*, asking in regretful indignation: "Has the British This or That come to *this!*" Or they wrote, in the serious reviews of which so many still survived, articles taking under their care, manners, the Arts, diplomacy, inter-Imperial trade, or the personal reputations of deceased statesmen and men of letters.

At other times, he will become the detached observer, reporting the external behavior of his actors, their speeches, gestures, and deeds — an angle of vision usually reserved for high dramatic moments. On occasion Ford moves in the other direction, completely entering the consciousness of a character in order to present his inward reflections.

This, Tietjens thought, is England! A man and a maid walk through

Kentish grass fields: the grass ripe for the scythe. The man honourable, clean, upright; the maid virtuous, clean, vigorous; he of good birth; she of birth quite as good; each filled with a too good breakfast that each could yet capably digest . . . Each knew the names of birds that piped and grasses that bowed: chaffinch, greenfinch, yellow-ammer (*not*, my dear, hammer! *ammer* from the Middle High German for "finch"), garden warbler, Dartford warbler, pied-wagtail, known as "dishwasher." (These *charming* local dialect names.) . . .[68]

Passages of interior monologue, however, are comparatively rare.

Most often Ford blends the public and private, simultaneously presenting objective event and the subjective reflection of a particular character, the perspective being as though partly within and partly behind its focal character. Very appropriately to his "public" aims, Ford's focus changes frequently, and includes Valentine, Sylvia, Macmaster, Edith Ethel, Mark, and, of course, Christopher.

Ford's variable use of third-person modes thus greatly helps him in creating a universe that is both broadly social and intensely personal. The remarkable depth and richness of personality of his main characters is clearly made possible by his entrance into their awarenesses. The method enables Ford — in fact, requires him — to explore and objectify in detail their inner rationales, ambitions, motivations, temperaments, and longings; and the reader, in consequence, observes them intimately in their deepest selves. At the same time, and as importantly, the reader also sees them externally, through the eyes of the omniscient and observant author and of the other characters. The impressive reality, for example, with which Christopher and Macmaster are introduced in the opening chapter owes its success particularly to the shift in focus between the two men. Not being the prisoner of their own consciousness (or, even for that matter, of the author's), Ford's people thus take on a remarkably rounded, solid dimension and an enhanced independent life.

Similarly, Ford's method increases the actuality of his public, objective milieu. Seen variously, the world grows impressionistically richer. And since most of the external events of the novel are transmitted to the reader not objectively alone but also colored by a single consciousness which is deeply engrossed in them, they gain enormously in interest, urgency, and drama.

One of the most striking illustrations of the dramatic effects made possible by Ford's shift of focus from character to character is in the opening chapter of Part Two — the stunning revelation to the reader that the immensely learned, intellectually arrogant Christopher has lost his memory from shell-shock. Instead of presenting the information from the focal point of view of Christopher, as in the two preceding chapters, Ford chooses to render the scene through Sylvia's eyes. By sealing off Christopher's consciousness from the reader and presenting him from the outside, he thus wins the full impact of surprise when the condition is revealed. And by showing the effect of the news on the consciousness of Sylvia, the person least sympathetic to him, the episode is doubly enhanced. Her shock and pity are all the more effective a medium for transmitting a kindred shock and pity to the reader.

The second major tool of composition, the time-shift, is made possible by the first and is probably even more fundamental. By the very fact of entering into the consciousness of a character, the author may freely range wherever he wishes within it — including its roomiest domain, the memory. (As Ford himself has said: "we are almost always in one place with our minds somewhere quite other.") [69] More than any other element, the time-shift is the source of the technical originality and freshness of the novel, making possible in large measure its broad and deep social picture, its exciting narration, and its remarkable verisimilitude.

Although the action of *Some Do Not* is concentrated, as we have seen, into two brief periods, the use of the time-shift, in which Ford switches between the present and the past, allows him to extend far beyond these confines. The opening chapter provides an excellent example: the immediate scene is aboard a train carrying Christopher and Macmaster southward from London to Rye. During the journey Macmaster works on the proofs of his monograph and at one point the pair heatedly dispute the merits of its subject. But in the course of the chapter the scene and the time often change. The reader observes Macmaster effectively moving in cultivated drawing rooms; both men dealing with the head of their department; Christopher in a scene with his mother and in another with his father. The two friends are also observed in several past conversations, in different London rooms, and in a hansom cab which that morning had taken them to their office. Ford's canvas plainly is stretched spatially no less than chronologically. Like his variable point of view, the time-shift thus enables him, if in another way, to combine space and depth.

A fictional method which frequently turns backward risks the serious hazard of becoming static and dull. But in Ford's management of the time-shift in *Some Do Not* — however it might be with a number of his other novels — the narrative is made only more exciting. This heightened interest, as in *The Good Soldier*, Ford accomplishes by launching many of his chapters at some advanced, and arresting, point of action and then gradually filling in the obscured picture with the relevant background. The reader's interest, having been immediately seized, is thus held firm by the very fact of being oriented.

One of the purest examples of Ford's method is the final chapter of Part One, which begins abruptly:

Jumping down from the high step of the dog-cart the girl completely disappeared into the silver: she had on an otter-skin toque, dark, that should have been visible. But she was gone more completely than if she had dropped into deep water, into snow — or through tissue paper. More suddenly, at least! In darkness or in deep water a moving paleness would have been visible for a second, snow or a paper hoop would have left an opening. Here there had been nothing.

The constatation interested him. He had been watching her intently and with concern for fear she should miss the hidden lower step, in which case she would certainly bark her shins. But she had jumped clear of the cart with unreasonable pluckiness, in spite of his: "Look out how you get down." [70]

Although the reader is reasonably sure that the couple are Christopher and Valentine, he knows little else — neither the time, the setting, what the characters are doing, nor why the girl has jumped. But as he continues to follow Tietjens' thoughts, which are as usual scientifically observant, the scene takes on clearer outlines (they are on a back-country road in the mist), the time is fixed (before dawn), and, after twelve pages, the reason for their journey and its earlier stages are finally filled in. Through it all, the reader is steadily drawn on.

The use of the time-shift and *in medias res* chapter openings is not new, of course, in Ford's work. But decidedly different is the way in which these devices are managed. In *The Good Soldier*, as we have seen, the action, covering many years, has already taken place and is transmitted through a first-person narrator in whose mind memories haphazardly arise; scenes rarely are as long as four pages. In *Some Do Not*, by reason of the third-person point of view and the unities of time, all action occurs in the present, since the past episodes are conceived as occurring immediately in the minds of a character; and the scenes are long and richly extended. One scene, in fact, develops continuously for a hundred and thirty-five pages, running through five chapters (comprising all but the last eight pages of Part Two). The technical problems, labor, and imagination required to achieve such feats successfully and artistically are enormous.

Ford's backward turnings — and thus in point of fact his forward narrative — are also invigorated by his trick of making the past events dramatic in themselves, each with its own vivid, carefully detailed setting, characterization, gesture, and dialogue. Past time, in short, is given the actuality of the dramatic present. More significant for narrative pace, these scenes, like the brief episodes of *The Good Soldier*, frequently are the crystallization or highlight of some dramatic, arresting, or revealing instant. Characteristic is Tietjens' engagingly comic conversation with his Yorkshire father in the opening chapter, which admirably serves to establish their particular style of man. Commenting that Christopher had spoken not more than twenty words to anyone about his wife's desertion, the author continues (the passage is quoted in its entirety):

Those had been mostly to his father, who, very tall, very largely built, silver-haired and erect, had drifted, as it were, into Macmaster's drawing-room in Gray's Inn, and after five minutes of silence had said:

"You will divorce?"

Christopher had answered:

"No! No one but a blackguard would ever submit a woman to the ordeal of divorce."

Mr. Tietjens had suggested that, and after an interval had asked:

"You will permit her to divorce you?"

He had answered:

"If she wishes it. There's the child to be considered."

Mr. Tietjens said:

"You will get her settlement transferred to the child?"

Christopher answered:

"If it can be done without friction."

Mr. Tietjens had commented only:

"Ah!" Some minutes later he had said:

"Your mother's very well." Then: "That motor-plough *didn't* answer," and then: "I shall be dining at the club."

Christopher said:

"May I bring Macmaster in, sir? You said you would put him up."

Mr. Tietjens answered:

"Yes, do. Old General ffolliott will be there. He'll second him. He'd better make his acquaintance." He had gone away.[71]

The time-shift, finally, aids Ford enormously in giving the book its remarkable sense of reality. Since experience at any given moment is always many-faceted, and human individuals are in the continual process of making meaning out of situations only partly clear, the method of time-shift, combined with advanced narrative beginnings, makes possible a strikingly life-like illusion of actuality. As details one by one slip into place, the reader, actively working to understand, becomes a creative participant, and his sense of direct, personal drama is greatly enhanced. Akin to the time-shift in creating this effect is another device: the simultaneous rendering, in the present, of disparate thought and action. Faced with an immediate, exciting physical difficulty, a character may be confronted at the same time with an intense, entirely different psychological challenge — as when Christopher, at the climax of the mist chapter, struggles both to control the frightened, rearing horse and to absorb the emotional shock of Valentine's "My dear," spoken to him at the very instant of the collision. Perhaps more than any other single quality, Ford's ability to create the illusion of life actually being lived imparts to *Some Do Not* its authentic literary distinction.

The success of the novel depends, however, on the masterful handling of tools other than point of view and time-shift. Of these, the most important involve the process by which the work moves through time — the relentlessness of its advance and the modulation of its effect. Principles of composition rather than devices, they cut across and in part draw on the other methods. Let us examine each in turn.

Like his other fine novels, *Some Do Not* beautifully illustrates the theory of *progression d'effet*. The novel moves purposefully forward in every word, growing faster and more intense as it proceeds. Every device or effect serves to advance the story and to develop the over-all plan. The movement of the mist chapter, for example, is not dictated principally by the requirements of exposition, as engrossing as that may be presented. The chief drama develops rather from the conflict within Christopher between his Yorkshireman's stolid observance of the proprieties and his desire to take a holiday from them. Although chronologically the action moves backward, emotionally it intensifies, bringing the lovers closer and closer together in feeling. Similarly in the opening chapter, Ford's division of the points of view between Christopher and Macmaster is not a mere tour de force of character presentation, the simple revelation of their different qualities through their contrasting responses to the same circumstances. Although the subject of their reflections overlaps, the progress of the action from the focus of Christopher to that of Macmaster is not in the slightest repetitive. Macmaster's thoughts further advance the situation. Even the division of the book into two separate parts enables Ford to satisfy the doctrine of *progression d'effet* that the narrative accelerate in speed and intensity as it advances. The very nature of the world of Part One is slower — an agrarian society at peace, while the world of Part Two is intrinsically faster and more agitated — urban, industrial, and torn by the emotions of war. Characteristically, Ford rounds out this onward, intensifying progress of his narrative with a quieter final chapter. A richly complex coda, it weaves together, by means of time-shift in the mind of Tietjens, all the various emotional strands of the book — its places, persons, and evocative lines of poetry, the social atmosphere of England and London, Macmaster's shamed betrayal, Christopher's love for Valentine and his self-denial — and so produces an understated, summatory close which is at once remarkably moving and aesthetically satisfying.

But the most fascinating example of Ford's sheer narrative finesse is his handling of the opening and closing of a tandem pair of chapters (Three and Four) in Part One. "At the slight creaking made by Macmaster in pushing open his door," Chapter Three begins abruptly, "Tietjens started violently." In the ensuing conversation we learn only that it is night and that as a result of the day's events General Campion is indignant at Christopher. The rest of the chapter and of Four develops what had happened, the former concentrating on Macmaster and his remembrance of the day and the latter, through an adroit transition, focusing on Christopher within that day. Throughout the second chapter, Christopher is shown as intently trying not to reflect upon his impending reunion with Sylvia, seeking to lose himself in mathematical calculations and a game of solitaire; and the opening of its final paragraph returns to Macmaster's sudden entrance into the room and Tietjens' violent start — which is described as giving Christopher "a really terrible physical shock." "He nearly vomited; his brain reeled and the room fell about," and the paragraph continues to the chapter's end:

He drank a great quantity of whisky in front of Macmaster's goggling eyes; but even at that he couldn't talk, and he dropped into his bed faintly aware of his friend's efforts to loosen his clothes. He had, he knew, carried the suppression of thought in his conscious mind so far that his unconscious self had taken command and had, for the time, paralysed both his body and his mind.[72]

The extremity of Christopher's reaction plainly is at variance with his behavior described earlier at the opening of Chapter Three, for then Christopher had only been discomforted at being seen to start

and immediately had entered into a long conversation with Macmaster. The inconsistency, however, is far from being a flaw; rather
it is a remarkable stroke of narrative economy. The reader, as Ford
knew, never feels any discrepancy. Not only do forty pages inter-
vene between the two moments, but the very nature of the method
of the time-shift does not require strict factual consistency. Less
bound in its mode, closer to poetry, its aesthetic principle is much
less "scientific" than the chronological novel; the consistency it demands is emotional. Thus, with masterly assurance Ford has made
one instance of startle achieve two dramatic purposes – to launch
with interest his backward-turning account of the day's events and
to enforce emotionally upon the reader the intensity of the burdens
pressing upon Christopher.

No less important than *progression d'effet* in *Some Do Not* is the
principle of variety. Ford's continual modulation of the unfolding
experience of the novel perpetually requickens its life by preventing
a dulling sameness of effect. Variety, in short, serves to make the
temporal movement of the narrative constantly new, fresh, and engaging. The elements of the novel which Ford varies for this purpose are many and are almost as complex in relation to one another
as the variations of sound—pitch, volume, timbre, tempo—available
to the musician. They include point of view; mood; personality;
time: past and present, objective and subjective; modes of rendering
experience: dramatic and novelistic, realist and impressionist; and
rhythm and surprise, both of language and action.

The virtuoso powers with which Ford has modulated and renewed the life of *Some Do Not* may be understood more clearly
through a closer look at a single section, which of necessity must
be more than usually technical and detailed. The intense fifth chapter which presents the Duchemin breakfast episode, one of the big
scenes of the novel, constitutes the crux of Part One, bringing together for the first time all four lovers. Its chief narrative end is to
dramatize the growth and crystallization of the passion between
Macmaster and Edith Ethel. Wishing to help Macmaster in his literary research, Mrs. Duchemin had arranged the meeting in the hope

that her husband's insane state might pass unnoticed. Instead the Reverend Duchemin violently disrupts the social occasion by provocatively uttering sexually charged phrases, even attempting to reveal intimacies between himself and his wife. On discovering the conditions under which Mrs. Duchemin must live, Macmaster's sympathy for her grows still stronger and, after her husband is led away, the pair exchange pledges of devotion.

The action of the chapter is divided into four parts or "movements," formally separated from each other by the particular angle of vision adopted. The first movement (six pages), which sets the scene and presents a revealing conversation between the two old friends, Valentine and Edith Ethel, is told strictly from the objective point of view. The chief purposes of the section are to set the scene and to characterize, and objectify, the two women who have been presented up to this point only through the eyes of their respective lovers. The second movement (nine pages), which groups the various guests, seats them at the breakfast table, and introduces the explosion of the Reverend Duchemin's obscene words, is more complex in its handling of point of view. Omniscient and objective at the outset, it soon slides into Valentine's consciousness, for a longer time into Christopher's, and then by way of an adroit objective transition, enters the key awareness of Edith Ethel, where the focus remains, except for a brief but important return to Christopher, until the end of the unit. The third movement (five and a half pages) which begins a few minutes in time before the close of the second, concentrates on a single awareness, Macmaster's, as he seeks to manage the unruly Duchemin. The fourth movement (four pages), in which the lovers pledge their troth, combines the objective and focal points of view, alternating between the detached author and the separate inner reflections of the impassioned pair, who agree to meet again at dusk.

This continual shifting of the angle of vision within the chapter is of key importance in achieving the variety of effect, but other elements are also significantly varied. Fundamental are the shifts between realism and impressionism and the contrasts of mood and dramatic intensity. The opening movement, the conversation between Valentine and Edith Ethel, is itself markedly different in method from the pages preceding it — which had depicted the aftermath of Christopher's golfing day and his violent upset at Macmaster's sudden entrance. The method of the earlier episode was impressionistic in character (telescoping several hours and tending toward vaguely outlined detail); the new section, on the other hand, is realistic and dramatic (objective, following clock time, and with sharply defined particularity). The earlier mood had been tense and, in the end, profoundly disturbing; the beginning of the new chapter is relaxed, conversational and decorative in atmosphere, with the interest deriving mainly from a simple contrasting of two very different women. The turmoil to come is only slightly hinted: no more than Macmaster or Christopher has the reader been let in on the true condition of the husband.

As the first section of the chapter contrasts with the pages before, so it does also with those that follow. The opening of the second movement returns to the impressionistic, but this time from the omniscient, not focal, point of view. It is a method, as managed, highly appropriate to presenting the atmosphere of a situation in which various people are politely and superficially meeting each other for the first time. By combining omniscience and impressionism, Ford is able to create the illusion of the quick elapse of time in which nothing vital is happening. But soon, as Ford enters the minds of Valentine and Christopher and then moves toward Edith Ethel, the method changes again, becoming more objective and realistic. (With these alterations, it should be pointed out, the reader's sense of the movement of time also varies: having hurried along impressionistically, it slows to the stretched-out subjective time of consciousness; then, when completely objective, it quickens to regular clock time; soon, however, it will slow again to agitated consciousness, only to change tempo once more — a process which continues, giving life to the experience, throughout the chapter, and, in fact, the book.) Essentially social comedy, the first half of the second movement continues, like the first movement, with comparative quiet. Its drama and interest derive largely from the characters' underlying evaluation of each other revealed as the internal focus changes.

But the second half of the movement, which shifts into Edith Ethel's consciousness, marks a decided change — not only from realism to impressionism but, even more strikingly, in tension and mood. Part of the dramatic conflict in the episode is provided by the various obstacles, such as Mrs. Wannop and Christopher, that stand in the way of Mrs. Duchemin's having Macmaster for herself. More intensely dramatic, however, is her desperate wish that her new guests will not discover her husband's condition. Her fearful panic as the polite structure begins to collapse dominates the mood of this half and is the more frightening and disturbing because, although permitted within her mind, the reader does not know the source of her terror. The knowledge is finally acquired through an entry into Christopher's consciousness, shortly before the end of the section, at the same time that he himself perceives the truth. Not only has Ford varied his method again from realism to impressionism, but he has also varied the kind of impressionism itself. Unlike the earlier passage in which the gathering of the guests was presented vaguely, this instance in Edith Ethel's mind is personal and well chosen to intensify the experience.

Thoroughly different again are the mood, method, and dramatic tension of the third movement. From the blurred sensibility of an emotionally distraught personality, the focus shifts to an individual, Macmaster, in whom the cool, rational principle is uppermost. The method thus turns realistic again. At the very entrance of the Reverend Duchemin — who now for the first time is presented clearly to the reader (having been before a voice speaking from behind table flowers) — Macmaster had become suspicious and alerted. Only disciplined intellect, he recognized, could save the situation. The intense drama of the third part springs, therefore, from Macmaster's determination to enforce his will on the demented man, which he does through the adoption of a donnish tone and a scholarly challenging of the accuracy of the clergyman's Latin. At one point, when for the moment Macmaster turns aside to exchange passionate confidences with Edith Ethel, Duchemin slips from check and becomes disruptive again. Only physical violence — a discreet jab to the kidney by the clergyman's attendant upon Macmaster's orders — ends the disturbance.

The mood and tension of the final movement alters again, is quieter and more romantic. From coolly resourceful manager, Macmaster becomes the tremulous poetic lover. And the section ends impressionistically, in still another change of method, on a rococo wave of delicate sensibility between him and Edith Ethel which spiritually echoes the description of the exquisite decor with which the chapter began.

Thus by modulating these various elements, and still others (such as prose rhythm which would here require too elaborate an analysis), Ford perpetually enlivens his action. At times, two or more of these separate elements may operate in conjunction, as we have seen, but the particular combinations are continually altering.

Not only is Ford's skill in varying his experience masterful within his chapters but also from chapter to chapter. Consider as example the splendid modulation of Part One. The opening chapter, divided in focus between two key characters, Christopher and Macmaster, begins leisurely and operates mainly on the principle of time-shift. But Chapter Two, which moves to Sylvia, her mother, and Father Consett in Germany, is dramatic and strictly chronological. The third chapter, on the other hand, returns to the time-shift, almost entirely in the mind of Macmaster, and its beginning (Christopher's startle) is not leisurely but abrupt. The next change, to the objective and public, begins before the section ends and continues into the next, but in time Ford enters Christopher's consciousness — not in retrospect but *during* the day. The method thus becomes chronologically impressionistic. Only at the end of Chapter Four, when the startle incident is rounded out, is the time-shift employed. The contrasting organization of Chapter Five, the breakfast episode, we have already seen in detail: the time-shift is not used at all; the focus is on at least four characters, not one; and the experience is more social or public in nature than personal or private. (Still another variation is its leisurely beginning.) The management of Chapter Six is again modulated: Ford focuses on the consciousness of a single character throughout (except for a brief entry into Valentine's awareness) and returns, though not *in medias res*, to the time-shift. For the first time in such a case, the action is divided in the middle by a change of scene and time. As important is the variance of mood between Chapters Five and Six, the first being extremely intense and exciting, the second, for much of the way, pastoral, lyric, and relaxed. In the final Chapter Seven, the mist episode, the form changes once more. Although Christopher continues as focus, this time the action is launched abruptly in the midst of things. And again Ford's principle of organization is fresh: unlike the earlier abrupt ("startle") opening of Chapter Three, in which the action that followed took place entirely in the past, this time the narrative not only looks back but also dramatically moves forward at the same time.

The richness and variety of *Some Do Not* derives also from its diverse, thick texture and atmosphere. Its surface is vigorous with splendid detail. Although this life-giving depth of treatment was considered earlier (in the discussion of Ford's full-bodied characters and of his English milieu and setting), it is apparent in countless other elements. Consider, as example, the revealing particularity of the quoted opening sentence of Macmaster's monograph — so rounded, judicious, and formally authoritative in tone, so calculated to impress:

Whether we consider him as the imaginer of mysterious, sensuous and exact plastic beauty; as the manipulator of sonorous, rolling and full-mouthed lines; of words as full of colour as were his canvases; or whether we regard him as the deep philosopher, elucidating and drawing his illumination from the arcana of a mystic hardly greater than himself, to Gabriel Charles Dante Rossetti, the subject of this little monograph, must be accorded the name of one who has profoundly influenced the outward aspects, the human contacts, and all those things that go to make up the life of our higher civilisation as we live it to-day. . . .[73]

Or Christopher's long telegram to Sylvia, which is given an extra touch of reality — beyond its biting opening words, *accept resumption yoke* — by its real misprint in transmission, *esoecially*. Or again in the prose, which (though essentially "simple" in style) is given atmospheric effectiveness not only by the already mentioned anglicisms, but also by the occasional use of uncommon, richly suggestive words like *tantalus, capercailzies, epergne, galantine, spikenard, glaucous, matutinal, pawkiness, tendential, fane, cockerel, dockleaf.*

One of Ford's two unmistakable masterpieces, *Some Do Not* inevitably demands comparison with his other, *The Good Soldier.* Written by the same novelist and sharing certain basic attitudes and themes, they are yet extraordinarily different works — in method, spirit, and the intensity and configuration of their emotion. Something of this contrast may perhaps be conveyed by observing that where *The Good Soldier* derives from the French tradition — it has, in fact, been called "the greatest French novel in English" — *Some Do Not* is, surprisingly, in the line of the English novel. Such classification should not, of course, be applied too strictly. It does not mean, as analysis makes clear, that the later work is wanting in the gallic concern with form which justifiably earned the earlier book John Rodker's description. What is indicated, rather, is that the pattern and experience of the novel has not been drawn with the excruciating tightness of *The Good Soldier.* Spacious and leisurely, the book is more easily accessible. It does not demand of the reader the very close attention required for the full understanding of *The Good Soldier.* Rather than the novel as poem, *Some Do Not* is the novel as novel. But the book also belongs in the native tradition because of its peculiarly English character and spirit — especially, its humor. For *Some Do Not* is a richly comic work — not in the ironic vein of *The Good Soldier,* which is a mordant, intellectual, French form of comedy, but in the warm English tradition of Fielding and Dickens. Christopher is tragic, of course, but he is also decidedly amusing, particularly when he is being very much the Yorkshireman, as in Part One. And Mark Tietjens is a genuine comic original in the line of descent of Dickens, almost a caricature with his mannered prominences, but conceived with such vitality that he thoroughly seizes the imagination. The book is full of comic surprise. Consider the dialogue, for example, that follows Christopher's adamant refusal, because his dead father had believed Ruggles' gossip, to accept any of his inheritance:

"You won't forgive father?" [asks Mark]

Christopher said:

"I won't forgive father for not making a will. I won't forgive him for calling in Ruggles. I saw him and you in the writing-room the night before he died. He never spoke to me. He could have. It was clumsy stupidity. That's unforgivable."

"The fellow shot himself," Mark said. "You usually forgive a fellow who shoots himself."

"I don't," Christopher said. "Besides he's probably in heaven and don't need my forgiveness. Ten to one he's in heaven. He was a good man."

"One of the best," Mark said. "It was I that called in Ruggles though."

"I don't forgive you either," Christopher said.

"But you *must*," Mark said — and it was a tremendous concession to sentimentality —"take enough to make you comfortable." [74]

The same comic unexpectedness as that of Mark's intense plea (so thoroughly *un*sentimental and so characteristically Mark) can be seen also in other places and characters in the book, particularly in the episodes involving Mrs. Wannop.

Ford's sense of the comic serves him even in some of his most serious and intense moments. After the horse has been struck in the mist, for example, and is badly bleeding, Christopher hurriedly instructs Valentine to get over the hedge and remove her petticoat to provide bandages for the wound. As the girl hastens up the bank, the watching Tietjens reflects: "She didn't go over the quickset as neatly as he had expected. No take off." [75] Christopher's quirky comic turn of mind thus provides a detail which both enlivens the experience and thickens its truth. Or the superb social comedy of the terrible moment when the Reverend Duchemin breaks from Macmaster's control and begins to shout obscenities. As though nothing unusual is taking place, the various guests determinedly make conversation with each other, "talking with polite animation and listening with minute attention." "To Tietjens that," comments the text, "seemed the highest achievement and justification of English manners!" [76]

Which of Ford's two finest novels, we must ask finally, is the greater? Critical judgment will vary with varying criteria, and it will be further made uncertain by the thoroughly different natures of the two works. But ultimately the greater achievement does seem to be *The Good Soldier. Some Do Not*, for all its high art, is not an unflawed work. The second chapter of Part Two, dealing with the dishonoring of Tietjens' checks, is, for example, inferior to the rest of the novel — the one place where the persecution Christopher suffers seems unconvincing, its details excessively piled on and unobjectified. On occasion, too, Ford is carelessly inconsistent: Valentine's brother changes name from Edward to Gilbert; Christopher's brothers, Ernest and James, become Curly and Longshanks; and the day of the action in Part Two shifts in mid-course from Friday to Monday. (None of these inconsistencies is particularly obvious, however.) A fastidious critic might observe also that the technical management of the second half is a trifle less subtle and various than the supremely artistic accomplishment of Part One — a value which only begins to assume aesthetic significance, however, after several readings. This novel, finally, is not quite as intensely piercing, intellectually or emotionally, as the earlier book. Meanings often lie deep in *Some Do Not* but the novel cannot equal *The Good Soldier* in its power to fascinate — to create the sense that the ultimate has not yet been reached, that meaning still lies beckoning within meaning to lure us on.

Readers who invoke other criteria than these no doubt will disagree. They may hold perhaps that no work of fiction should require more than one reading. Or, more seriously, that a novel should be a novel, not a poem. Or that character creation is nine tenths of the novelist's genius and that *Some Do Not* is filled with the more full-bodied cast. But however any individual verdict may go between this pair of superb works, one conclusion is clear: Ford has written two masterpieces which are successful, abundantly, in the two great traditions of the novel. He more than earned the right of being addressed as "Cher Maître."

vi

AND AFTER

A MAJOR writer's early and inferior novels are of considerable importance to the critic. They anticipate the future, and in
nascent form they sound the themes and formulate the situations to
which the greater novels to come will give life and body — as we
have seen. But when in the canon of a novelist's work there is a
dying fall and a group of unsatisfactory productions follows the
creative peak, the task of the critic becomes less fruitful and his
temptation to dwell on them small. So it is with the five novels
written by Ford after the Tietjens series: *A Little Less Than Gods*
(1928); *When the Wicked Man* (1931); *The Rash Act* (1933);
Henry for Hugh (1934); and *Vive Le Roy* (1935). Wanting in
literary importance, they require no elaborate analysis.

In technique, the five reveal little, save in diction and cadence,
not already described. The principles of *progression d'effet*, impressionism, and the frequent modulation of effect are used, and,
as in each of Ford's post-war novels, the time-shift. But the management of these techniques is not creative. Ford's characters fail
to come alive, seem too often mere surfaces intensely driven by
motivations — compulsions really — which are both queer and unplaced. If passion is the essential mark of Ford's great character creations, these books unhappily reduce passion to a dead formula.
From this failure, it inevitably follows that the narrative will suffer,

a condition scarcely improved by Ford's lax handling of the other elements of fiction. As in the later Tietjens books, the stream-of-consciousness technique is used monotonously; and setting, prose, and atmosphere are not shaped artistically.

Creatively poorer than the apprentice novels, this quintet of books seems the tired product of a novelist who had ceased to care about the medium — written apparently to satisfy his publishers, but without conviction. Ford's public reference to *When the Wicked Man* as "a silly novel" (in the "author's note" to the English edition) plainly reveals its unimportance to him. Indeed, during the period in which he wrote these books — 1928 to 1935 — and afterwards, Ford's main creative energies went rather into composing his volumes of reminiscence: *Return to Yesterday* (1932), *It Was the Nightingale* (1933), and *Portraits from Life* (1937). (The first two memoirs were, in fact, constructed on Ford's novelistic principles, and he himself preferred to term them "novels," partly to disarm complaints against his casualness toward fact.)

Yet, seen against the entire body of his work, these final novels are not without a certain interest, since they further establish that in his novels Ford consistently endeavored to reflect his world. Strikingly different in atmosphere from his Edwardian and early Georgian novels, the five very decidedly mirror their own times: the impact of the Great War, the collapse of moral values during the twenties, alcoholism, narcotic addiction, and promiscuity, the widespread emphasis on pleasure, the crash of the stock market, the world depression. Ford's own exiled life is revealed in the choice of settings, which instead of England are the French Mediterranean, Paris, New York; and American characters and even attitudes largely have supplanted English ones. (There would seem justice, incidentally, in connecting Ford's decline in these works with his personal separation from England — a deep resource and vital stay of his inner life, as we know. Radically unrooted himself, he clearly conveys his alienated condition in these novels.) The accelerating breakdown of a civilization is the subject particularly of *When the Wicked Man* and *The Rash Act* and its sequel, *Henry for Hugh* — the "rash act" being, of course, suicide, expressive symbol of moral bankruptcy, both in individuals and in a civilization. But the other two novels are also products of their period. Ford's criticism of the ambitions of Napoleon, and other public leaders, in *A Little Less Than Gods* mirrors, for example, the often articulated reaction of the twenties against the "great men" — politicians and generals — who make pawns of their fellow mortals. And *Vive Le Roy*, with its invented struggle for the rule of France between Communists and Royalists, dramatizes in its conclusion still more directly Ford's own "solution" to the world dilemma.

Ford's first historical novel in fifteen years, *A Little Less Than Gods*, takes as its subject the final months of the Napoleonic enterprise. It introduces such personages "a little less than gods," as Napoleon himself, Tsar Alexander, Wellington, Metternich, and Marshal Ney. But the central figure of the novel is George Feilding, a young, generous, honor-wishing, and impetuous English officer of good family who is in love with a waiting-woman of Napoleon's miniature court on Elba. A worshiper of Bonaparte ("this unjustly caged eagle") and a prisoner on parole, the young man accompanies the Emperor during the descent on France, and the march to Paris. After Waterloo, he is tried by the English crown for treason and, disgraced, plans to continue his life in America. The young man's reversal of attitude by the end of the book from adoration to hostility toward Napoleon and the other heroes — including an accomplished, absolutely self-sufficient, arrogant English *milor* (the world's richest commoner) — becomes not Feilding's alone, but the reader's as well.

Of Ford's historical novels *A Little Less Than Gods* is probably his most grandly romantic, in part explained by the glory-cherishing nature of its hero. But the large effect is enhanced by still other elements: by Feilding's intense, romantic love for the waiting-woman, Hélène de Fréjus, who is, in shocking fact, his half-sister; and by the self-redeeming sacrifice of Hélène's much older husband (a cynical financier), who, Sidney Carton–like, chooses to die before the Bourbon firing squad in place of Marshal Ney.[1]

The novel is uneven, however, and peculiarly lacking in unity.

The narrative during the first hundred pages is told in straightforward chronology and is surprisingly stock in its characters and
speeches. But afterwards, the tale suddenly adopts the method of
the time-shift — to the decided benefit of credibility, excitement,
and poetry. Beginning dully, the book thus ends by being romantic
and large-visioned, even moving.

This Napoleonic tale, it should be noted, was originally to have
been a collaboration with Conrad. But in the end, after Ford had
apparently abandoned the field to the older writer for a time, the
pair decided to undertake the venture separately. In 1924, in a
letter to Ford, Conrad reported that he did not expect that his
novel would leave Elba, so that they would not be in competition.
At his death, later that year, Conrad's version was far from complete: published as *Suspense*, it runs to three hundred pages, yet
still seems no more than introductory. The two novels have little
in common beyond a period and place; and the figures, atmosphere,
and approach are different in very characteristic ways. But even
incomplete, Conrad's work has the greater distinction.

Probably the chief accomplishment of *When the Wicked Man*,
Ford's next novel, is its capacity for rendering the fatigues and
inner ravages of a hard-driving business life. Through the awareness of its central figure, Joseph Notterdam, the reader gets a vivid
impression of the consequences of an existence built year after year
on commercial compromise, cut-throat competition, too much
drink, kept women, and general rootlessness. Quite successfully,
Ford has conveyed the feeling of a life of strain piled upon strain,
of little friendship or affection, in which past actions and present
commitments bar the tired spirit from the clear, fresh light which
it desires.

Beyond this achievement, however, there is not much to com-
mend. The course of Notterdam's relationships with three different
women, which makes up much of the action, is mechanical and
tedious. The trio of females are in fact an uninspired reworking of
the types in *The Good Soldier*. Notterdam's wife, the Scots-born
Elspeth, has many of the determined, self-contained, agonized qual-

ities of Leonora. Lola Porter, the hoydenish widow of an author born in the same English town as Notterdam, is a Florence, appropriately altered to conform to the style of the twenties, including a gangster inamorato. And his secretary, the Tennessee-born Henrietta Faulkner Felise, "Nicolete au clair visage," is essentially a Nancy: young, fresh, tortured, direct of heart. No more persuasive or urgent is Notterdam's relationship with his long-time partner and rival, the millionaire brick man and realtor, Bill Kratch, who has long loved Notterdam's wife and who is in fact the father of his children.

Like *When the Wicked Man, The Rash Act* is most successful at creating an atmosphere, the social and moral decay of the twenties and of the early depression years. Its texture is crowded with examples of the dissolution of an age: drink, illicit sex, drugs, Lesbianism, boredom, despair. But the fable in which these details are placed again is queer, unintentionally farcical, and overly special.

The fantastic story, which takes place on the French Mediterranean, involves two male characters who look alike and bear almost the same names. One, an American and the focal character of the novel, is named Henry Martin Aluin Smith. The other, an Englishman, is Hugh Monckton Allard Smith. Both had been at Oxford at the same time, had served in the same British regiment during the war, and had had Scandinavian mistresses by whom they have been discarded. And both are simultaneously planning to commit suicide. The chief contrast is financial. On bad terms with his overbearing, businessman father (there seems an echo here of Hart Crane), Henry Martin is down and out. The Britisher, on the other hand, is the head of the leading automobile industry in England, one of the few firms to survive the stock market crash with ease. His motive for doing away with himself is not lack of money, but failure in love, together with shattering headaches. The Englishman succeeds in taking his life, but his American counterpart fails and assumes instead the identity of the dead man. As a result, Henry Martin becomes burdened both with his own problems (he loves a cocaine-peddling beauty-shop operator, a New York French girl named Eudoxie, who has penetrated his impersonation), and those of the dead Hugh Monckton, whose name he does not wish to discredit. These added burdens include not only illness and a literal headache but also a French "mistress," with whom (it is characteristically Ford) the Englishman had never slept and in whom Henry Martin is not interested. In this situation the novel ends.

Ultimately the book seems pointless. Its literal, realistic level is neither convincing nor interesting, and the psychology and motivation of its people, particularly Henry Martin, are peculiar in the extreme. And, looked at symbolically, the nature of the characters and the plot in which they are involved seem to lack general relevance. Is some public comment being made perhaps about the English and American souls and the non-triumphant supplanting of one by the other, as in *The Good Soldier*? Henry Martin and his relationship to Hugh Monckton show faint traces, in fact, of John Dowell and his somewhat awed feeling for Edward Ashburnham. (Continually citing the epitaph of an ancient Roman boy, *Saltavit. Placuit. Mortuum est*, the American ruefully reflects that he himself has danced but never given pleasure.) In *The Rash Act*, however, the symbols seem uncontrolled and without force. Dowell's symbolic suggestiveness derives as much as anything from the reader's actually knowing little about his American life. Henry Martin's career, on the other hand, is given at considerable length, so that his characterization, which is the chief one of the novel, demands a more realistic treatment than it gets. Only in the narrow terms of what seem to be Ford's private obsessions — his exile from his native country, his finding of a more favoring home in America (even while spending much time each year in France), and his spiritual rejection of England — does the story seem to take on significance. But such a limited personal response is scarcely sufficient to make the novel meaningful, certainly not when burdened by its many technical weaknesses.

The next year Ford published a sequel to *The Rash Act*, called *Henry for Hugh* (1934). All but unreadable, the novel continues the career of Henry Martin and includes a challenging confrontation with Hugh Monckton's aunt, who accepts him as her real nephew. It is only at the end, while she is dying, that the Englishwoman learns the truth, and then she acknowledges him anyway, since he has given her much pleasure. By this time, Henry Martin has discovered that he is, through common Continental grandparents, actually Hugh Monckton's cousin, his nearest living relative, in fact, and thus heir. *Henry for Hugh*, it might also be remarked, is a demonstration of the time-shift and the interior monologue at their nadir.

A major source of the unpleasant quality of these two novels and of *When the Wicked Man* lies in their creator's hardened sensibility. Ford's prose has assumed a harsh, pseudo-tough character. Its rhythms are often staccato. Its diction is studded with slangy, coarse, and, worst of all, dated words, like *lech*, *swell* as an adjective, *caboodle*, *s.a.* (for sex appeal). Its images are cheaply flashy: "The motionless silver of the sea was ruffled in irregular streaks like watered satin." The boat "became vivid — a melon slice of incandescent white, a curved stripe of scarlet." And the writing, which has little freshness of perception or sensitivity, lacks genuine poetry. A similar criticism of Ford's work in this period has already been made about his revision of *Ladies Whose Bright Eyes*, published in 1935. Shorn of connectives, cadenced grace notes, and resting places, the delicate romantic texture of the original was turned into a narrative with a similarly hard, unappealing atmosphere. In novels dealing with contemporary social deterioration, such a "tough" method might appear defensible, but only superficially. For an essential poetry is all the more needed, to provide an implicit judgment on spiritual bankruptcy: a tension between a described actuality and the ideal which is thoroughly meaningful.

(The reader, incidentally, may note the persistent treatment in these novels of the theme of the look-alike, or double — the *Doppelgänger* motif. Obvious are Baron de Fréjus and Marshal Ney, the two H. M. A. Smiths, and — in *Vive Le Roy* — the Duke of Orléans and Walter Leroy. But Joseph Notterdam is also haunted by the sense, and on occasion the mysterious sight, of his *Doppelgänger*, who might, indeed, be Nostradamus. Nor is this motif of doubling — or at least of a pairing very close to it — new in Ford's writing. His novels abound in it, in fact. In his earlier work, the doubles are usually brothers: George and Gregory Moffat in *The Benefactor*; Don Collar Kelleg and his Italian half-brother in *An English Girl*; the Bettertons in *The Portrait*; the Bloods in *Mr. Fleight*; the Lovells in *The Young Lovell*; the Jessops in *The Marsden Case*; and, of course, Christopher and Mark Tietjens. Even the relationship of John Dowell and Edward Ashburnham is brotherly. ("He seems to me like a large elder brother," says Dowell of Edward, "who took me out on several excursions and did many dashing things.") At times the introduction of these twin characters, whether brothers or doubles, functions toward some total meaning. But at others they would seem to exist primarily to satisfy an obsession of their creator. Inevitably, these recurring patterns suggest something of a serious division in the psyche of their author. Conrad, at least at one period, would seem to have had a similar malady, and to have drowned the "miserable scorpion" "in the inkwell of his writing desk" through the composition of his brilliant *Doppelgänger* tale, "The Secret Sharer." Perhaps the only places where Ford himself mastered the material of his inner division was in *The Good Soldier*, where the motif is fugitive rather than overt, and in *Some Do Not*, where it has been schematized expressively.)

The last of these novels, *Vive Le Roy*, might be called a loose blend of detective story and political fantasy and dramatizes Ford's political and sociological solution to the world crisis. The presentation of the action is characteristically oblique. Revolution and counter-revolution have swept France. The Communists, having overthrown the Republic, in turn have been dislodged by the Royalists, who are led by the young Duke of Orléans, the newly claimed King of France. As Walter Leroy, a youthful American doctor and the central character of the book, prepares to sail from New York for France, the political situation is still uncertain. (The new monarch, according to one report, has been assassinated while walking among his subjects; twenty-four hours later, however, the report is denied.) With him Leroy carries money, hidden in the uncut pages of a Simenon detective novel, for delivery to the

French Communists. Not a Communist himself, the unpolitical American has undertaken the mission to oblige friends, and out of a vague democratic disapproval of kings. On board ship also are M. de la Penthièvre, one of the chief royalist advisors, who is struck with the resemblance between Walter and his monarch; Penketh-man, a former Scotland Yard inspector, now associated with the League of Nations; and a youthful painter named Cassandra. On arriving in Paris, the young doctor attempts to deliver the book, and disappears. Entirely by suggestion the reader learns that the king actually was slain and that Walter Leroy, to judge from a brief glimpse of him later in the royal car, has sadly consented to take his place. (Thus, the title.) The young American apparently has been moved by M. Penthièvre's (and Ford's) vision of the feudal ideal of human life on a small, simple, local scale, under the benevolent guardianship of a king.

As a novel, *Vive Le Roy* is probably too slow-moving to be suc-cessful. Nevertheless, it is the most attractively written of the five post-Tietjens novels, revealing a sense of control and distance which the others lack. And it is free of their harshness of style. At its end, too, it is able to manage once more that genuine, mutedly moving note of Ford's melancholy stoicism — for the last time in his fiction.

DOWN STREAM AND UP

MY DEAR FRIEND; it is, our profession, truly a dog's trade. . . . You will write, and you will write. . . . And no one, no one in the world will understand, either what you wish to say, or what you have given in effort, in blood, in sweat. And at the end you will say to yourself: It is as if I had rowed all my life in a boat, on an immense river, in an impenetrable fog. . . . And you will row and you will row and never, never, will you see a mark on the invisible banks that will tell you if you are going upstream or if the current bears you along . . . and you will know penury; cold nights, without coverings; bitter food, and sleep haunted by regrets. And you will never find, not ever during all of your life, one soul who can say if in the end you are the greatest genius of the world . . . Or for that matter if you are the vilest, most odious descendant of . . . Ponson du Terrail . . .[1] (Englished from Ford's French written at Conrad's death)

Our exploration of the writing of Ford the novelist is almost at an end — its stretch traversed, and his imaginative world, in its many shapes and shades, closely inquired into. We have seen his analysis of what a novel should do, and be; the genres in which he wrote; his vision of life and the world; the evolution of his characters and the growth of his powers; and, most importantly, the individual novels themselves: their what and their how. Of all this, no summary is needed.

What must engage us instead are certain larger questions: points

of artistic propriety and priority, and of ultimate worth. How —
we now need to ask — did Ford Madox Ford fare as a novelist?
In which directions, both down and upstream, and to what places,
did he journey in his craft? Do his own novels disparage his view
of fiction? — or do they vindicate it? And finally — a question
which must not be slid over — how do they compare with those
of other novelists?

In Ford's books there is very much to celebrate — and in the end
that fact is the major fact, overriding and crystalline. Superbly endowed as a novelist, an exciting master of narrative, of character,
of texture, and of language, Ford was merely being objective about
his talents and himself when he wrote:

My brain, I think, is a sort of dove-cote. The thoughts from it fly
round and round, seem about to settle and circle even further than
before and more and more swiftly. I try in the end to let them come
home with the velocity and precision of swifts that fly at sixty miles
an hour into their apertures that you would say could not let them
through. I hope thus to attain to a precision of effect as startling as
any Frenchman who is forever on the make. Perhaps I do.[2]

And, when he was in phase, the precision and piercingness of his
work are unequaled.

But, in truth, Ford was not forever on the make. And he failed,
as we have seen, very much of the time to live up to his genius.
Indeed, the most striking single impression which a survey of his
many novels is likely to arouse in the critic is that of waste, of
great and remarkable gifts far too often unused. Put beside *The
Good Soldier* and *Some Do Not*, those works of superlative artistry, his other novels even at their most impressive are pale creations. With the result that, unlike his avowed masters — Flaubert,
James, Conrad — Ford did not, in fact, produce a sizable body of
distinguished work. The causes of this wastage of a high talent
have already been looked at: his need to write for a livelihood (in
forty-seven years, seventy-six books), which all too often prevented him from giving the necessary time and care; and his acutely
self-doubting nature, indolent and excessively conscious of the
Preacher's words on vanity. Only rarely did Ford feel that per-

sonal audacity, that conquering boldness, essential to the artist if he is to set out on the original conception, and hard execution, of a masterpiece. The creative force of self-discipline and of will was somehow diseased at the root.

But this failure can also be located, in a measure, in Ford's very doctrines of fiction themselves. For when combined with his un-selfconfident spirit, a number of them would appear, in fact, to have been more fettering than expressive — to have locked Ford in a prison of imperatives whose artistic rigors he could rarely sustain. The theories of *constatation* and of the "affair," for example, seem to have justified Ford too often in the writing of books that were ineffectively organized or inadequately detailed, on the principle that their value as mirror was enough. But like the time-shift, the interior monologue, and free verse, the novel as "affair" runs the serious risk of being formless and without tension: a mere tedious cross-cutting of life, unless its author controls his texture and narrative with imagination and with extreme attention to craft. And since Ford often failed to exert this full care, as he himself admitted, his works were weakened all the more.

Nor by temperament was Ford especially well equipped to be a penetrating historian of his times. He was too exclusively literary, and no doubt too uninterested, to saturate himself in the affairs of the world. Although he was sensitive to them, his concern was not — on the accumulated evidence of the bulk of his novels — that of a deeply versed, broadly informed, or particularly incisive student. Flaubert's ranging knowledges and his tenacity in research, which made a book like *L'Éducation sentimentale* (which operates, in fact, on the principle of *constatation*) so achieved and culturally acute, were only rarely Ford's. Instead, he relied on his "impressions." Quite frequently Ford's insights into his time are fundamental — and, as norms against which to test our ways, they are extremely valuable. But the consequence of his approach and temperament was that the cross-section of life he did cut was too often thin, both intellectually in the grasp of the genuine complexities of the problems of modern life, and aesthetically in the presentation of the texture and "feel" of his milieu.

Thus, too, with his fixed fidelity to the Flaubertian doctrine of the aloof, non-commenting novelist. From every account, Ford in person was a vivid and extremely appealing figure, a first-rate conversationalist, and a delightful story-teller. But this vivacious, highly gregarious side of himself was by the doctrine of aloofness very largely, and very noticeably, barred from his novels — and had to find its outlet elsewhere, in a multitude of idiosyncratic memoirs and autobiographical articles. Hence at those times when Ford's craft was uncreative, the rule of impersonality only made the work the more featureless, so that it lacked that deeper "personality" which Ford knew was essential to any literary work, Flaubertian or Thackerayan. Conrad similarly found himself a prisoner of the doctrine of detachment, but in his shrewdness early recognized that his particular genius and personality needed commentary — demanded that he guide the reader along the road, set the scene, and help him to understand the inner meaning of the journey. To gain this privilege, while technically adhering to his Flaubertian code, Conrad was thus driven to the device of the first-person narrator, which he employed in the bulk of his most characteristic work. Like Conrad, and like Thackeray (whom he was inclined to ridicule for it), Ford also was something of a "Prince of Comment." Only rarely, however, did he exercise that privilege. *The Inheritors*, *The Good Soldier*, and *The Marsden Case* are his only novels in the first person. Later in his career Ford would seem to have understood, at least in part, the strait jacket in which the doctrine of impersonality had placed him. His memoirs of the thirties, *Return to Yesterday* and *It Was the Nightingale*, which he in fact called "novels," mark a decided step toward liberation. Ford's engaging presence in these books, together with their intriguing structure, designed according to his novelistic principles, endows them with far greater verve, interest, and importance than the novels he wrote in the same period, and as creative works they surely will endure far longer. Thus it is that by adhering to methods inappropriate to his own nature, Ford comes under the charge, it would seem, of having been an unwise and uncritical victim of orthodoxy.

A final limitation of Ford's work might also be named, by some critics at least — the possibly limited relevance for today of their central ideas and vision. The matter is a complex one and subject to constant reinterpretation in the light of an endlessly changing present. But it probably must be allowed that Ford's *thought*, by and large, is likely to seem less pertinent to the essential concerns of the modern reader than that of authors such as Flaubert, Conrad, Lawrence, Joyce, or even James, with his moral imagination. Repelled by the present, even in a measure by the very conditions of life itself, Ford nostalgically looks too much to the past perhaps to say many meaningful things to men caught up by the problems of living in a drastically altered here and now. A genuine novelist as thinker, like a Conrad or a Lawrence, will strive to grapple with the present conditions of man, and will attempt, however partially or aberrantly, to create out of them an image of a more significant way of being. There is considerable truth, if not all, in R. P. Blackmur's observation that Ford was a writer in love with the defeat of the past for the sake of that defeat.[3] If Ford was a moralist, he was but infrequently a working one. Too often his vision of the good life was merely traditional, more code than morality. At heart, indeed, Ford was not a moralist or a "historian" of his times at all; rather, like Edward Ashburnham or John Dowell, he was a ritualistic sentimentalist. Upon the thorns of life he had fallen, and, like Shelley, he bled. And at its core this, when his work was most expressive, was Ford's message. The contrast with his collaborator is marked. The younger man's immense respect for the older derives as much as anything, one feels, from his recognition that Conrad — with his differing Byronic vision of life as voyage — possessed an inner force he himself lacked. "For suffering is the lot of man," Ford had written in his concluding peroration to *Romance*. And Conrad had added, significantly (Ford himself cited the fact with admiration): "but not inevitable failure or worthless despair which is without end — suffering, the mark of manhood, which bears within its pain a hope of felicity like a jewel set in iron."[4] Between the two streams of romanticism epitomized by these two men, probably more readers are likely to respond, in the abstract at least, with greater sympathy to Conrad's than to Ford's.

These, then, are some of the limitations of Ford and his fiction. Because of them, and in particular the absence of a sizable body of distinguished work, the critic must conclude that Ford belongs to a lesser place in the pantheon of novelists than, say, Flaubert, James, Conrad, or Joyce. Lacking their ultimate dedication to their calling (he is surely no austere "high priest" of the novel) and on but two occasions truly first-rate, Ford cannot be spoken of as a giant of fiction. That fact would seem clear. But — and here is the chief point of this study — neither is Ford a pygmy, or a mere literary camp-follower. If not "the greatest genius of the world," he most decidedly was not "the vilest, most odious descendant," either of Ponson du Terrail — or of the Flaubertian tradition. It is time, then, to reverse our coin, and to look at Ford's strengths and his very real achievements.

Ford's lesser novels, to begin with, if paler than his best, are by no means without worth or admirable qualities. A respectable number are sensitive and very accomplished, as we have seen; and several, within the range of their ambitions, are genuine works of art. Nor can Ford's novels, for all his dependence on them for his livelihood, be charged with sensationalism or cheapness of subject. If not always richly created, they are never unserious in aim, never mere potboilers directed at a simple reader's pocketbook. Only *Ring for Nancy* is an "entertainment," and for writing this "frivolous" work, its author was decidedly apologetic.

But, of course, Ford's permanent importance as a novelist will be based, in the end, on his best work — on his two strikingly different masterpieces: *The Good Soldier*, a brilliant small-group novel in the French tradition, mordant and ironic and intensely concentrated in form, subject, and passion; and *Some Do Not*, deriving more from English roots; broad in social scope; populated with a diverse cast of fully drawn, appealing characters; and more relaxed, humorous, and leisurely in spirit. On this pair of works, his reputation will solidly rest. If Ford is a "lesser" novelist, is not actually a "giant" of English fiction like James or Conrad, he has never-

theless written, in these two volumes, certainly one and perhaps
two novels richer and fuller in their accomplishment than any
created by James or Conrad — books which for years to come will
more deeply stir and give pleasure to the literate reader. Let us
see why.

At his best, Ford is superior to Conrad because he is, by lengths,
the finer artist. The work of his one-time collaborator is, in fact,
peculiarly heavy. Splendid and deeply imaginative it may be, but
it is also sluggish and ponderous. The reader must often literally
force himself to press on; and it can be seriously, as it should be
honestly, asked how many of Conrad's novels have been begun
but never finished. Compare the lumbering quality of the Marlow
books, for example, with the similar time-shift, first-person narrative of *The Good Soldier*, which is so subtly modulated, swift, and
gripping, and, above all, so poignant with sentient life. And a comparison of *Some Do Not* with any of the older writer's narratives
in the third person yields the same conclusion. Of which novel of
Conrad's can it be said, as it may of Ford's, that he had composed
a long work whose tensions were as finely adjusted as that of the
lyric poem or the short tale? *The Secret Agent* comes closest perhaps, but how much of "felt life" does one actually find in it?
Conrad, in fact, was peculiarly unable to impart to his characters
a feeling of an inner life, except perhaps in moments of physical
crisis. Instead they are static figures who have been given an external vividness by description, symbol, and setting. Almost no-
where in Conrad's work can one find a character with the genuinely created, *living* quality of Christopher Tietjens, of Valentine Wannop, of Nancy Rufford, of Leonora Ashburnham, of Sylvia Tietjens, of Edward Ashburnham, of John Dowell. (Razumov,
of course, is a splendid exception, but only when still in Russia.)
As an analyst of human psychology, Conrad was extremely subtle,
probably more penetrating than Ford, but his characters remain
inert and essentially abstract, for Conrad was not a creator of human beings who live in process. The reader who advances beyond
the surface attractions of Conrad's narrative of adventure is almost certain to be quickened to astonishment by the extraordinary

mythic imagination at work, and by his perception of the author's remarkable power of will and mind. But in judging Conrad's creations it too often is forgotten that this deeper admiration normally forms after the reading rather than during, and that its appeal is primarily cosmic and intellectual. Both *The Good Soldier* and *Some Do Not* are better novels as novels than any of Conrad's because they have a greater inner life and because the experience of reading them is richer and more various, more genuinely "real," more pleasing, and, finally, much more moving.

The superiority of Ford at his best to James needs to be placed, of course, on different grounds, for as artist of the novel James was superb. If at times, as in *The Portrait of a Lady*, his books were overspun, the fact can largely be blamed on the contemporary fashion for long works. But undeniably James knew how to mount and develop his fiction, had a first-rate sense of form, and a masterful command of variety and pace. In the technique of the novel, he has, in fact, few peers in any language. James's deficiency as compared with Ford is not his art but the limited depth of emotion in his work. In nuances of civilized feelings, James is admirably expressive, subtly and excitingly addressing himself to the conscious intelligence. But in the rougher, more passionate places of human experience he does not walk. His tragedies lack the force, the rage of spiritual terror and anguish. James does not shake the reader in the deeper places of the spirit. And it is precisely in Ford's ability to do this in both of his masterpieces that his superiority lies. His work possesses, in short, a power and depth of emotional expression which James at times may suggest (Conrad never at all) but does not actually sound.

And so we return here at the end to that uniqueness in Ford which we observed at the outset. Passion and art — "agony and cat's cradle" — are fused in his work to a degree unparalleled by other novelists, winning for his books a depth and an intensity, and a beauty of order, which are astonishing. And thus we see at the same time also the ultimate vindication of Ford's novelistic doctrines. If his adherence to certain of his fictional principles would seem to have unneedfully weakened his less ambitious work, it cannot be argued in any final sense that Ford was wrong, since his two masterpieces (as well as the best of his other novels) were also products of them. The theories of *constatation*, of the "affair," of the exhaustion of aspects, have undeniably enhanced the cultural penetration, the significance, and the richness of these works — works which, in their crystallization of a momentous shift in the course of history and of man, provide remarkable, permanently captured images of their era. And the doctrine of aloofness has almost surely given these volumes their sense of self-existing, objective reality; by it Ford has won that crucial aesthetic distance which gives to a work of art its own organic life, complex and resonant, freed from reference to a creator. Had Ford varied from his principles in writing his lesser novels they may have been more attractive and very probably would have increased his public reputation and sales. It is scarcely likely, however, that they would have caught certain essentials, had the abiding truth, or the penetrating reality of his triumphs. It may be even wondered, indeed, whether Ford, if he had been less single-minded in his devotion to his aesthetic assumptions, would have developed the command of technique that, when the afflatus came, enabled him to create his masterpieces.

In certain important ways, Ford's career may be compared to that of Coleridge, including the intimate association for several years with a literary genius of strong personal character of whom each was in awe, and with whom the relationship eventually cooled. To understand Coleridge properly the critic will have to study and describe much that is vague, rambling, and even tedious, and he will sigh at the waste of the great talent that might have produced such abundant chefs-d'oeuvre. But in the end there remains that small core of astonishing, achieved work that has made Coleridge's reputation. So with Ford. It is one thing to deprecate a career foundered on the wreck of a weak character. It would be quite another to forget that some of Ford's vessels reached port, laden with riches and sufficient amply to make his fortune — that Ford did, after all, transcend himself. Our final attitude toward his work, therefore, should be to acknowledge their shortcomings but to concentrate upon his achievements. One work of art, only one, is enough to distinguish any man's name. And Ford has written not one but two. If he is not a great novelist — and even of that who at this date can feel certain — he is at least a very important one, a major artist whose masterworks are sure to take a permanent place in that rather small group of actively read and returned to novels in English. As with Thackeray, as with Hardy, as with Lawrence, the lesser productions will be forgotten. But the fruit of his career will remain.

NOTES, BIBLIOGRAPHY, AND INDEX

NOTES

1 Ford the Novelist: Anguish and Cat's Cradle

[1] The name of Ford Madox Ford was Ford Madox Hueffer, of course, before 1919. That year, in a move unparalleled in a major writer, he had his name legally changed. By this date he had already published nineteen novels (including *The Good Soldier* and two collaborations with Conrad), as well as twenty-eight other books, and was widely known. [2] H. G. Wells, *Boon* (New York, 1915), p. 135. [3] Ezra Pound, "Homage to Ford Madox Ford," *New Directions in Prose and Poetry* (Norfolk, Connecticut, 1942), p. 480. [4] For an account of the centrality of England as subject matter in Ford's work, and of his own complex, uneasy relation to his native country, see Chapter II. [5] Ford's attitudes toward the society of his time are examined more closely in Chapter III. [6] Ford Madox Ford, *A Call* (London, 1910), p. 274. [7] Ford Madox Ford, *Henry James* (London, 1913), p. 163, hereafter cited as *James*. [8] *James*, p. 161. [9] Ford Madox Ford, *Joseph Conrad: A Personal Remembrance* (Boston, 1924), p. 225, hereafter cited as *Conrad*.

[10] Ford Madox Ford, *Thus to Revisit* (New York, 1921), p. 44, hereafter cited as *Revisit*. [11] Ford Madox Ford, "On Impressionism," *Poetry and Drama*, II (June and December, 1914), 328. [12] *Revisit*, p. 44. [13] *James*, p. 161. [14] Ford Madox Ford, *It Was the Nightingale* (Philadelphia, 1933), p. 212, hereafter cited as *Nightingale*. [15] Caroline Gordon, "Homage to Ford Madox Ford," *New Directions in Prose and Poetry* (Norfolk, Connecticut, 1942), p. 475. [16] Ford Madox Ford, "Joseph Conrad," *The English Review*, X (December, 1911), 76–77. [17] Ford Madox Ford, *The Critical Attitude* (London, 1911), p. 33. [18] *Conrad*, p. 223. [19] *Critical Attitude*, p. 26. [20] *Critical Attitude*, pp. 27–28. [21] *Critical Attitude*, p. 28. [22] Ford Madox Ford, *The English Novel* (Philadelphia, 1929), p. 29. [23] Ford Madox Ford, *Portraits from Life* (Boston, 1937), p. 134. [24] *James*, pp. 53–54. [25] *English Novel*, pp. 132–133. [26] *English Novel*, p. 132. [27] *Revisit*, p. 36. [28] *Critical Attitude*, pp. 34–35. [29] *Revisit*, p. 96.

[30] "On Impressionism," p. 323. [31] *English Novel*, p. 135. [32] *Critical Attitude*, p. 58. [33] *Revisit*, p. 49. [34] *Critical Attitude*, p. 64. [35] *James*, p. 14. [36] *Nightingale*,

p. 212. [37] *Critical Attitude*, pp. 37–39. [38] "On Impressionism," p. 333. [39] Ford Madox Ford, "Techniques," *The Southern Review*, I (July, 1935), 32. [40] *Conrad*, p. 206. [41] Ford Madox Ford, "Preface," *Stories from de Maupassant* (London, 1903), p. 13. [42] *English Novel*, p. 121. [43] *Revisit*, p. 52. [44] *Conrad*, pp. 214–215. According to Ford, Conrad held that a habit of good cadence could be acquired by the study of models (Flaubert being a favorite); he himself believed that everyone has his own natural cadence from which he cannot escape. [45] *Revisit*, p. 52. [46] *Conrad*, p. 208. Ford's admiration of Hudson extended to several other writers in the field. An oft-cited favorite was the Gilbert White who wrote *Natural History and Antiquities of Selborne* (1789). Another, about whom he wrote eloquently and revealingly in the *transatlantic review* (p. 504): "a tribute to what I thought then — and I think it still — *sui generis* the most beautiful book in the world: Samuel Smiles' *Life of a Scottish Naturalist*. I found this book by chance a year ago, bought it for sixpence and recognised at once that my intimate cadence, the typical sentence that I try all my life to create, that I hear all the while in my ear and only once in a blue moon am aided to write, is to be found always in the recorded speeches of Thomas Edward. His sentences have a dying fall, a cadence of resignation. He will write of dotterels on the wet sands, of spoonbills labouring in the immense engineering feat of turning over a great dead fish, of foxes in their homes on the faces of the sea-cliffs — and it is as if you were hearing a *nunc dimittis* spoken without pomp or self-consciousness." [47] Ford Madox Ford, *Return to Yesterday* (New York, 1932), p. 61, hereafter cited as *Yesterday*. [48] *Yesterday*, p. 287. [49] *Conrad*, p. 192.
   [50] "On Impressionism," p. 323. [51] "Joseph Conrad," p. 76. [52] *Conrad*, p. 199. [53] "On Impressionism," p. 174. [54] "On Impressionism," p. 167. [55] See Herbert Muller, "Impressionism in Fiction: Prism vs. Mirror," *The American Scholar*, VII (Summer, 1938), 355–367. Muller points out that the term was borrowed from the example of the French impressionist painters, who, discarding intellectual preconceptions, sought to render their immediate, naive sensory impressions — to practice, as they saw it, a more meaningful realism. As impressionists in fiction, Muller also includes Conrad, Crane, Sherwood Anderson, Mansfield, Faulkner, and Wolfe. Joseph Warren Beach, in his chapters on Impressionism in *The Twentieth-Century Novel* (1932) cites Conrad, Lawrence, and Dorothy Richardson (in an ascending order of purity), but describes a writer like Virginia Woolf as an "expressionist" (that is, one whose aim is not representation but the symbolic expression of inner meaning or essence). The disagreement between these scholars develops from premises which differ according to their particular critical aims. For the present purposes, Beach's distinction is not required. [56] *Conrad*, pp. 136–137. [57] "On Impressionism," pp. 173–174. [58] *Conrad*, pp. 192–194. [59] Stella Bowen, *Drawn from the Life* (London, 1941), p. 79, hereafter cited as Bowen.
   [60] Bowen, p. 163. [61] Bowen, p. 80. [62] "On Impressionism," p. 326.

II The Historical Novels

[1] David Garnett, *The Golden Echo* (London, 1953), p. 64. [2] Douglas Goldring, *Trained for Genius* (New York, 1949), p. 69, hereafter cited as *Trained*. [3] Ford Madox Ford, *Joseph Conrad: A Personal Remembrance* (Boston, 1924), p. 22. [4] *Conrad*, p. 6. [5] *Conrad*, p. 23. [6] *A Conrad Memorial Library: The Collection of George T. Keating* (New York, 1929), p. 133. [7] *Conrad*, p. 43. [8] *Conrad*, p. 47. [9] *Conrad*, pp. 42–45.

[10] *Trained*, p. 76. [11] Joseph Conrad and Ford Madox Ford, "A Note on *Romance*," *The Nature of a Crime* (London, 1924), pp. 105–106. [12] Joseph Conrad and Ford Madox Ford, *Romance* (New York, 1923), pp. 372–373. [13] *Romance*, pp. 530–532. [14] "Appendix," *Nature of a Crime*, pp. 115–116. [15] "Appendix," *Nature of a Crime*, pp. 108–109. [16] *Romance*, p. 118. [17] Ford Madox Ford, *Return to Yesterday* (New York, 1932), p. 198, hereafter cited as *Yesterday*. [18] *Yesterday*, p. 181. [19] Ford Madox Ford, *It Was the Nightingale* (Philadelphia, 1933), p. 74.
[20] Ford Madox Ford, *Collected Poems* (New York, 1936), pp. 80–82. [21] *Trained*, p. 168. [22] Ford Madox Ford, *The Critical Attitude* (London, 1911), p. 29. [23] Ford Madox Ford and Violet Hunt, *Zeppelin Nights* (London, 1915), p. 285. [24] *Trained*, p. 179. [25] *Yesterday*, pp. 167–169. [26] Historical novels were, of course, highly popular with English readers, and between 1880 and 1910 a great flood of them appeared. Ford's own work seems chiefly influenced by two trends in the historical novel which developed in the later 1800s – the revival of medievalism (as in Morris's prose romances), and a greater emphasis on literary craftsmanship (Flaubert's *Salammbô* and Stevenson's novels). [27] G. Jean-Aubry, *Joseph Conrad, Life and Letters* (New York, 1928), II, p. 67; dated February 20, 1908. [28] Ford Madox Ford, *Privy Seal* (London, 1907), p. 116. [29] *Privy Seal*, pp. 115–116.
[30] Ford Madox Ford, *The Fifth Queen* (London, 1906), p. 28. [31] *Privy Seal*, pp. 116–117. [32] *Fifth Queen*, p. 40. [33] *Fifth Queen*, p. 239. [34] Ford Madox Ford, *The Fifth Queen Crowned* (London, 1908), p. 257, hereafter cited as *Queen Crowned*. [35] *Queen Crowned*, pp. 307–310. [36] *Privy Seal*, p. 244. [37] *Fifth Queen*, p. 197. [38] *Queen Crowned*, p. 16. [39] *Queen Crowned*, pp. 118–119.
[40] "I amassed a great deal of information about Henry VIII," he later commented about his researches, "and wrote three long novels all about the Defender of the Faith. But I really know — so delusive are reported facts — nothing whatever. Not one single thing! Should I have found him affable, or terrifying, or seductive, or royal, or courageous? There are so many contradictory facts; there are so many reported interviews, each contradicting the other, so that really all that I *know* about this king could be reported in the words of Maupassant . . . introducing one of his characters. . . . 'C'etait un monsieur à favoris rouges qui entrait toujours le premier.' And that is all I *know* about Henry VIII. – that he was a gentleman with red whiskers who always went first through a door." ("On Impressionism," p. 171.) [41] *Fifth Queen*, p. 20. [42] *Privy Seal*, pp. 238–239. [43] Herbert Butterfield, *The Historical Novel: An Essay* (Cambridge, 1924), pp. 36–37. [44] Ford Madox Ford, "On Impressionism," *Poetry and Drama*, II (June and December, 1914), 171. [45] *Fifth Queen*, p. 26. [46] *Queen Crowned*, p. 312. [47] *Queen Crowned*, pp. 193–217. [48] *Queen Crowned*, p. 201. [49] The book was published to coincide with the tricentennial celebration of the event, and was the first of Ford's independent novels issued in the United States.
[50] Ford Madox Ford, *Ladies Whose Bright Eyes* (London, 1911), p. 130, hereafter cited as *Ladies*. [51] *Ladies*, p. 257. [52] *Ladies*, p. 357. [53] *Ladies*, p. 361. [54] *Ladies*, pp. 142–143. [55] *Ladies*, p. 362. [56] Ford Madox Ford, *The "Half Moon"* (London, 1909), p. 333. [57] *Ladies* (1911), p. 67. [58] Ford Madox Ford, *Ladies Whose Bright Eyes* (Philadelphia, 1935), p. 70. [59] *Zeppelin Nights*, p. 138.
[60] *Zeppelin Nights*, p. 138. [61] *Conrad*, p. 186. [62] *Zeppelin Nights*, p. 138. [63] *Conrad*, p. 186.

III Novels of Social Satire

¹ Edgar Jepson, *Memories of an Edwardian* (London, 1937), p. 134. ² Joseph Conrad and Ford Madox Ford, *The Inheritors* (New York, 1923), pp. 9–10. ³ *James*, p. 60. ⁴ Ford Madox Ford, *An English Girl* (London, 1907), pp. 252–254. ⁵ Ford Madox Ford, *Mr. Fleight* (London, 1913), p. 21, hereafter cited as *Fleight*. ⁶ *Fleight*, pp. 124–125. ⁷ *Fleight*, p. 125. ⁸ Ford Madox Ford, *Mr. Apollo* (London, 1908), p. 235, hereafter cited as *Apollo*. ⁹ *Fleight*, p. 158. ¹⁰ *Fleight*, p. 162. ¹¹ *Apollo*, pp. 36–37. ¹² *Apollo*, p. 191. ¹³ Ford Madox Ford, *The Simple Life Limited* (London, 1911), p. 18, hereafter cited as *Simple Life*. ¹⁴ *Simple Life*, p. 49. ¹⁵ *Simple Life*, pp. 27–28. ¹⁶ *Simple Life*, p. 56. ¹⁷ *Simple Life*, p. 29. ¹⁸ *Simple Life*, p. 26. ¹⁹ *Simple Life*, p. 77.

²⁰ *Simple Life*, p. 93. ²¹ *Simple Life*, pp. 141–144. ²² *Simple Life*, p. 187. ²³ *Simple Life*, p. 319. ²⁴ *Simple Life*, p. 213. ²⁵ *Simple Life*, p. 44. ²⁶ *Fleight*, pp. 43–44. ²⁷ Robert Lowell, "Ford Madox Ford, 1873–1939" *Encounter*, II (April, 1954), 32. ²⁸ *Apollo*, p. 121. ²⁹ Ford Madox Ford, *The New Humpty-Dumpty* (London, 1912), pp. 75–76.

³⁰ *Yesterday*, p. 92. ³¹ *Simple Life*, pp. 213–214. ³² *Simple Life*, p. 371. ³³ *Conrad*, p. 51. ³⁴ *Conrad*, p. 124. ³⁵ *Conrad*, p. 154. ³⁶ *Conrad*, p. 149. ³⁷ *Conrad*, p. 153. ³⁸ *Conrad*, p. 141. ³⁹ Joseph Conrad and Ford Madox Ford, *The Inheritors* (New York, 1923), p. 210.

⁴⁰ *Inheritors*, p. 53. ⁴¹ *Conrad*, p. 187. ⁴² Ford Madox Ford, "Joseph Conrad," *The English Review*, X (December, 1911), 68. In the Dreyfus case, Ford was on the clerical side (*Between St. Dennis and St. George: A Sketch of Three Civilizations* (London, 1915), p. 78; *Yesterday*, p. 277). ⁴³ *Inheritors*, p. 102. ⁴⁴ *Fleight*, p. 2. ⁴⁵ *Fleight*, p. 213. ⁴⁶ *Fleight*, pp. 193–194. ⁴⁷ *Fleight*, p. 3. ⁴⁸ In the portrayal of Mr. Fleight's mentor, Ford provides, it would appear, an excellent illustration of his comment in *The Critical Attitude* (pp. 34–35) that the author in his novel may create himself as a character and that in his objectivity he may even "psychologise himself as a villain . . . marring fine destinies and making evil fortunes." Similarly, another persona, himself as "generous but naturally unsound," would seem to be Count Macdonald. ⁴⁹ *Fleight*, p. 213. ⁵⁰ Et comme il était très fort, courageux, temperant, avisé, il obtint sans peine le commandement d'une compagnie. ⁵¹ *Fleight*, pp. 292–293. ⁵² Later in his career Ford transcended his early genteel anti-Semitism and was among the first to speak out against the Nazis. In *It Was the Nightingale* (1933), for example, he wrote: "The layman hates the artist as the atrocious Mr. Hitler hates learning. Indeed the layman regards the artist as a sort of Jew." And he continued by pointedly praising Heine as "the greatest of German poets." (P. 10.) ⁵³ *Return*, pp. 261–268; *Trained*, p. 114. ⁵⁴ *Apollo*, p. 32. ⁵⁵ *Apollo*, p. 60. ⁵⁶ *Apollo*, p. 294. ⁵⁷ *Apollo*, p. 297. ⁵⁸ *Apollo*, pp. 304–305. ⁵⁹ *Apollo*, pp. 287–288. ⁶⁰ *Apollo*, p. 94. ⁶¹ *Apollo*, pp. 105–112. ⁶² *Apollo*, p. 222. ⁶³ *Apollo*, p. 81. ⁶⁴ *Apollo*, pp. 168–169. ⁶⁵ *Apollo*, p. 299. ⁶⁶ *Apollo*, pp. 306–310. ⁶⁷ *Apollo*, p. 119. ⁶⁸ *Apollo*, p. 125. ⁶⁹ *Apollo*, pp. 193–196.

⁷⁰ *Apollo*, pp. 269–270. ⁷¹ *Apollo*, p. 307. ⁷² In Ford's London is sounded, interestingly enough, the same note, in almost the same manner, as Eliot's in *The Waste Land* — but fourteen years before it. Compare the following, for example, with the "Unreal City" section of the later work: "Girls slapped young men hard blows on the back, and screamed half, half laughed; men burdened with babies melancholily pushed perambulators against their hips; women bore before them distended string bags; . . . But where a canal beneath a bridge ran across this high road, the crowd, the shops, and the stalls came alike

to an end; and standing on a pavement almost vacant, the stranger awaited the missionary. . . . The long canal stretched away into the distance a slate-grey surface with little patches of thin vapour arising beneath the translucent haze, between slate-grey and undistinguished houses and spindly trees whose foliage had no shimmer because of the film of soot that covered each leaf. . . . The stranger, standing on the peak of the bridge, looked back at the crowd that, serried and jostling, in the narrow space between the traffic and the house-fronts, appeared like a section of dark and troubled fluid in a test tube." (Pp. 38–41.) [73] *Apollo*, p. 290. [74] *Apollo*, p. 118. [75] *Apollo*, p. 244.

IV Novels of Small Circles

[1] In the subtitle of *The Benefactor: A Tale of a Small Circle* and in the "Epistolary Epilogue" of *A Call* (p. 304). [2] Conrad, pp. 186–187. [3] Ford Madox Ford, *The Benefactor* (London, 1905), p. 48. [4] *Benefactor*, p. 32. [5] *Benefactor*, p. 25. [6] *Benefactor*, p. 51. [7] *Benefactor*, p. 36. [8] *Conrad*, p. 188. [9] *Benefactor*, p. 187.

[10] *Benefactor*, p. 216. [11] *Benefactor*, p. 346. [12] *Benefactor*, p. 180. [13] *Benefactor*, p. 39. [14] *Benefactor*, pp. 76–77. [15] *Benefactor*, p. 278. [16] *Benefactor*, p. 335. [17] *Benefactor*, p. 44. [18] *Benefactor*, p. 105. [19] *Benefactor*, p. 67.

[20] *Benefactor*, p. 118. [21] Ford Madox Ford, *A Call* (London, 1910), p. 122. [22] *Call*, pp. 15–17. [23] *Call*, p. 30. [24] *Call*, p. 33. [25] *Call*, p. 230. [26] *Call*, p. 210. [27] *Call*, p. 140. [28] *Call*, p. 203. [29] Joseph Conrad and Ford Madox Ford, *The Nature of a Crime* (London, 1924), p. 10, hereafter cited as *Crime*.

[30] December 4, 1924, p. 826. [31] *Crime*, p. 7. [32] Ford Madox Ford, *Ring for Nancy* (Indianapolis, 1913), p. 29, hereafter cited as *Nancy*. [33] *Nancy*, p. 281. [34] Ford Madox Ford, "Dedicatory Letter to Stella Bowen" (dated January 9, 1927), *The Good Soldier* (New York, 1951), pp. xvii–xxii, hereafter cited as *Soldier*. [35] Letter to Percival Hinton, quoted by Douglas Goldring, *Trained*, p. 245. [36] Ford Madox Ford, *Portraits from Life* (Boston, 1937), p. 217. [37] Robie Macauley, "The Good Ford," *The Kenyon Review*, XI (Spring, 1949), 277. [38] Mark Schorer, "An Interpretation," *Soldier* (1951), pp. v–xv. For an extended defense of Mr. Schorer's position, see Richard A. Cassell, *Ford Madox Ford: A Study of His Novels* (Baltimore, 1961), pp. 148–201. [39] *Soldier*, p. 70. For convenience, this and the ensuing quotations from *The Good Soldier* are cited from the 1951 edition. (The 1957 paperback version is identical.)

[40] The text does not warrant Robie Macauley's interpretation that the other women in Edward's life were merely substitutes for his true love, Leonora — that the Ashburnhams "can love each other only through a third person" (p. 276). Edward's positive feeling for his wife is never deeper than respect; all else about her repels his spirit. Mr. Macauley's assertion that Ford by his original title meant to say "that the saddest story is the perpetual story of love between man and woman, love that can never quite arrive at understanding and decays" is, as far as it goes, valid enough. But this theme does not require any notion of a third person intermediary between the Ashburnhams. Unjustified also is his statement that Leonora's character is as "equally right and wrong, equally good and evil" (p. 275) as Edward's. For a while, no doubt, that is part of Ford's dramatic illusion; it is not what he is saying. [41] *Soldier*, p. 242. [42] From "In the Neolithic Age" in *Barrack Room Ballads*. [43] *Soldier*, p. 164. [44] *Soldier*, p. 15. [45] *Soldier*, p. 78. [46] *Soldier*, pp. 28, 250. [47] *Soldier*, pp. 21–23; see also pp. 7, 12, 14, 46, 67. [48] This deeper, more sympathetic and human side of Dowell Mr. Schorer entirely ignores; in his reading, Ford's narrator is

merely a mindless, self-deluded fool, worthy of a passionate scorn. [49] *Soldier*, p. 33.
[50] *Soldier*, p. 49. [51] *Soldier*, p. 103. [52] *Soldier*, p. 94. [53] *Soldier*, pp. 253–254.
[54] *Soldier*, p. 61. [55] *Soldier*, p. 110. [56] *Soldier*, p. 85. [57] *James*, p. 82. [58] *Soldier*, p. 185. [59] *Soldier*, pp. 238–239.
[60] *Soldier*, p. 256. [61] *Soldier*, p. 28. [62] *Soldier*, p. 162. [63] *Soldier*, p. 251. [64] *Soldier*, p. 235. [65] *Soldier*, pp. 91–92. [66] *Soldier*, p. 51. [67] *Soldier*, p. 33. [68] *Soldier*, p. 239. [69] *Soldier*, pp. 44–45.
[70] *Soldier*, p. 32. [71] *Soldier*, pp. 12–13. [72] *Soldier*, p. 79. [73] *Soldier*, p. 39. [74] *Soldier*, p. 252. [75] *Soldier*, p. 42. [76] *Soldier*, p. 110. [77] *Soldier*, p. 239. [78] *Soldier*, p. 220. [79] *Soldier*, p. 115.
[80] *James*, pp. 25–27. In addition Ford quoted in an appendix eight pages from James's two versions. [81] *Nightingale*, p. 212. [82] *Soldier*, p. 11. [83] *Soldier*, p. 5. [84] *Revisit*, p. 44. [85] *Soldier*, p. 86. [86] *Soldier*, p. 250. [87] *Soldier*, p. 211. [88] *Soldier*, p. 57. In Mr. Schorer's analysis, Edward is simply a libertine, having neither dignity nor depth and subject to the same distressingly hard scorn which marks his approach to Dowell. The reader would not even discern that Edward, not the narrator, is the central figure of the novel. [89] *Soldier*, p. 105.
[90] *Soldier*, p. 12; see also p. 164. [91] *Soldier*, p. 254. [92] *Soldier*, p. 234. [93] *Soldier*, p. 71. [94] *Soldier*, pp. 18–19. [95] *Soldier*, p. 120.

v Tietjens, the Great War, and England

[1] *Some Do Not . . .* (1924), *No More Parades* (1925), *A Man Could Stand Up –* (1926), *The Last Post* (1928), published together for the first time by Knopf in 1950 as *Parade's End*. (The points of ellipsis and the dash in the titles of two of these novels may be noted; for practical reasons – typographical appearance, readability, and the avoidance of distraction – the author has chosen not to use these marks in the main body of this study.) [2] *Soldier*, pp. xviii–xix. [3] Bowen, p. 109. [4] *Nightingale*, p. 199. [5] *Nightingale*, p. 214. [6] Ford Madox Ford, *No Enemy* (New York, 1929). *No Enemy*, Ford wrote, is "not a novel but my own reminiscences of the war written just after and, as to one chapter [doing] part of the writing under fire." "The Letters of Ford Madox Ford," *The Saturday Review of Literature*, XXIV, No. 15 (August 2, 1941), 14. [7] *Trained*, p. 223. [8] The autobiographical element of the novel, apparent in the character of Jessop, can be seen also in the references to a hill farm with a "view," anti-German hysteria among the English which plagued Ford personally, and in the situation he described in *Return to Yesterday*, which corresponds with events in the novel: "I wrote a shadow play for Mme. Strindberg and had to act it myself in place of the lovely actress who should have done it. A too ardent admirer of Mme. Strindberg had stolen the manuscript because he could not bear to let my play be produced." (P. 411.) [9] *Nightingale*, pp. 65–66.
[10] *No More Parades*, pp. 306–307. For convenience, this and the ensuing quotations from the four Tietjens volumes are cited from the 1950 omnibus edition, *Parade's End*. [11] The bulk of his observations appear in *It Was the Nightingale*, but these may be supplemented with his remarks in the epistolary dedications to the last three novels of the cycle. [12] *Nightingale*, p. 215. "I sit frequently and dream of writing an immense novel in which all the characters should be great masses of people – or interests. You would have Interest A, remorselessly and under the stress of blind necessities, slowly or cataclysmically overwhelming Interest Z. Without the attraction of sympathy for a pic-

turesque or upright individual. It ought, I have felt for years, to be done. But I doubt if I shall ever get to it. More power, then, to the elbow of the man who eventually tackles the job." [13] *Nightingale*, p. 209. [14] *Nightingale*, pp. 215–216. [15] *Nightingale*, pp. 217–218. [16] *Nightingale*, pp. 218–219. [17] *Nightingale*, pp. 219–220. [18] *Trained*, p. 95. [19] *Revisit*, the dedicatory letters to the Tietjens volumes, *Yesterday*, and *Nightingale*. [20] *Revisit*, p. 59. Facts about Marwood, Goldring records, are difficult to discover. Whether he was actually a Yorkshire "squire" is uncertain, but he definitely was educated at Clifton, a public school (which Tietjens attended), secured an Exhibition at Trinity College, and did in fact have a remarkable encyclopedic mind. A Cambridge contemporary (Archibald Marshall, according to *Trained*, p. 95) declares, however, that Marwood fell ill in his second year, and, since he went down without a degree, was never in the running for a Senior Wranglership, as Ford used to assert, nor was he a Fellow. [21] *Nightingale*, p. 208. [22] *Nightingale*, p. 222. [23] "Dedicatory Letter" to *No More Parades* (New York, 1925). [24] "Dedicatory Letter" to *The Last Post* (New York, 1928). [25] "Dedicatory Letter" to *A Man Could Stand Up* (New York, 1926). [26] "Dedicatory Letter" to *The Last Post*. [27] "Dedicatory Letter" to *A Man Could Stand Up*. [28] "Dedicatory Letter" to *No More Parades*. [29] *Nightingale*, p. 80. [30] *Nightingale*, p. 151. [31] *Trained*, p. 58. [32] *Yesterday*, p. 167. [33] *Revisit*, p. 96. [34] "Reality to Romance: A Study of Ford's *Parade's End*," *College English*, XVII, No. 8 (May, 1956), 445–450. [35] The memory of it arouses in her a groaning anguish ("She had to invent a chronic stitch in her heart to account for this groan which ended in a mumble and seemed to herself to degrade her") and yet, at the same time, she feels a dreadful desire to re-experience that feeling: "the longing for the brute who had mangled her, the dreadful pain of the mind . . . but . . . not with Drake" (*Some Do Not*, p. 149). [36] *Some Do Not*, p. 201. [37] Ford himself tells us that externally she was based on Dorothy Minto, an English actress he admired, who had once played the part of a suffragette. [38] The motif of brothers is common in Ford's novels, but the only character like Mark is Gregory Moffat in *The Benefactor*, especially in the affection he feels for his brother, whom he considers capable of great accomplishments. [39] In portraying Macmaster Ford invited a curious connection with himself. Like his character, he had published a monograph on Rossetti (in 1902; it dealt with his painting rather than his poetry). And in *Nightingale* he notes that his opening scene in the railway carriage, between Macmaster and Christopher, was modeled on a trip he had taken with Marwood (p. 227). Macmaster's betrayal of Tietjens is similar also to Etchingham-Granger's of Churchill in *The Inheritors* — a novel which, to judge from Ford's remarks, appears to have involved some personal revelation.

[40] Calling *Maisie* "the book by that very great writer that most 'matters,' " Ford, in *No Enemy*, goes on to try to convey the quality of the work: "this is the story of a child moving amongst elemental passions that are veiled. But, of course, elemental passions can never be veiled enough not to get through to the consciousness, if not to the intelligence of the child in the house. So, in an atmosphere of intrigues, divorces, prides, jealousies, litigations, conducted as these things are conducted in this country, by what it is convenient to call 'the best people,' Maisie always 'knows.' She knows all about concealed relationships, as she knows all about intrigues, processes, and the points of view of old family servants. It is, of course, a horrible book, but it is very

triumphantly true." (P. 178.) [41] *Nightingale*, p. 217. [42] *No Enemy*, pp. 202–203. [43] *Some Do Not*, p. 178. [44] *Nightingale*, p. 225. "I do not think that I have any desire for personal liberty. In the army I had been ordered about and had found it agreeable because, having no personal responsibilities to ponder over, my mind was free. I asked really nothing better." (P. 100.) "I would, for my personal comfort, far rather go through another similar war than face an eternity of writing endless books" (p. 225). [45] *Nightingale*, pp. 225–226. [46] *Parade's End*, p. xxi. [47] Letter quoted in *The Saturday Review of Literature* (August 2, 1941), 14. [48] "Tietjens had walked in the sunlight down the lines, past the hut with the evergreen climbing rose, in the sunlight, thinking in an interval, good-humouredly about his official religion: about the Almighty as, on a colossal scale, a great English Landowner, benevolently awful, a colossal duke who never left his study and was thus invisible, but knowing all about the estate down to the last hind at the home farm and the last oak; Christ, an almost too benevolent Land-Steward, son of the Owner, knowing all about the estate down to the last child at the porter's lodge, apt to be got round by the more detrimental tenants; the Third Person of the Trinity, the spirit of the estate, the Game as it were, as distinct from the players of the game; the atmosphere of the estate, that of the interior of Winchester Cathedral just after a Handel anthem has been finished, a perpetual Sunday, with, probably, a little cricket for the young men." (*No More Parades*, pp. 365–366.) [49] "Along with cricket. There would be no more parades of that sort. Probably they would play some beastly yelping game. . . . Like baseball or Association football." (*No More Parades*, p. 366.)

[50] *Nightingale*, p. 237. [51] *Nightingale*, p. 239. [52] Ford tells in *Nightingale* of the day he returned to using a pen. While sailing to Paris, he read the typescript of one of his books and found its prose horrible: "I cut out miles of passages intended for one or another of those secretaries. As if with a chaff-cutter I cut into five or six sentences that, fluidly, I had composed on my new Corona. . . . Even nowadays I almost cry when I see the back of that book and of others written in New York at about the same period. So I have locked all my own books that I possess into a press of which I have mislaid the key." (P. 242.) [53] *No More Parades*, p. 387. [54] *A Man Could Stand Up*, p. 503. [55] *No More Parades*, p. 291. [56] *No More Parades*, p. 296. [57] *No More Parades*, p. 500. [58] *No More Parades*, pp. 307–308. [59] *A Man Could Stand Up*, p. 559.

[60] *A Man Could Stand Up*, p. 552. [61] *A Man Could Stand Up*, p. 562. [62] *A Man Could Stand Up*, p. 564. [63] *A Man Could Stand Up*, p. 572. [64] *The Last Post*, pp. 704–705. [65] *Some Do Not*, p. 75. [66] *Some Do Not*, p. 187. [67] *Some Do Not*, p. 144. [68] *Some Do Not*, p. 105. [69] Ford Madox Ford, "On Impressionism," *Poetry and Drama*, II (June, 1914), 174.

[70] *Some Do Not*, pp. 124–125. [71] *Some Do Not*, pp. 6–7. [72] *Some Do Not*, p. 80. [73] *Some Do Not*, p. 14. [74] *Some Do Not*, pp. 217–218. [75] *Some Do Not*, p. 140. [76] *Some Do Not*, p. 100.

vi And After

[1] In the epistolary dedication, Ford noted that he had based his account on a report that Ney had escaped execution in the White reaction and had fled to America.

vii Down Stream and Up

[1] Ponson du Terrail (1820–1871) was a hack writer of serial fiction — *Exploits de Rocambole* being his most celebrated, and interminable, work. (Had

Ford been writing for an English audience instead of a French one, his equivalent would have been Hall Caine.) The quoted passage is the final paragraph of an essay written for the *Journal Littéraire* (August 16, 1924); the article is reprinted in the appendix to *Conrad* (pp. 271–276), where it appears in its original French. It remained untranslated, Ford said, because it expressed "more emotion than the English language will bear." The remark is provocative — and illuminating, since it throws into vivid relief Ford's own, almost unparalleled, achievement as a novelist writing in English. The speaker in the passage is imagined to be Conrad, but the voice is distinctly Ford's. The theme expressed, however — tastes in emotion apart — fits with equal appropriateness the hard careers and lives of both men. ² *Nightingale*, p. 254. ³ R. P. Blackmur, "The King over the Water: Notes on the Novels of F. M. Hueffer," *The Princeton University Library Chronicle*, IX (April, 1948), 126–127. ⁴ Joseph Conrad and Ford Madox Ford, "Appendix" to "A Note on *Romance*," *The Nature of a Crime* (London, 1924). (The American edition incorrectly assigns Conrad's words to Ford, and vice versa.)

BIBLIOGRAPHY

Novels by Ford

The Shifting of the Fire. London: T. Fisher Unwin, 1892.
The Inheritors: An Extravagant Story. With Joseph Conrad. London: Heinemann, 1901.
Romance. With Joseph Conrad. London: Smith, Elder, 1903.
The Benefactor: A Tale of a Small Circle. London: Brown, Langham, 1905.
The Fifth Queen: And How She Came to Court. London: Alston Rivers, 1906.
Privy Seal: His Last Venture. London: Alston Rivers, 1907.
An English Girl: A Romance. London: Methuen, 1907.
The Fifth Queen Crowned: A Romance. London: Nash, 1908.
Mr. Apollo: A Just Possible Story. London: Methuen, 1908.
The "Half Moon": A Romance of the Old World and the New. London: Nash, 1909.
A Call: The Tale of Two Passions. London: Chatto and Windus, 1910.
The Portrait. London: Methuen, 1910.
The Simple Life Limited ("By Daniel Chaucer"). London: Lane, 1911.
Ladies Whose Bright Eyes: A Romance. London: Constable, 1911; Philadelphia: Lippincott, 1935 (revised).
The New Humpty-Dumpty ("By Daniel Chaucer"). London: Lane, 1912.
Ring for Nancy: A Sheer Comedy. Indianapolis: Bobbs-Merrill, 1913. (Published in England in 1912 as *The Panel*.)
Mr. Fleight. London: Howard Latimer, 1913.
The Young Lovell: A Romance. London: Chatto and Windus, 1913.
The Good Soldier: A Tale of Passion. London: Lane, 1915; New York: Boni, 1927; New York: Knopf, 1951, 1957.
The Marsden Case: A Romance. London: Duckworth, 1923.
The Nature of a Crime. With Joseph Conrad. London: Duckworth, 1924; New York: Doubleday, 1924.
Some Do Not . . . London: Duckworth, 1924; New York: Seltzer, 1924.
No More Parades. London: Duckworth, 1925; New York: Boni, 1925.
A Man Could Stand Up —. London: Duckworth, 1926; New York: Boni, 1926.

The Last Post. London: Duckworth, 1928; New York: Literary Guild of America, 1928.

A Little Less Than Gods: A Romance. London: Duckworth, 1928; New York: Viking, 1928.

No Enemy: A Tale of Reconstruction. New York: Macauley, 1929.

When the Wicked Man. New York: Liveright, 1931; London: Cape, 1932.

The Rash Act. New York: Long and Smith, 1933; London: Cape, 1933.

Henry for Hugh. Philadelphia: Lippincott, 1934.

Vive Le Roy. Philadelphia: Lippincott, 1936.

Parade's End (The four Tietjens novels in one volume: *Some Do Not . . . , No More Parades, A Man Could Stand Up –, The Last Post*). New York: Knopf, 1950.

Other Works by Ford

The Brown Owl: A Fairy Story. London: T. Fisher Unwin, 1892. (Actually published in October, 1891.)

The Feather. London: T. Fisher Unwin, 1892.

The Questions at the Well (poems). London: Digby, 1893. (Published under the pseudonym "Fenil Haig.")

The Queen Who Flew: A Fairy Tale. London: Bliss, Sands, and Foster, 1894.

Ford Madox Brown: A Record of His Life and Work. London: Longmans Green, 1896.

The Cinque Ports: A Historical and Descriptive Record. London: Blackwood, 1900.

Poems for Pictures. London: John MacQueen, 1900.

Rossetti: A Critical Essay on His Art. London: Duckworth, 1902.

"Preface," *Stories from De Maupassant.* Translated by E. M[artindale]. London: Duckworth, 1903.

The Face of the Night (poems). London: John MacQueen, 1904.

The Soul of London: A Survey of a Modern City. London: Alston Rivers, 1905.

Hans Holbein the Younger: A Critical Monograph. London: Duckworth, 1905.

The Heart of the Country: A Survey of a Modern Land. London: Alston Rivers, 1906.

Christina's Fairy Book. Pinafore Library. London: Alston Rivers, 1906.

From Inland (poems). London: Alston Rivers, 1907.

The Spirit of the People: An Analysis of the English Mind. London: Alston Rivers, 1907.

England and the English: An Interpretation (Omnibus volume containing *The Soul of London, The Heart of the Country,* and *The Spirit of the People*). New York: McClure, Phillips, 1907.

The Pre-Raphaelite Brotherhood: A Critical Monograph. London: Duckworth, 1907.

"The Future in London," *London Town Past and Present,* by W. W. Hutchings. London: Cassell and Company, 1909, Vol. II, pp. 1094–1110.

Songs from London (poems). London: Elkin Mathews, 1910.

Memories and Impressions: A Study in Atmospheres. New York: Harper, 1911. (Published in England as *Ancient Lights and Certain New Reflections: Being the Memories of a Young Man.* London: Chapman and Hall, 1910.)

The Critical Attitude. London: Constable, 1911.

High Germany (poems). London: Duckworth, 1911.
"Joseph Conrad," *The English Review* (December, 1911), 68–83.
Collected Poems. London: Goschen, 1913.
Henry James. London: Secker, 1913; New York: Boni, 1915.
The Monstrous Regiment of Women (suffragette pamphlet). London: Women's Freedom League, 1913.
"On Impressionism," *Poetry and Drama*, II (June and December, 1914), 167–175, 323–334.
When Blood Is Their Argument: An Analysis of Prussian Culture. London and New York: Hodder and Stoughton, 1915.
Between St. Dennis and St. George: A Sketch of Three Civilisations. London: Hodder and Stoughton, 1915.
Antwerp (poems). London: Poetry Workshop, 1915.
Zeppelin Nights: A London Entertainment. With Violet Hunt. London: Lane, 1915.
On Heaven and Other Poems. London: Lane, 1918.
"A House: A Modern Morality Play," *The Chapbook*, No. 21 (March, 1921).
Thus to Revisit: Some Reminiscences. New York: Dutton, 1921.
Mister Bosphorus and the Muses: Or a Short History of Poetry in Britain. London: Duckworth, 1923.
Women and Men. Paris: Three Mountains Press, 1923.
Joseph Conrad: A Personal Remembrance. London: Duckworth, 1924; Boston: Little, Brown, 1924.
"Introduction," *Transatlantic Stories*. Selected from *transatlantic review*. London: Duckworth, 1926.
A Mirror to France. London: Duckworth, 1926.
New Poems. New York: Rudge, 1927.
New York Essays. New York: Rudge, 1927.
New York Is Not America: Being a Mirror to the States. London: Duckworth, 1927; New York: Boni, 1927.
The English Novel: From the Earliest Days to the Death of Conrad. Philadelphia: Lippincott, 1929; London: Constable, 1930.
"Introduction," *The Life and Strange Surprising Adventures of Robinson Crusoe of York, Mariner*, by Daniel Defoe. San Francisco: The Grabhorn Press, 1930, pp. iii–xiv.
Return to Yesterday. London: Gollancz, 1931; New York: Liveright, 1932.
"Pound and 'How to Read,' " *The New Review*, II (April, 1932), 39–45.
It Was the Nightingale. Philadelphia: Lippincott, 1933; London: Heinemann, 1934.
Provence: From Minstrels to the Machine. New York: Lippincott, 1935; London: Allen and Unwin, 1938.
"Techniques," *The Southern Review*, I (July, 1935), 20–35.
Collected Poems. New York: Oxford University Press, 1936.
Great Trade Route. New York: Oxford University Press, 1937; London: Allen and Unwin, 1937.
Portraits from Life: Memories and Criticisms. Boston: Houghton Mifflin, 1937. (Published in England as *Mightier Than the Sword*. London: Allen and Unwin, 1938.)
The March of Literature from Confucius to Modern Times. New York: Dial, 1938; London: Allen and Unwin, 1939.

Works Relevant to Ford

For a more complete bibliography on Ford, the reader is referred to the pages of *English Fiction in Transition (1880–1920)*, edited by Helmut E. Gerber, particularly the following two issues: I (1958), 2–19; and IV, No. 2 (1961), 11–29. Chiefly engaged in compiling and annotating these listings have been Helmut E. and Helga S. Gerber, Frank MacShane, Richard A. Cassell, Charles Green, Richard J. Herndon, Richard W. Lid, and Richard M. Ludwig. The most comprehensive bibliography on Ford, not as yet in print, has been compiled by David D. Harvey.

Aldington, Richard. *Life for Life's Sake*. New York: Viking, 1941.

Allen, Walter. *The English Novel: A Short Critical History*. New York: Dutton, 1955.

Baines, Jocelyn. *Joseph Conrad*. London: Weidenfeld and Nicolson, 1959.

Baisch, Dorothy Ruth. "London Literary Circles, 1910 to 1920: With Special Reference to Ford Madox Ford, Ezra Pound, D. H. Lawrence, and Virginia Woolf." Ph.D. dissertation, Cornell University, 1950.

Bartlett, Paul Alexander. "Letters of Ford Madox Ford," *Saturday Review of Literature*, XXIV, No. 15 (August 2, 1941), 3–4, 14.

Beach, Joseph Warren. *The Method of Henry James*. New Haven: Yale University Press, 1918.

——. *The Twentieth-Century Novel*. New York: Century, 1932.

Blackmur, R. P. "The King over the Water: Notes on the Novels of F. M. Hueffer," *The Princeton University Library Chronicle*, IX (April, 1948), 123–127.

Bowen, Stella. *Drawn from the Life*. London: Collins, 1941.

Butterfield, Herbert. *The Historical Novel: An Essay*. Cambridge: University Press, 1924.

Cassell, Richard A. *Ford Madox Ford: A Study of His Novels*. Baltimore: Johns Hopkins University Press, 1961.

Conrad, Jessie. *Joseph Conrad and His Circle*. New York: Dutton, 1935.

——. *Joseph Conrad as I Knew Him*. London: Heinemann, 1926.

Conrad, Joseph. *Collected Works of Joseph Conrad*. Garden City, New York: Doubleday, Page, 1925. I. *Almayer's Folly. The Inheritors: An Extravagant Story*, by Conrad and F. M. Hueffer. II. *An Outcast of the Islands*. III. *The Nigger of the "Narcissus."* IV. *Lord Jim*. V. *Typhoon, and Other Stories*. VI. *Youth, A Narrative, and Two Other Stories*. VII. *Romance*, by Conrad and F. M. Hueffer. VIII. *Nostromo*. IX. *The Secret Agent*. X. *A Set of Six*. XI. *Under Western Eyes*. XII. *A Personal Record* and *The Mirror of the Sea*. XIII. *'Twixt Land and Sea: Tales*. XIV. *Chance*. XV. *Within the Tides: Tales. Tales of Unrest*. XVI. *Victory*. XIX. *Notes on Life and Letters*. XXI. *Suspense*.

——. *Conrad to a Friend: 150 Selected Letters from Joseph Conrad to Richard Curle*. Edited with an introduction and notes by Richard Curle. Garden City, New York: Doubleday, Doran, 1928.

——. *Last Essays*. Introduction by Richard Curle. Garden City, New York: Doubleday, Doran, 1926.

——. *Letters from Joseph Conrad, 1895–1924*. Edited with an introduction and notes by Edward Garnett. Indianapolis: Bobbs-Merrill, 1928.

——. *Letters to William Blackwood and David S. Meldrum*. Edited with an introduction and notes by William Blackburn. Durham, North Carolina: Duke University Press, 1958.

——. *The Sisters.* Introduction by Ford Madox Ford. New York: Crosby Gaige, 1928.

A Conrad Memorial Library: The Collection of George T. Keating. New York: Doubleday, Doran, 1929. (Ford wrote the introduction to the section on *The Inheritors*, pp. 74–83.)

Crankshaw, Edward. "Ford Madox Ford," *The National Review*, CXXXI (August, 1948), 160–167.

——. *Joseph Conrad: Some Aspects of the Art of the Novel.* London: Lane, 1936.

Dreiser, Theodore. "The Saddest Story," *The New Republic*, III (June 12, 1915), 155–156.

Edel, Leon. *The Psychological Novel: 1900–1950.* Philadelphia: Lippincott, 1955.

Firebaugh, Joseph J. "Tietjens and the Tradition," *Pacific Spectator*, VI (Winter, 1952), 23–32.

Garnett, David. *The Golden Echo.* New York: Harcourt, Brace, 1954.

Goldring, Douglas. *South Lodge: Reminiscences of Violet Hunt, Ford Madox Ford and the English Review Circle.* London: Constable, 1943.

——. *Trained for Genius: The Life and Writings of Ford Madox Ford.* New York: Dutton, 1949. (Published in England as *The Last Pre-Raphaelite.* London: MacDonald, 1948.)

Gorman, Herbert. "Ford Madox Ford: A Portrait in Impressions," *The Bookman*, LXVII, No. 1 (March, 1928), 56–60.

——. "Ford Madox Ford: The Personal Side," *The Princeton University Library Chronicle*, IX (April, 1948), 119–122.

Gose, Elliott B. "Reality to Romance: A Study of Ford's *Parade's End*," *College English*, XVII, No. 8 (May, 1956), 445–450.

——. "The Strange Irregular Rhythm: An Analysis of *The Good Soldier*," *PMLA*, LXII (June, 1957), 494–509.

Greene, Graham. *The Lost Childhood and Other Essays.* New York: Viking, 1952.

Guerard, Albert J. *Conrad the Novelist.* Cambridge, Massachusetts: Harvard University Press, 1958.

——. *Joseph Conrad.* New York: New Directions, 1947.

Hackett, Francis. *Henry the Eighth.* New York: Liveright, 1929.

Hicks, Granville, Caroline Gordon, and others. "Homage to Ford Madox Ford: A Symposium," *New Directions: 1942.* Norfolk, Connecticut: New Directions, 1942, pp. 443–494.

Hueffer, Oliver Madox. *The Book of Witches.* London: Nash, 1908.

Hunt, Violet. *I Have This to Say.* New York: Boni and Liveright, 1926. (Published in England as *The Flurried Years.* London: Hurst and Blackett, 1926.)

Jean-Aubry, G. *Joseph Conrad, Life and Letters.* New York: Doubleday, Page, 1928, 2 vols.

Jepson, Edgar. *Memories of an Edwardian and Neo-Georgian.* London: Richards, 1937.

Kenner, Hugh. *The Poetry of Ezra Pound.* Norfolk, Connecticut: New Directions, 1951.

Lowell, Robert. "Ford Madox Ford, 1873–1939" (poem), *Encounter*, II (April, 1954), 32.

Lubbock, Percy. *The Craft of Fiction.* London: Cape, 1921.

Macauley, Roble. "The Good Ford," *The Kenyon Review*, XI (Spring, 1949), 269–288.

MacShane, Frank. "The Pattern of Ford Madox Ford," *The New Republic*, CXXXII (April 4, 1955), 16–17.

Marrot, H. V. *The Life and Letters of John Galsworthy*. London: Heinemann, 1935.

Meixner, John A. "The Saddest Story," *The Kenyon Review*, XXII (Spring, 1960), 234–264.

Muller, Herbert. "Impressionism in Fiction: Prism vs. Mirror," *The American Scholar*, VII (Summer, 1938), 355–367.

Naumburg, Edward, Jr. "A Catalogue of a Ford Madox Ford Collection," *The Princeton University Library Chronicle*, IX (April, 1948), 134–165.

———. "A Collector Looks at Ford Madox Ford," *The Princeton University Library Chronicle*, IX (April, 1948), 105–118.

Putnam, Samuel. *Paris Was Our Mistress: Memoirs of a Lost and Found Generation*. New York: Viking Press, 1947.

Schorer, Mark. "An Interpretation," *The Princeton University Library Chronicle*, IX (April, 1948), 128–133; *Horizon*, XX (August, 1949), 132–138; *The Good Soldier*. New York: Knopf, 1951; 1957, pp. v–xv.

Steegmuller, Francis. *Flaubert and Madame Bovary*. New York: Viking, 1939.

Walter, E. V. "The Political Sense of Ford Madox Ford," *The New Republic*, CXXXIV (March 26, 1956), 17–19.

Wells, H. G. *Boon, The Mind of the Race, The Wild Asses of the Devil, and The Last Trump*. Being a First Selection from the Literary Remains of George Boon, Appropriate to the Times. Prepared for Publication by Reginald Bliss . . . With an Ambiguous Introduction by H. G. Wells. New York: Doran, 1915.

———. *Experiment in Autobiography: Discoveries and Conclusions of a Very Ordinary Brain (Since 1866)*. New York: Macmillan, 1934.

Wilson, Edmund. "Flaubert's Politics," *The Partisan Reader: 1934–1944*. New York: Dial, 1946.

Wimsatt, William K., Jr., and Cleanth Brooks. *Literary Criticism: A Short History*. New York: Knopf, 1957.

Young, Kenneth. *Ford Madox Ford*. London: Longmans, Green, 1956.

Zabel, Morton Dauwen. *Craft and Character in Modern Fiction*. New York: Viking, 1957.

INDEX